THE
BUDDHA'S
WIZARDS

THE BUDDHA'S WIZARDS

MAGIC, PROTECTION, AND HEALING IN BURMESE BUDDHISM

THOMAS NATHAN PATTON

Columbia University Press
New York

Columbia University Press
Publishers Since 1893
New York   Chichester, West Sussex
cup.columbia.edu

Library of Congress Cataloging-in-Publication Data
Names: Patton, Thomas Nathan, author.
Title: The Buddha's wizards : magic, protection, and healing in Burmese
  Buddhism / Thomas Nathan Patton.
Description: New York : Columbia University Press, 2018. | Includes
  bibliographical references and index.
Identifiers: LCCN 2018010997 (print) | LCCN 2018033294 (ebook) |
  ISBN 9780231547376 (electronic) | ISBN 9780231187602 (cloth : alk. paper)
Subjects: LCSH: Buddhism—Burma. | Burma—Religious life and customs. |
  Wizards—Burma. | Occultism—Burma.
Classification: LCC BQ438 (ebook) | LCC BQ438 .P38 2018 (print) | DDC
  294.3/43309591—dc23
LC record available at https://lccn.loc.gov/2018010997

Columbia University Press books are printed on permanent and
durable acid-free paper.
Printed in the United States of America

Cover design: Milenda Nan Ok Lee
Cover image: U Bho Thi Library, Thaton, white parabaik ms 1.
Photo courtesy D. Christian Lammerts.

For my Triratna*: Oiyan, Rosalie, and Anneliese*

CONTENTS

ACKNOWLEDGMENTS

would not have been able to complete this book had it not been for the kindness of many people. It has been my very good fortune to have had Anne Blackburn as my teacher, mentor, and friend over these many years. I thank her for believing that the research for this book was worth pursuing, which encouraged me to continue with this study. The book has greatly benefited from Anne's guidance, keen insights, and good judgment. A great debt of gratitude also goes to Erik Braun, Lilian Handlin, D. Christian Lammerts, and Alicia Turner. Erik not only read most of this manuscript in earlier drafts but also went out of his way to thoughtfully answer my numerous questions related to publishing and academia in general. Lilian read the entire manuscript with care and offered both excellent suggestions and images that helped improve the quality of this book. Christian provided motivation for this project from its initial stages and has been more than generous in sharing with me any source he has come across. Alicia has always been willing to drop what she was doing to offer sound advice whenever I needed it. The intellectual and personal support that all of the above people have given me over the course of this project cannot be overstated. Their friendship and academic camaraderie have meant much to me, and I have turned to them on countless occasions for moral support and drawn on their vast knowledge of Buddhism and Burma studies, which they have shared selflessly. This book would have never even gotten off the ground had it not been for the enduring and generous help I received from friends and colleagues in Myanmar. My friend and research assistant, Toe Win, accompanied me on many research trips and, with the help of his mother, nursed me back to health on the many occasions I fell ill. Some of my fondest memories in Mandalay are of us relaxing, sipping tea at one of the local tea shops. Soe Kyaw Thu selflessly and diligently collected and shared dozens of crucial documents for this study, as well as introduced me to numerous individuals who follow the *weizzā* path. Likewise, Dr. Tin Maung Kyi shared valuable and rare sources with me and explained, with care and patience, the intricate world of the *weizzā*. Dr. Than Tun Sein took time out of his busy schedule on several occasions to drive me to remote *weizzā* places of interest and shared with me his knowledge about particular *weizzā* saints. Daw Mi Mi and Daw Khin Soe Aye were like older sisters to me and always made sure I was adequately fed and in good health. The nuns of Maukathiwon Thilashin Kyaung allowed me to stay in their nunnery on multiple occasions.

I began this project while still a doctoral student at Cornell University and, therefore, would like to acknowledge the support and mentorship of the faculty of the Cornell Southeast Asia Program and the Department of Asian Studies, particularly Brett de Bary, Thak Chaloemtiarana, Tamara Loos, Jane Marie Law, Stanley O'Connor, San San Hnin Tun, Eric Tagliacozzo, and Keith Taylor. From my very first semester as a graduate student, Daniel Gold was supportive and encouraging, providing sound advice at every step of the way. Andrew Willford's brilliance and kindness have been an inspiration, and our long chats over the years have been instrumental in developing this book. Magnus Fiskesjö provided valuable comments on chapter 4. While at Cornell, other people also helped me a great deal. I thank Claudine Ang, Jack Chia, Lawrence Chua, Pamela

Corey, Jane Ferguson, Nina Hien, Samson Lim, Rosalie Metro, Lorraine Patterson, Trais Pearson, Cuong Pham, John Phan, and Erick White. Beyond Cornell and Myanmar, I am indebted to many friends and colleagues. Yin Ker shared with me sources related to the *weizzā* that she came across. Conversations with Niklas Foxeus, as well as his own research on the *weizzā*, have been an inspiration. Min Zin Oo sat with me on many occasions, helping me to decipher some of the more cryptic of *weizzā* texts. Bo Bo Lansin provided me with rare *weizzā*-related images. In my early stages of research, Kyaw Myaing taught me the basics of the *weizzā* path. Mi Khin Khin Soe generously supported a follow-up research trip in 2011. Patrick Pranke, Keiko Tosa, Bénédicte Brac de la Perrière, and Guillaume Rozenberg gave sound advice regarding undertaking fieldwork related to the *weizzā* in Myanmar. Chie Ikeya's advice was invaluable during the initial stages of writing. John Ferguson invited me to his home during his last days and shared with me fascinating stories and documents regarding his research on *weizzā*. Janet Gyatso, Kimberley Patton, and Donald Swearer patiently answered my numerous research-related questions. Jason Carbine, Erik Davis, Jane Lapeña, Brooke Shedneck, and Luke Thompson have also given me valuable assistance. Very special thanks go to Justin McDaniel, who generously read the entire manuscript with great care and provided suggestions, comments, and critiques that helped me turn my initial manuscript from something I was merely content with to something I am now truly proud of. Richard Fox also read the entire manuscript, and his input has much improved the work and motivated me to rethink the ways I translate some of the Burmese terms into English. Anne Hansen also read large chunks of the book, provided detailed comments, and was the person who first encouraged me to look at the role of affect in Burmese Buddhism. Thanks go also to Juliane Schober and Steven Collins, who read most of this work and gave sage advice at various points of writing and research. Julia Cassaniti offered excellent suggestions on an earlier draft of the book.

My colleagues at the City University of Hong Kong have been very supportive. Toby Carroll and Bradley Williams have been good friends since the day I arrived, and Mark Thompson has continued to be a trusted mentor. Thanks also go to Birgit Bunzel Linder, Paul Cammack, Nan Choi, Federico Ferrara, Ruben Gonzalez Vicente, Jonathan London, Alina Ortwein, Justin Robertson, Sean Starrs, and Nicholas Thomas.

My research was funded by a Fulbright-Hays Fellowship from the U.S. Department of Education. Intensive Burmese language instruction was conducted thanks to the Blakemore-Freeman Fellowship. I have also received generous financial assistance from the Cornell University Graduate School, Cornell Southeast Asia Program, Mario Einaudi Center, and U.S. Department of State. I would like also to express my appreciation to the College of Arts and Social Sciences and Department of Asian and International Studies at the City University of Hong Kong for additional fellowships and research funding that insured this project came to a timely completion.

I would also like to thank the team at Columbia University Press for helping to bring this book to publication: Publisher of Philosophy and Religion Wendy Lochner for taking a chance on my book; Associate Editor Lowell Frye for overseeing its production; Production Editing Manager Leslie Kriesel for carefully copyediting the text and making useful suggestions; and Senior Designer Milenda Lee for creating the book's cover. Thank you as well to Do Mi Stauber for painstakingly indexing the book.

My family: parents, Tom and Kathy, and sister, Jacklyn. They continually encouraged me to do what I love, no matter how unpopular it was at the time. They have been a constant source of love, concern, support, and strength all these years. I would like to express my heartfelt gratitude to them.

My friends Christopher Keyser, Christopher Mack, and James Snyder have been an endless source of strength over the years.

An enormous amount of thanks goes to my in-laws. They provided warm and loving homes for me over the years of my writing this book. I am grateful to have such supportive family members.

I thank my daughters, Rosalie and Anneliese, for motivating me to finish this project in good time, especially as you asked me on a daily basis: "Is your book done yet, Daddy?"

Most of all, I thank my wife, colleague, and best friend, Oiyan Liu, who shared with me the adventures and headaches of research, writing, and teaching even while she had her own research, writing, and teaching to do. Being lucky enough to meet her during the first month of my graduate program and experiencing the ups and downs of graduate school and postgraduate life together is worth more than completing one hundred books. She continues to be my greatest source of strength and encouragement.

A NOTE ON ABBREVIATIONS

In citing my interviews, I used a number and letter notation system to protect the source's privacy and to give the reader essential information about the source. For example, the code "Interview KM-M-35" means:

Interview = face-to-face interview
Pers. comm. = informal discussion
Correspondence = communication via letters or emails
KM = fictional initials for the source, but consistent throughout so that the reader will know who is saying what
M = sex (man; W = woman)
35 = age
? = I was unable to ascertain that specific information

I have not altered the personal information of interviewees who appeared in popular religious magazines. If known, their name, sex, age, and city of residence are presented as they appear in the interview and follow the same abbreviation format as above, with the addition of the magazine title in which the interview appears.

A NOTE ON TRANSLITERATION

Scholars working with Burmese typically write a Burmese word with a phonetic transcription that approximates its pronunciation rather than the ALA-LC Romanization system used by the Library of Congress (LOC) for cataloging Burmese-language book holdings. Transliterating according to pronunciation helps to avoid rendering words with diacritics that bear little resemblance to how they sound. For example, "Yangon" is written "Ranʻ kunʼ" in strict LOC transliteration. In the body of the text, I use the phonetic transcription, but for sources that appear in the bibliography, I give the LOC transliteration so that anyone who wants to find those sources in the library can do so. John Okell (1971) recommended a "standard conventional transcription system" to phonetically write Burmese words, which I use for the body of the text.

INTRODUCTION

P assing out from a 105-degree fever, I collapsed onto the floor of my Burmese language tutor's home after a late dinner. What happened thereafter was mostly a blur, but I was eventually able to piece together the following series of events. The Buddhist nunnery in which I was living was twenty miles away, too far for me to get to in my current state. I had forgotten to bring my passport with me, thus making it impossible for me to stay at a hotel for the night. In 2006, it was against the law for a foreigner to spend the night at the home of a local. Fearful that the local authorities would learn that a foreigner was illegally staying at his home and unable to find a doctor at such a late hour, my tutor had an idea. Propping me up in the back of his motor scooter, he drove me to his parents' home nearby. "You'll be safe there," I remember him saying. "My father has developed a severe case of paranoia and has turned his home into a walled fortress in fear of imaginary robbers."

When we arrived, his parents were sleeping. My tutor woke them while I sat on their sofa in agonizing pain. I overheard the father refuse me refuge because he feared I was a CIA agent who had been drugged by an enemy. The father was very sure of this, as he "saw it in American movies many times." I let out a moan of pain, and after much negotiation, he finally relented and said I could stay, so long as it was outside the main house.

I awoke at 4:00 a.m. My fever had broken, and I was feeling well enough to get up and walk around. I had a vague idea where I was and desperately wanted to get back to my apartment. I tried to open the door, but to my surprise, I found it was locked from the outside! It was still dark, and no one in the compound was awake yet. I managed to carefully work my hand through a jagged hole in the window and unbolt the door. Exiting the room, I was shocked to see that they had put me in a storage closet and laid me down on a mattress placed atop sacks of rice.

As I crept out, the guard dogs woke up and immediately surrounded me. Their barking woke up my tutor's father, who, in a matter of seconds, was at the front door brandishing a knife. I told him that I was leaving. I thanked him for letting me sleep in his storage closet and said that I really needed to get home. With a snarl he went back into his dark room and reluctantly reappeared with the key, the dogs still surrounding me. He unlocked the gate, and I scampered away into the night. My adrenaline was pumping, and I just wanted to get out of there. I was also afraid the police would come.

Because it was so early in the morning, there was no public transportation up and running to bring me back to my apartment. The only place for me to go was a monastic compound adjacent to the house. There was already a large group of people gathered at the compound to do their morning rituals of chanting, meditating, and offering food to monks. Exhausted and ill, I felt helpless, alone, and on the verge of tears. Shuffling over to a quiet corner, I sat down crossed-legged, closed my eyes, and fell asleep sitting up.

I awoke a couple of hours later covered in sweat from the heat of the morning sun. Disoriented and thirsty, I looked around me and noticed that while I was sleeping, someone had placed a small laminated photo of an old man on my bag. Although I did not know who this person was, I remembered seeing images of him throughout my travels in the country.

That afternoon I checked myself into a hospital in Mandalay. I was diagnosed with dengue fever and remained in the hospital for a week. On the second day of my stay, I showed my doctor the small laminated photo of the old man and asked him who he was. The doctor held the photograph, and with a smile on his face replied, "This is Bo Min Gaung. He is a *weizzā*. How would you say this in English? A Buddhist wizard." As he passed the photo around the room to the nurses and orderlies, they all began chatting in earnest about this Bo Min Gaung. I immediately became fixated on the words "Buddhist wizard," and my fever-induced dreams became filled with images of Merlin the magician, Gandalf the Grey, and Harry Potter wearing Buddhist monk robes.

I quickly became known throughout the ward as the foreigner curious about *weizzā*. Over the next several days, nurses, orderlies, doctors, and patients stopped by my bed to tell me personal stories about their encounters with these wizards. There was the doctor who told me of a little girl suffering from an incurable disease who was cured when a *weizzā* wrapped his cloak around her. Then there was the nurse who recounted the dream she had of a wizard-saint giving her winning lottery numbers. I too became part of the web of stories circulating about Bo Min Gaung. In my short time at the hospital, people began telling my story and entreated me to share it with others: a foreigner, far from home and suffering from illness, was visited by a *weizzā*, which ultimately led to his healing and initial interest in the *weizzā*. My story became just another of dozens of such tales I heard during my hospital stay.

To this day, I interpret the situation much differently than those I spoke with. For me, it was a coincidence that, marked by the intensity of the situation in which it occurred, took on life of its own. By the time I was discharged, I was fascinated by these wizards and the people who say their lives were touched by them, and over the next ten years, I set about traveling the country, collecting more stories about the *weizzā*. To those I spoke with in the hospital, it was a moment when, to use Robert Orsi's words, "the transcendent broke into time."[1]

Admittedly, magical wizards with supernatural powers flying around the world healing the sick, taking over the minds and bodies of men, women, and children, and defending the religion from the forces of evil did not fit with the vision of Buddhism that I had when I first began doing research in Myanmar. But this is exactly what I encountered in a country where the majority of people abide by Theravada Buddhism—a form of Buddhism often perceived, by people both in and outside of the religion, as stoic and staid, lacking religious devotion and elements of the supernatural.

Based on a decade of fieldwork in Myanmar and a cross-disciplinary approach (religious studies, anthropology, history), this book explores the last one hundred years of Burmese Buddhists' devotion to Buddhist wizards, known in Myanmar as *weizzā*, to argue that understanding their protective power in the lives of the devout is the key to understanding their persistence in the modern period.[2] The wizards who are believed to possess such magic, and their devotees who harness it, are thought to manipulate the natural world around them to enact real changes. To make this point, I situate religious narratives, magical practices, and ritual works involving Buddhist wizards and their devotees within a broader landscape of Burmese Buddhist traditions and contemporary social dynamics in Myanmar, as well as within the more intimate setting of devotees' lives.

I explore the performance of Buddhist thought and ritual through practices of magic, spirit possession, image production, sacred protection, and healing through a variety of genres and media to learn about the construction, contestation, and maintenance of the Burmese Buddhist wizard-saint phenomenon specifically, and religion in contemporary Myanmar more broadly. Potency, especially the power to affect the world, explains the continuing presence of wizards in the lives of Burmese devotees, and by examining the intimate bonds that devotees form with various wizard-saints, I show that these relationships and the perceived benefits gained from them are formed in an ongoing, dynamic relation with the realities and structures of everyday life in particular times and places. The devotees' experiences reveal insights into the interface between ordinary individuals and a larger network of forces—social norms and expectations, religious constructs, economic and political pressures, and historical conditions—and how these forces are expressed through the bonds formed with the wizards. For instance, the wizards' protective power and devotees' visionary experiences can take on aggressively affective tones in moments of political crises and social upheaval. Moments of being possessed by a wizard or having wizard-laden dreams during periods of familial or medical hardships are thought to imbue the devotee with certain supernatural powers that can be used to change their lives for the better. Therefore, *weizzā* devotees do not simply act; they narrate themselves as actors in an attempt to make sense of the world they live in. The stories they tell and interpret are part of their engagement with the world, and it is necessary to study beliefs and practices together with the people who use these ideas in the definite circumstances of their everyday lives.

Although the Buddha is considered dead and the Pāli Canon of Buddhist scriptures closed, revelation is still ongoing for those devotees who enter into relationships with Buddhist wizard-saints. The *weizzā* appear in dreams, in visions, in person, or through spirit mediums to impart new teachings, meditation practices, magical spells, iconography, and, in some cases, supernatural powers. I examine the experiences, perceptions, and revelations that have arisen from these relationships to show that they develop from a specific set of social and practical engagements and draw upon particular cultural repertoires. Moreover, this book investigates *weizzā* devotees' visionary and emotionally charged experiences that occur at their interfaces with the wizards to show how both the felt anomalous nature of such experiences and the attribution processes through which they are considered special are shaped into religious ideas and stable teachings and institutions in contemporary Myanmar.

AFFECTIVE TURN TO RELIGION

In this book, I trace the intimate bonds between wizard-saints and their devotees to argue that seeing religion in these relational terms allows for a great deal of fluidity and variation. Not everyone has the same kind of connections, needs, or aspirations in their religious practices, and examining these personal relationships can uncover the experiences devotees consider central to their lives, along with the varied rituals and practices that make up their personal religious expressions.[3] From this approach, we can begin to understand contemporary patterns of religiosity in Myanmar. Grappling with the complexities, apparent inconsistencies, heterogeneity, and untidiness of the range of religious practices that people in any given culture partake in and find meaningful and useful is valuable, for it reveals important things about religious traditions and the ways people incorporate them into their daily lives that we might not otherwise recognize.

Focusing on relationships, experiences, and expression leads, then, to "affect." I attempt to understand how it "feels" to be in a relationship with a wizard-saint. The study of affect is, at its heart, the study of people and their relationships. By using "affect," I am referring to the name we give those intuitive forces "beneath, alongside, or generally *other than* conscious knowing, that drive [a body] to act and be acted upon."[4] Affect includes nonverbal modes of transmitting feelings and influence between bodies and how they influence the ways bodies flow into relationships with other bodies.[5] As we will see throughout this book, this refers to more than just human bodies or even sentient bodies. *Weizzā* devotees enter into relationships with, affect, and are affected by immaterial bodies (spirits, apparitions, and dreams), and material bodies (images, statues, and pagodas). In this sense, affect makes up the relations the devotees create and by which they are created.

When I use the term "affect," I am also referring to emotion.[6] Indeed, I would argue that emotion is such a central component of peoples' religious lives that, following the advice of John Corrigan, "the study of religion must attune itself to the emotional realities of its practitioners if it is to grasp the complex textures of lived religion."[7] For many *weizzā* devotees, the recognition of the emotional tone of the relationship they have with the wizard-saint is a religious goal in itself. I came to see that the stories devotees share about their relationships with the *weizzā*, the images and objects they use to remind them of or interact with the *weizzā*, and even the dreams and visions they experience of certain *weizzā* evoke a wide range of emotions, and are, to use Jennifer Scheper Hughes's words, "bearers of affective memory." The means by which devotees interact with the *weizzā* are "repositories of emotion" whereby religious feelings are encoded in these affective bodies themselves.[8]

While affect theory has recently been applied to a number of fields of research, including cultural studies, sociology, neuroscience and cognitive science, gender and sexuality studies, and politics, it has rarely been applied to religious studies. The only full-length work employing affect theory in the study of religion is Donovan Schaefer's recent book, *Religious Affects*.[9] I have been particularly influenced by Schaefer's affective turn, especially in asking, "In what ways is religion . . . about the way things feel, the things we want, the way our bodies are guided through thickly textured, magnetized worlds?"[10] Following Schaefer, I argue that people's religious beliefs and practices are intimately tied with their bodies. Such embodied, affective processes and responses are instant and instinctive, working at both the conscious and unconscious levels.[11] The affective turn in religious studies is important because it provides a means, outside of language, texts, and beliefs, for examining the transmission and operation of power,[12] which, in this book, pertains to the power of protection: protection of the Buddha *sāsana* (the teachings of the Buddha and the institutions and practices that support them), protection of the mental and physical well-being of *weizzā* devotees, and protection of the nation of Myanmar. Acknowledging that power resides in "the body's affects" and that one's religion is intimately interwoven "with a complex of material sensations emerging out of an affectively driven, embodied practice" highlights "the many modes in which religion, like other forms of power, feels before it thinks, believes, or speaks."[13]

While this book is both an affective and an emotive turn to the study of Buddhism in contemporary Myanmar, it constitutes a material and pictorial turn as well. *The Buddha's Wizards* provides some of the first forays into the study of Burmese Buddhist material and visual culture. Indeed, as Justin McDaniel points out in his study of material and visual culture in Thai Buddhism, the "stuff" through which beliefs are articulated have been "overlooked in the study of religion, even in many studies in the growing field of material culture and religion," and Burmese Buddhist studies is no exception.[14] Burmese Buddhist meditation and monasticism have been popular subjects for scholars of religion in Myanmar, but given that the majority of Buddhists in the country neither meditate nor ordain as monastics, it is surprising that more attention has not been given to statues, chromolithographs, photographs, Buddhist telling beads, amulets, religious magazines, and pagodas, among other "stuff," that matter a great deal to everyday Buddhists.

Inspired by the work of David Morgan, I show how material and visual objects help create and preserve the worlds in which the wizard-saints and their devotees reside. The objects and images devotees use in their engagements with the *weizzā* are, in Morgan and Promey's words, "nonverbal articulation of space, property, the past, present, and future, kinship, status, value, power, authority, friendship, alliance, loyalty, affection, sentiment, order, ethnicity, class, race, gender, sexuality, eating, dying, birthing, aging, memory, and nationhood—among other things."[15] I take this approach one step further, however, by applying affect to the study of the "lives" of religious bodies and the ways these bodies evoke and shape emotion in those they come into contact with.[16] As I mentioned above, these bodies do not refer to sentient beings only. In chapters 3 and 5, for instance, we will encounter material and visual objects that, although not sentient, are nonetheless understood by *weizzā* devotees to possess energy and agency. This "vital materialist" approach, as Jennifer Scheper Hughes refers to it, attributes "agentic potency" to objects that are not merely symbolic representations of internal mental states but have the power to affect "social relations, behaviors, and outcomes" and are "subject-actors within particular religious communities" in their own rights.[17]

Finally, the affective turn to religion allows me to "become attentive to the nimbus of affects whose dynamics move along and make worlds, situations, and environments."[18] To this end, I am choosing to look at affect at the intersection of *weizzā* devotees' experiences that arise from interaction with material and visual objects; from dreams and visions; and from encounters with *weizzā* in apparitional or flesh-and-blood forms. Using Ann Taves's theoretical work on anomalous experiences, I have chosen to focus on those experiences, feelings, visions, etc. that *weizzā* devotees themselves consider anomalous and worth taking note of. The Burmese words that devotees use to describe the emotionally charged experiences that arise from their unions with the *weizzā* can be translated into English as "unusual," "strange," and "special," and their relationships often involve gaining "supernatural powers" as a result of "following a path." Likewise, Taves's recent work on religious studies theory reframes religious experiences as those that people deem "anomalous," "strange," or "special" and are often associated with "nonordinary powers" that are attributed to a goal-oriented "path." Some experiences, sensations, feelings, and emotions are more important than others and are what devotees share with one another in person, in hospital rooms, on internet websites, and in the pages of monthly magazines. The importance lies in their anomalies, or "things that people consider special because they are strange or unusual or in some way violate people's ordinary expectations."[19] This "specialness" encapsulates what both the reader and my interlocutors may have in mind in terms of what might be considered magic, paranormal, spiritual, and mystical.[20] Applying Taves's theory involving unusual events, places, objects, and experiences, the book explores both the felt anomalous nature of such experiences and the attribution processes through which these experiences are considered special and, in some cases, shaped into religious ideas and stable teachings and institutions in contemporary Myanmar. As a result, this book contributes to Taves's call for "a cognitively and/or affectively based typology of experiences often deemed religious."[21] And this opens up potential comparative work with other religious traditions whose devout experience similar kinds of anomalies.

SOURCES AND FIELDWORK

In sources most scholars would have ignored, I hear life-giving voices. And I hope that these voices will deepen readers' respect for the individuals who appear in this book. Readers may even recognize in them the voices of devout men and women from any number of religious traditions around the world, and perhaps even from their own lives. I hope to show that what these devotees have to say is important: providing us with a window into the personal lives of Burmese Buddhists, their families and friends, their religious lives, and their relationships with otherworldly saints who have a very immediate presence.

My model for undertaking a study of lived religion in Myanmar takes seriously the Burmese devotees' beliefs and practices on their own terms and for their own sake. And while I attempt to approximate the worldview of the people whose lives are enriched by the *weizzā*, I offer a synoptic narrative, as Jennifer Scheper Hughes defines it: "a comprehensive view of events pieced together from disparate and varied perspectives [where] multiple voices, including scholarly ones" are allowed to flesh out the lives and practices of *weizzā* devotees.[22] I try whenever possible to give the devotees the last word, for their relationship with the *weizzā* makes them, in my view, the ultimate authority—not because I believe them to possess some direct and unmediated access to divine forces but rather, "it is this very contingency that makes theirs the privileged voice."[23]

My examination, then, deals with people who develop strong bonds with these wizard-saints and who share a common set of practices, stories, and beliefs regardless of their organizational affiliation, and therefore differs from previous works on the *weizzā*. Niklas Foxeus (2011) gave us an in-depth historical and ethnographic analysis of a single *weizzā* organization in upper Myanmar, especially focusing on the chief members and their writings. Guillaume Rozenberg's (2015) anthropological examination of a specific *weizzā* cult and its leaders was a similarly narrow study. My project is more synchronic in range, about the *weizzā* phenomenon as it is found broadly in contemporary Myanmar, especially as it relates to healing and devotional practices, while at the same time a diachronic examination of how such beliefs and practices developed over the past century. This book is certainly concerned with some of the more prominent wizard-saints (one of whom, Bo Min Gaung, will appear continually throughout these chapters), but it is centrally a study of the people whose lives are touched by them. These people may not belong to an organized *weizzā* association or engage in any practices directly related to the goals of an aspiring *weizzā*, but as the forthcoming chapters reveal, they still align themselves with the *weizzā* path, or at least acknowledge that the practices and beliefs of the wizard-saints play important roles in their lives.

The research for this book was carried out in the cities of Mandalay and Yangon and their environs while I was living in Myanmar for extended periods of time between 2006 and 2011. I engaged in additional fieldwork during subsequent trips to the country in 2013, 2014, and 2016. Much of the research is based on interviews, conversations, and correspondences with the devotees—all together making up the most important foundation of primary sources. And in many ways, this source material shaped how the research unfolded. My overall interview method was not to hide my own intentions but rather to reveal to my interlocutors what I was thinking and, in turn, not edit their responses. I took seriously their claims of the realities, relationships, and results of the *weizzā* they relished telling me about. I attempted to interweave the apparatus of anthropology, history, religious and cultural studies, and at times psychology in a nonintrusive manner while allowing the lives and voices of the devotees to remain in the foreground. Thus this study, while not acknowledging the reality of the *weizzā*, does not attempt to reduce my interlocutors' religious experiences to merely mental fabrications. When retelling devotees' stories I have tried to preserve as much as possible each individual's style and idiosyncrasies in translating the words into English, a language only a handful spoke or wrote. I give sustained attention to the voices and writings of and about individual devotees and the *weizzā* themselves.

In addition to testimonies of the devout, long-term participant observations during periods of time when I was an ordained Buddhist monk in Myanmar, and a plethora of traditional historical sources (manuscripts, travelers reports, murals, chronicles) from the nineteenth to the twenty-first centuries, *The Buddha's Wizards* draws on popular Buddhist periodicals, scores of magazines, personal journals, and even websites that focus on the *weizzā* and their devotees, thus offering a study of Burmese Buddhism in general, and Buddhist magical practices in particular, that use these popular media. As I demonstrate through rich narrative analysis, the stories, interviews, and even magical spells that appear in these sources offer unique narrative spaces in twentieth- and twenty-first-century Burmese religious life, an avenue where the difficulties and complexities of the intersection of religion and modern life are unambiguously disclosed. Through these media, we see what really matters to Burmese Buddhists—which of their popular traditions are remembered and transmitted, and how aspects of these social processes of transmission and memory affect how the beliefs surrounding the wizards change, develop, and endure.

CHAPTER OUTLINE

The chapters in *The Buddha's Wizards* are arranged so that the book moves thematically and chronologically. Thematically, each chapter is a window into how and why the *weizzā* and their devout interact to enact change in the world around them. The book looks at different displays of magic, visionary experiences, and spirit possession to address the themes of protection, religious propagation, wish fulfillment, healing, and political manipulation. Chronologically, it begins in the late nineteenth century, tracing the possible origins and evolution of the figure we now refer to as *weizzā*. The book continues with a discussion of the initial formation of wizard-saint associations as a response to threats from colonial rule and moves on through the twentieth century and the beginning of the twenty-first century to show how devotees' relationships with wizard-saints transformed in response to the changing sociopolitical situation.

Chapter 1 begins with an introduction to the *weizzā*, their powers, and their appearances in the world as understood by their devotees. Drawing upon historical accounts from Burmese Buddhist popular magazines, biographies of wizard-saints, and devotional tracts, the chapter concentrates on the power of protection by showing how the wizard-saints and their devotees believe that they have been, and still are, on the frontline in the battle for both Myanmar's and Buddhism's survival against perceived forces of evil. The chapter examines how the wizards and their devotees organize paramilitary secret associations, or what I call "Buddhist Salvation Armies," whose goals are to use Buddhist rituals and magic spells to fend off, and in some instances violently destroy, their targets. Since the early twentieth century, groups of Burmese Buddhist wizards and their followers have taken on the duty of guarding the Buddha's *sāsana* from colonial, ideological, and religious threats. *Sāsana* (the teachings of the Buddha and the institutions and practices that support them) and how it should be sustained in the face of its inevitable demise has been a central concern of these societies expressed in their textual, oral, and visual representations. In particular, the chapter analyzes the factors and strains of discourse that have shaped religious motivations for national defense (both violent and metaphysical) and how these wizard societies have responded to different historical circumstances and perceptions of threats by colonial, ideological, and non-Buddhist forces.

In chapter 2 I analyze how an old man named Bo Min Gaung (1885–1952) with severe psychological disorders could have risen to the rank of "Chief Wizard," second only to the Buddha, in such a short period of time. The chapter focuses on this most revered Burmese wizard-saint in order to understand what about this figure, and others like him, inspires such faith and devotion among everyday Burmese. Drawing from biographies of Bo Min Gaung, interviews with people who knew him personally, and the experiences of his devotees, the chapter examines the biographic process through which the figure of Bo Min Gaung has been created in publicly circulating oral and written sources to show that his devotees expand his biography through their own experiences of him. I discuss how his elevation to the status of wizard-saint was tied up with the events of World War II when Allied air forces bombed his village, Japanese soldiers attempted to assassinate him, and Burmese Communist insurgents imprisoned and interrogated him. From these events, his devotees began to transform his biography after the war into something very personalized, with an expansiveness of the past, present, and future linked to their understanding of their own experiences, karmic biography, and aspirations. The chapter ends by explaining how the selective appropriation of visual images of Bo Min Gaung and physical engagement with these images reveals another dimension of the personalized relationship to the saint, as well as revealing how Bo Min Gaung as icon becomes a powerful focus for personalized affect.

Evoking visions, possessions, and healing, chapter 3 examines the Burmese cultural atmosphere in which magazines, devotional literature, and other forms of popular media all recognize, endorse, and publicize the ways certain Buddhist wizard-saints interact with their mostly female devotees to heal specific illnesses. The chapter argues that these female devotees becoming possessed by a saint and carrying out his bidding can be seen as a creative yet culturally sanctioned response to restrictive gender roles, a means for expressing otherwise illicit thoughts or feelings, and an economic strategy for women who have few options beyond traditional wife or daughter roles. Young women who can channel the spirit of a powerful male *weizzā*, for example, are able to renegotiate the often silent and passive roles assigned to them by the religious and medical culture by setting the experience of sickness into a new narrative framework where the wizards are the source of all healing. Women express their own needs and desires and, through their relationship with the saints, find the strength to insist on them. On another level, illness is recast as a sacred drama in which the healing power is understood to come ultimately from the wizard-saints, whether they are entreated or not. Though the women never directly challenge the social structures that oppress them, through the power of their wishes and within the flexible parameters of devotional practice, they are able to enact significant and positive changes in their lives and the lives of those around them.

In the spring of 1958, on a small farm in western New York State, the first Burmese Buddhist monk to ever set foot in the United States erected the very first Theravada pagoda on American soil. It wasn't any ordinary pagoda. It was a *weizzā* pagoda that the monk had constructed at the behest of Bo Min Gaung, the wizard-saint who figures throughout this book. In chapter 4, I focus on the main themes raised in the preceding chapters, namely, *sāsana* protection, the cult of Bo Min Gaung, and devotees' anomalously embodied experiences of the wizard-saints, in order to examine the roles they play in the lives of devotees who engage in one of the most common, yet powerful, activities thought to help manifest the wizard-saints' teachings here in the world: pagoda construction. Devotees dedicate extensive amounts of time, energy, and especially money—perhaps more than to any other activity—to erecting pagodas in various parts of Myanmar and, as the Burmese diasporic communities continue to grow, the world. Such religious structures are believed to protect the Buddhist religion and its adherents wherever they may reside, help harness and make physically manifest the wizards' power here on Earth, and help usher in a new era of peace and prosperity.

Chapter 5 takes up issues of *weizzā* devotion marginality in contemporary Myanmar by examining reasons for expressed hostility and mistrust toward the wizard phenomenon from segments of Myanmar's governmental and ecclesiastical authorities, and how such notions have begun to change in light of a renewed interest in the wizard-saints among large segments of the affluent lay population. I proceed with an examination of the belief among devotees that the most powerful Burmese Buddhist wizards have used their magic to manipulate the recent political and societal turn of events in Myanmar. Like a Burmese-style Illuminati, the wizards are thought to have clandestinely orchestrated a series of events starting with the 1988 nationwide popular pro-democracy uprising and continuing with the opening up of Myanmar today, and to be ultimately responsible for the political, social, and economic transformations that have taken place.

THE
BUDDHA'S
WIZARDS

1

VANGUARDS OF THE *SĀSANA*

In 1906, a Burmese Buddhist wizard-monk who possessed supernatural powers walked right into the British-occupied Mandalay Palace. Thinking him to be mad, the Indian soldiers who were there under British command at the time ordered the monk to leave. When he refused, the soldiers began beating him with their batons. However, the more they struck the monk, the calmer he became and the angrier the soldiers got. The monk said to them, "It does not hurt me, but it hurts you."

Suddenly, each time one of the soldiers hit the monk, a sharp pain was felt by all the soldiers! Asking for his forgiveness, the soldiers ceased hitting the monk and bowed to him, paying their respects. Seeing this, the British commanders became angry and sent their biggest, strongest soldier to deal with the monk. This soldier beat the magic monk mercilessly, but the monk only said, "It does not hurt me, but it hurts you." Like the others, this soldier felt pain each time he struck the monk. The soldier put down his weapon in reverent awe.

The British commanders then had the monk arrested and placed in a jail cell, and over time, the British head minister of this regiment became amazed at the monk's demeanor and abilities. In prison, he never saw the monk lie down, eat or drink, or try to hurt or kill any insects, and he never lost weight even though he never slept or ate. Eventually, even this British head minister felt such respect for the monk that he too got down on his knees to pay his respects. As soon as the minister finished bowing, the wizard-monk said, "Okay, my work here is done," and suddenly disappeared from the jail cell.

The above is a popular story that was (and continues to be) shared among *weizzā* devotees as an example of how they and the wizard-saints they emulated could imagine themselves engaging external, non-Buddhist powers that threatened their country. Central to this story for those who told it was the message that, despite facing hostile forces, the Buddha's *sāsana* (the teachings of the Buddha and the institutions and practices that support them) would continue to flourish thanks to the intervention and protection of the wizard-saints and their followers.

Weizzā, their devotees, and the organizations they belong to have always been primarily concerned with ensuring that the Buddha *sāsana* continued to thrive in Myanmar, and ideally, throughout the world. The *sāsana*, and how it should be sustained in the face of inevitable decline, has meant different things to different people, and even different things to the same person or group, depending on context. To illustrate this tension between endurance and change, this chapter explores ideas of the life cycle of the *sāsana* and how they intersect with *weizzā* activities, particularly how ideas about *sāsana* responsibility to wider communities of Buddhists become expressed through the intersection of *sāsana* and *weizzā*. We will begin by looking at early notions of *weizzā* and explore how the evolution of this figure has been tied to the ways devotees and organizations have understood their roles in *sāsana* protection and propagation.

WHAT IS A *WEIZZĀ*?

Probably the first appearance of the word *weizzā* outside of Myanmar can be found in *Reisen in Birma in den Jahren 1861-1862*, by the

German ethnologist Adolf Bastian. Describing images he sees sculpted on a boat, Bastian writes that "a stone seat meant for preaching monks to sit upon had, at its corners, a *naga* (serpent), *galon* (dragon), a *weizzā* (sage or magician), and King Koyopamingyi."[1] Shortly after, Adoniram Judson, in his 1893 *Burmese-English Dictionary*, glosses the word following the traditional Pāli meaning of "knowledge or wisdom." But he also includes the meaning of "one possessed of certain miraculous powers," following from his understanding of the term *weizzā-dho* (the Burmese pronunciation of the Pāli, *vijjādhara*). James George Scott makes reference in his 1910 book to *weizzā* as "good people" who can be divided into distinct types according to their specialties. He also notes that the word can simply refer to wisdom or knowledge, as well as the sorcery studied by those on the *weizzā* path.[2] The term appears a short time later in George Orwell's 1934 *Burmese Days*, although often denoting a charlatan or expert in legerdemain who "was said to have appeared from nowhere and to be prophesying the doom of the English power and distributing magic bullet-proof jackets."[3]

Just what kind of figures these writers were referring to is not clear. As there has traditionally been no systematized set of beliefs, practices, or attire distinguishing *weizzā* from other members of society, there must have been something about the appearance of these men that caused the writers to identify them as *weizzā*. Looking at how *weizzā* have been portrayed in earlier eras may give us a clue as to what such European writers encountered. When the king asked his religious advisor, Lord Lek-way-naw-yata, about *weizzā*, the advisor responded by citing an instance in the commentary to the *Dhammapada* where a *weizzā* appears, thus supporting the claim that *weizzā* and their practices are indeed part of the Buddha *sāsana*.[4] The *weizzā* in this story, the advisor says, is an example of a "Small *Weizzā*" (P. *Cūḷa-gandhari-mantat*) who has the ability to fly. Around this same period, the figure of a superhuman *vijjādhara* appears in an eighteenth-century Mon chronicle where a monk by the name of Gavampati was, in a previous life, born from the eggs that resulted from the sexual union of a *weizzā* and a serpent princess.[5]

In addition to the above-mentioned texts, there are hundreds, if not thousands, of manuscripts that may make no explicit mention of *weizzā* but are nonetheless associated with beliefs and practices of wizard-saints and that, as Christian Lammerts, a specialist in the Burmese manuscript tradition, writes, "one would expect to constitute the primary field of research for anyone interested in understanding the history of these traditions."[6] One is the *Kappālaṅkāra*, a palm-leaf manuscript about the *weizzā* that was allegedly compiled by a monk during the first century CE and is extant in an eighteenth-century Pāli-Burmese commentarial version. The text, which is still referenced in a wide range of contemporary *weizzā* sources, is meant to explain the meaning and varieties of a number of magical diagrams and spells used for a wide range of aims, such as achieving immortality, gaining supernatural powers, and averting danger.[7]

Iconographic representations of *weizzā* are rare, but there are instances in eighteenth- and nineteenth-century mural paintings. Wearing white robes and turbans, they resemble modern day *bodaw*—literally, "noble grandfather," religious mendicants who are almost always associated with the *weizzā* phenomenon in contemporary Myanmar. Others are portrayed wearing brown robes like that of a Burmese hermit (S: *rishi*; B: *ya-they*; T: *ruesi*). The list of beings at the bottom of a nineteenth-century mural painting, for example, portrays the *weizzā* as a white-clad figure nearly identical to that of a *bodaw*: "The Buddha entered *nibbāna* [nirvana] and his body was cremated. Monks, laypeople, Sakka, *devas, nagas, galons, weizzā,* and *zawgyi* came and paid homage." The *weizzā* being referred to is the figure in the center of the image wearing a white robe and turban (see fig. 1).[8] In an eighteenth-century mural that depicts a final scene from the *Bhuridatta Jataka*, the central figure is dressed in a brown hermit's robe and wears the characteristic hat (B. *dauk-cha*) of a hermit, and is referred to as *bodaw ya-they*, a conflation of the two figures mentioned above.[9]

Images of *weizzā* began to appear with increasing regularity as the use of *parabaik* (paper folding books) and other types of manuscripts became more widespread starting in the nineteenth century. Such manuscripts are important sources for understanding the historical development of the *weizzā* phenomenon as well as what scholars observe in contemporary Myanmar among Burmese Buddhists who associate themselves with the *weizzā* path. Until fairly recently, perhaps as late as the early twentieth century, *weizzā* were portrayed as four types of semidivine beings, not unlike *devas* and *nats* (see figs. 2, 3, and 4), that were associated with each of the four *weizzā* techniques (mastery of iron work, medicine, sacred diagrams, and alchemy). At other times they were portrayed wearing nineteenth-century military-style uniforms and associated with other kinds of *weizzā* who possess an array of supernatural powers.

The *weizzā* as we know him today most likely had his genesis in the anticolonial *min-laung* ("embryo king") and medicine man of the nineteenth and twentieth centuries. The period immediately following the annexation of Upper Myanmar by the British in 1885 was marked by insurrection. Immediately upon the dissolution of the monarchy, a host of charismatic individuals attempted to expel the British and protect the Buddhist religion, and in the process, make themselves rulers. Monks, hermits, *bodaw*, and medicine men all vied for power and quickly began exerting their influence over ever-growing groups of people, which quickly roused the concern and ire of the colonizers. British forces began, with increasing regularity, to fight against a whole host of religious, millennial, and paramilitary groups who rallied around the mission of protecting the Buddhist religion and expelling the British, often through supernatural means.

Sometime in the early to mid-twentieth century, however, such representations were replaced as understandings of what constituted a *weizzā* evolved. A *weizzā* came to include any human being—monastic, hermit, or lay—who who has gained supernatural powers and transformed him- or herself into a semidivine being through specific practices of alchemy, manipulation of cabalistic squares, or mastering of sacred verses (see fig. 5). The wizards who are understood to possess such power are thought to manipulate the natural world around them to enact changes for the benefit of their followers and the Buddha's *sāsana*. At the time of death, the *weizzā* exits this world to an otherworldly abode where they remain to help those in need and guard the Buddha's dispensation. *Weizzā* are also known in Burmese as "htwet yat pauk" beings. The compound *htwet yat pauk* can be understood and explained in two ways. For some, it means "to reach (*pauk*) the place (*yat*) of exit (*htwet*)," in reference to the "exit" both from the cycle of rebirths and toward nirvana. A second gloss is "to exit (*htwet*)" the cycle of rebirths—"to stop" (*yat*) rounds of rebirths—"to break out" (*pauk*) from the current earthly state. Such transformation is done in one of two ways: leaving dead (B. *athey-htwet*) or leaving alive (B. *ashin-htwet*). Those who attain *weizzā*-hood by the first method undergo a dying process similar to what an ordinary human being would experience, except that the spirit, or *nān*, leaves the body free to dwell where it wishes. Those who become *weizzā* in the latter way leave this world with their physical bodies intact to dwell in a nonhuman abode.[10]

ENCOUNTERING THE *WEIZZĀ*

Devotees usually come across *weizzā* for the first time in one of several ways: seeing a statue, picture, or prayer card of a particular *weizzā* hung at a pagoda, shrine, or someone's home; reading about them in a magazine or book; hearing about them from someone else, a family member, friend, or even a stranger with whom the *weizzā* had a brief encounter; or having a visual, aural, or mental experience of a *weizzā* either directly or through a medium. The defining characteristic of these first encounters need not be extreme need or despair, and the interaction may not have a profound impact on the person at that particular moment. In fact, many times a person would not even recognize the wizard-saint who had visited them until much later—either realizing the identity of the *weizzā* themselves or having it revealed to them by someone else, usually a fortune-teller. Only later, when a person faced a particular hardship in life, did their previous encounter with the *weizzā* present itself in all its profundity. During such intensely charged periods of suffering when a *weizzā* would appear to offer help, the person could always trace it back to their first ever encounter with that particular wizard-saint. Regardless of the circumstances, the first realization of such intervention in the life of the devotee was, to borrow Robert Orsi's words, "an emotional moment marked in memory and experience both by the intensity of its need and the suddenness of the saints' interventions," and those I spoke with and read about could remember these occasions in great detail.[11] "For years I would have a recurring dream of an old man telling me he would watch over and protect me," one Buddhist nun related to me. "He was distinguished, and I could tell he was powerful. But I had no idea who he was. When I was going through an especially sad period in my life, though, this older man appeared to me again in a dream, and it was then that I suddenly realized that he was a *weizzā*."[12]

A *weizzā* is believed to manifest himself (for the *weizzā* is always a male) to his human devout in several possible forms.[13] A devotee usually perceives the presence of a *weizzā* in dreams or through ritualized trance states. Devotees may also communicate with the wizard-saints through auditory or visual signs, bodily sensations, meditative states, telepathy, divination, prayer, and various forms of inspiration. Once cultivated, the relationship between a devotee and a *weizzā* can last a lifetime. All of these experiences are considered anomalous, because they are so extraordinary and, for the most part, so unexpected that those who have had them could hardly believe it. This was especially true of those who had been *weizzās*' most ardent critics. As with conversion stories the world over, the structure of *weizzā* convert accounts shared with me and in the pages of popular magazines and websites goes along the lines of: I was not a follower of a *weizzā* or the *weizzā* path, and in many cases was hostile to those who were, but a *weizzā* intervened in my life to help me in some way, whereupon I decided to become a devotee of this wizard-saint. The *weizzā* are unknown yet intimately recognizable, and their arrival has the quality of a perfectly timed appearance. The story I shared at the beginning of this book about the appearance of Bo Min Gaung in my life would certainly fit this genre of conversion narrative, except that I did not end up becoming a *weizzā* devotee. "Good enough," said one Bo Min Gaung follower when I shared this story with him. "Because you are an academic, Bo Min Gaung spoke to you in a language you can understand. When your *pāramī* (purification leading to enlightenment) increases, he will return and you will believe."[14]

It is not expected that devotees will have vivid aural or visual experiences of the *weizzā* power working in their lives, although this is common. In fact, many of the wizard-saints' most ardent devotees have never encountered *weizzā* through the more direct methods of possession or dreams. Nonetheless, they believe the *weizzā* communicate directly with them, either through mental communication or from feelings they receive at various times throughout their life. "The *weizzā* work on a different frequency than what us humans work on," Zaw Min, a computer engineer, explained to me. "Think of a radio. We are like a radio whose function is to tune in to the same frequency that the *weizzā* work on." Continuing with this radio analogy, I asked how one can turn one's "dial" to tune in to the *weizzā*'s transmission waves. "It's not that there is a standard frequency," he answered, "which makes it all the more difficult to tune in. But through various practices, one can develop the mind in such a way as to make it receptive to the radio waves being emitted by the *weizzā*."[15] Such "tuning in" to the *weizzā* wavelength was a constant refrain among my interlocutors when discussions arose about how best to make contact. Again, this tuning in can be active or passive. Some whose *pāramī* is particularly advanced are, by their very nature of purity, already in tune with the *weizzā* and merely need to acknowledge it and embrace the workings of the *weizzā* within themselves. For the majority of devotees, like the head nurse of a hospital in Yangon, communicating with the *weizzā* is accomplished "by putting up one's antenna. Anyone can have access to their *weizzā*, so long as they practice lots of meditation to help develop the faculties necessary to be in touch with him."[16] It is not just the *weizzā*'s spirit that can make contact with the human world. A *weizzā* can appear in his physical form as well. Whether they have left this world alive or via death, all *weizzā* possess the power to manifest themselves materially. Although a *weizzā* may currently exist as a spiritual being, he can, it was explained to me, touch and grasp things, as well as manifest his bodily features to people.[17] The large number of corporeal encounters with *weizzā* over the past fifty years has warranted the development of a peculiar practice of setting up beds for them to rest upon should they decide to pay a visit to the human realm. In many *weizzā* shrine rooms around the country, devotees install beds in private rooms reserved specifically for the use of their patron *weizzā*.[18] Elaborately and haphazardly decorated with a wide assortment of religious paraphernalia,[19] these rooms are often found in homes and monasteries that affiliate themselves with a particular *weizzā* or lineage. As shown in fig. 6 from a monastery outside of Yangon, beds are made up with the expectation that they will be slept in should the *weizzā*, whose picture is hung just above the headboard, decide to visit. These "guests" often stay just one or two nights before moving on to their next destination.[20] But they are thought to leave signs of their nocturnal presence for the devotees that are collected as evidence of close connection with their wizard-saint. Ruffled comforters, creases in the sheets, food and drink missing from the previous night's offerings, displaced objects, and an assortment of pleasant smells are just some of the signs accepted by followers as indications that they have been visited by a *weizzā*.[21]

An elderly couple from Yangon who attributed their considerable wealth to the long-standing relationship they enjoyed with the *weizzā* Bo Min Gaung invited me to stay in their home for one night. Convinced that I would obtain data crucial to the successful completion of this book, Daw Pan Nu and U Saw Win had me sleep in the shrine room that they had made on the top floor of their suburban home. It was reserved for "VIP guests," as they put it, and contained one such bed to be used by Bo Min Gaung or any other *weizzā* that happened to be passing through. As I entered the room for the first time, I was struck by its stale, eerie quality. Dimly lit by a naked light bulb, it was lifeless and cold. And while it took several minutes for my eyes to become adjusted to the dark so I could take notice of all that was there, "I saw more of them in the first moments than might be supposed."[22] The room was overflowing with once splendid gold and silver religious objects that had lost their shine from disuse. Although it appeared tidy, layers of dust and cobwebs covered everything. The flowers, cooked rice, and green tea that had been placed upon the offering table were fresh, but that was the extent of any new life that may have been there. I walked over to the offering area and, seeing the couple nod to each other, set down my cot on the spot where I would be sleeping that night.

My hosts proudly told me that Bo Min Gaung visits them occasionally, and the proof was that the tea and water they offered him on the altar would be half gone when they entered the room the next morning. Although usually expressing the utmost respect for my interlocutors about their practices and beliefs, I could not help but jokingly remark to the old couple that I felt like a little kid on Christmas Eve waiting to catch a glimpse of Santa Claus. "Ah, but the difference here is that Santa Claus is fake, while the *weizzā* are real," Daw Pan Nu quickly admonished me with a scowl before turning off the lights and leaving the room.[23]

Admittedly, I felt somewhat uncomfortable about sleeping in this room where a saintly nocturnal visitor could potentially appear. It was already late in the evening, and after an hour or so of wishing that I was lying in my bed back home, I eventually fell asleep. Sometime in the middle of the night, however, I was awoken by a clatter coming from atop the Bo Min Gaung altar. It was a loud bang that sounded like metal pans smashing against one another. The hair on the back of my neck stood up from fear. After what seemed like fifteen minutes of fumbling for my flashlight, I immediately shone it in the direction of the sound. Completely unfazed by the light were two small mice lapping up the water from one of the shallow bowls placed there for Bo Min Gaung. They had apparently knocked down a metal serving tray on their way to the water. Not wanting to deprive them of sharing in the offering and thus possibly accruing merit to help them out of their animal state, I let them be and fell fast asleep, laughing to myself that for a split second, I thought that perhaps Bo Min Gaung really had come to visit.

The next morning when Daw Pan Nu entered the room to wake me for breakfast, the first thing she did was approach the altar. "Look! Come here! *Abha* ("grandfather," as she affectionately called Bo Min Gaung) did come! He told me he would come sometime this week. Isn't it amazing?"

Not sure what she was referring to, I crawled over from my cot to see her admiring, as if it were a precious gem, one of the shallow bowls of water she had set out the night before.

"See, the water in this bowl is almost all gone," she said, beaming.

"Wow, that is amazing," I said. "It's too bad I was here the whole night and didn't see him."

Any evidence of a possible *weizzā*'s presence in the human world is taken very seriously. Nothing, no matter how small or seemingly insignificant to an outside observer, is what it appears to be. One cannot fathom the ways *weizzā* work in the world, and such small tokens are therefore taken as evidence by the devout that they have a special bond with their wizard-saint. Such "traces" or "imprints," as Patrice Ladwig calls them with reference to immaterial beings' presence in the world, "might indicate the places where they appear, the materiality of the ritual items to deal with them, or . . . the offerings they receive."[24] And although the *weizzā* may not have appeared to them in more obvious visual or aural ways, followers are confident that if a time comes when they are in dire need of help, their *weizzā* will come to their aid.[25]

I heard of countless instances like the one described above, and as may be obvious by now, I am not concerned with interrogating the empirical validity of the claims made in these accounts. Rather,

I am interested in how they function as part of a larger process of identity construction in which the unpredictable actions of the *weizzā* continually introduce new levels of meaning into the lives of their devotees. Over time I came to realize that it is the shared experiences of these same occurrences, witnessed over decades, in different locales and among diverse groups of people, that devotees recount when attempting to describe the essence of their relationships with the *weizzā*. These are the incidents that matter to them, the ones they relate over and over to one another (and to ethnographers like myself). When I described the incident to a Burmese friend of mine who does not believe in anything about the *weizzā* phenomenon, thinking he would go on one of his usual rants about the absurdity of such beliefs, he surprised me by asking in all seriousness, "How do you know that Bo Min Gaung had not transformed himself into a mouse in your presence, especially as he knows you may have some doubts about his power?"[26]

THIRD CATEGORY

Becoming a *weizzā* requires years of rigorous and disciplined training to master a specific form of technical knowledge aimed at gaining supernatural powers for manipulating the physical and psychical world around them to, ideally, help others, propagate the *sāsana*, and eventually attain nirvana. *Weizzā* achieve this state through any number of methods that include alchemy, meditation, recitation of sacred spells, and drawing magical diagrams.[27] The literal translation of the Pāli word (*vijjādhara*) from which *weizzā* derives gives an accurate idea of a *weizzā*: "a master of wisdom" or even "master of spells." Those who aspire to this mastery are said to traverse the "*weizzā* path" (B. *weizzā lam*), and systems for classifying and ranking *weizzā* can be found in the writings of famous monks, popular magazines, and websites. There is no ecclesiastical governing body that dictates and oversees the *weizzā* and their devotees, which leads to quite a bit of innovation and regional difference among followers and the associations they belong to. I agree with Niklas Foxeus that due to "its eclecticism there is no authoritative version of *weizzā* path systems/cosmology/practices, etc., and it is difficult to point to a discrete set of beliefs or practices common to all practitioners. Nevertheless, some general ideas seem to be shared widely."[28] One such idea is the *weizzā* hierarchy. At the bottom of the ranking is the "Common (P: *Janapada*) *Weizzā*," who uses knowledge of alchemy, sacred diagrams, spells, Vedic knowledge, etc. to obtain supernormal powers to be used for mundane (P: *lokiya*) affairs, especially pertaining to matters involving finance, love, and prognostication. Next is the "Small (P: *Cūḷa*) *Gandhārī Weizzā*," a mid-level *weizzā* who has mastery over the same arts as the Common *Weizzā* but uses his powers for supramundane (P: *lokuttara*) affairs. Such *weizzā* include the mercury and iron *weizzā* who have devoted their practices to alchemy; the medicine *weizzā* whose practices involve the creation and mastery of various indigenous medicines and elemental properties; sacred diagram *weizzā* whose practice is centered on the creation and manipulation of cabbalistic squares and other diagrams made up of syllables and the quintessence of holy text; and the mantra *weizzā* who, like the sacred diagram *weizzā*, creates and adapts sacred verses (see fig. 7). Perhaps the most widely known "small" *weizzā* in Myanmar is in the form of the *zawgyi* figure (see fig. 8). Dressed in red robes and turban, carrying a long walking stick that is used as a magic wand of sorts, and proficient in alchemy and magic, the *zawgyi* is often considered synonymous with the *weizzā* path, even though he is not considered the highest power.[29] The highest authority is the "Great (P: *Mahā*) *Gandhārī Weizzā*"—a high-level *weizzā* who engages in concentration (P: *samatha*) and insight (P: *vipassana*) meditation and who has fulfilled *pāramī*, which allows him to become a chief disciple of the future Buddha or even a buddha himself in the future.[30] Such *weizzā* usually have some mastery of one or more techniques of the lower *weizzā*, as that is what would have elevated them to the state of *Mahā Gandhārī Weizzā*, imbued with the complete set of ten superpowers.[31] Throughout this book, I focus particularly on devotees' interactions with *Mahā Gandhārī Weizzā*. Such systems of classification are not always as neat as represented here or by those involved in the *weizzā* tradition. There is some overlap among the different kinds of *weizzā* (a lower-level *weizzā* may do higher-level *weizzā* practices and vice versa). And until one reaches the level of *Mahā Gandhārī Weizzā*, there is always the danger of backsliding in spiritual attainment (this usually is a result of succumbing to sexual desires).

When the term *weizzā* is used, it can also refer to wisdom or the mastery of some form of knowledge and not necessarily to a wizard-saint being. For example, someone who has expertise in the creation and use of spells is known as a *mantra weizzā*, and those who have dedicated themselves to mastering the art of medicine are called "medicine (B: *hse*) *weizzā*." This all bears striking similarities to, and no doubt shares a common origin with, the *wisa* of the Thai-Lao of northeast Thailand and the *mo wiset* of Thailand, all of whom are experts in incantations and specialized knowledge to obtain supernatural powers and control a variety of spirits.[32] Like the word *weizzā*, the terms for these religious specialists in other parts of mainland Southeast Asia all originate from and are local pronunciations of the same Pāli word, *vijjā*. We must, therefore, take care not to assume that anyone who dabbles in the art of spells, alchemy, or sacred diagrams aspires to become a wizard-saint. Buddhists in Myanmar who collect and use spells, for instance, are not limited to *weizzā* and their devotees. There is a whole cottage industry of male and female specialists (B: *hsaya*; *hsaya-ma*) in spells, medicine, sacred diagrams, alchemy, etc. who make their living using such knowledge for other peoples' protection and good luck. For instance, the practices of medicine and sacred diagrams are also commonly represented as associated with astrology and fortune-telling (B: *bedin*) and astronomy (B: *nakkhatta*), and the boundaries between *weizzā* and astrology professionals have often overlapped, as they do today. Moreover, the hermits (S: *rishi*; B. *ya-they*; T: *ruesi*) of Myanmar and Thailand are also intimately linked to practices that can be associated with the path of the *weizzā* (see figs. 9 and 10). I would venture to guess that this is why, insofar as they were regarded as practitioners of these worldly arts, the hermits, seen as the mythic authors of the *bedin* (Vedic) tradition, have been connected with the *weizzā* (though certainly there are different genealogies behind these figures yet to be unraveled).[33]

While the figure of the *weizzā* is found in Pāli literature, we should also be aware of the resonance of *weizzā* traditions with South Asian *vidyādhara* and *siddha* traditions, *mantra/yantra* practices, and even Taoist alchemical traditions.[34] The character and cult of the semi-divine *vidyādhara* of South Asia can be traced back to at least the beginning of the Common Era and continued to be popular in Indian literature throughout the medieval period. With regard to alchemy, as there were no mercurial cores indigenous to India (and Tibet), mercury had to be brought in from elsewhere in the subcontinent. David White, in his work on alchemical traditions of South Asia, says that Tibetans got their mercury from Chinese traders who most likely would have gone overland via the supposed ancient overland trade route linking Szechuan with India via Yunnan, Myanmar, and Assam, and goes on to suggest that a highly alchemical tradition intermingling elements from across South and East Asia arose in Myanmar in about the fifth century.[35] I would not suggest that all varieties of these practices had a necessary connection with discourses concerning *vijjādhara*, but rather that there is a relation that has yet to be adequately explored.

The *weizzā* can be considered a "third category" of religious practitioner somewhere between monastic and layperson, but it is a bit complicated. Unlike a monk, nun, or hermit, a *weizzā* is not ordained into the role. A *weizzā*, rather, has both a social status and a state of being attained after years of diligent study, living morally, and having a bit of karmic luck from previous lives. Whereas a monk, nun, or hermit undergoes an ordination ritual separating himself from lay life, a *weizzā* is something that any person can become regardless of their position in life.[36] A *weizzā* attains his status and state of being through an ontological transformation whereby his very biological and mental conditions are altered, giving him supernatural abilities that include flight, longevity, and healing, among others. Such a transformation is akin to what is thought to occur with an Indian Tantric *siddha* who, as David White states, "has through his practice realized his dual goal of superhuman powers and bodily immortality."[37] It is as if an alchemical change takes place in the body and mind whereby the aspiring *weizzā* reaches a state where a "critical mass has been reached and a chain reaction triggered," ultimately imbuing them with the wisdom and powers of a *weizzā*.[38]

Weizzā (or aspiring *weizzā*) is not a professional religious vocation, as is the case with monks, nuns, and hermits in Myanmar, and a *weizzā* can be from any position in society. Although there are no well-known or revered female *weizzā*, women do have the capacity to become *weizzā*, similar in theory to a female being able to become an *arahant*. Although the majority of *weizzā* are monks, as we will see in chapter 2, the most popular, Bo Min Gaung, was a layman. Some people following the *weizzā* path or aligning themselves with a particular *weizzā* group or wizard-saint might wear special clothes that identify them as a practitioner: donning brown or white robes or wearing counting beads around the neck, for example. For the most part, however, there is nothing outwardly different to distinguish someone aspiring to *weizzā* status from others around them. Japanese scholar of *weizzā* associations Keiko Tosa argues that people following the *weizzā* path have an alternative Buddhist belief that enables them to "pursue more enthusiastic practice than that of an ordinary lay person."[39] Individuals who are thought to have attained *weizzā*-hood often have cults formed around them from which new lineages, practices, and ideas are developed and disseminated.[40] In the end, however, the *weizzā*, as Rozenberg points out, "is an essentially ambiguous figure, a paradoxical and troubling one,"[41] possessing characteristics so distinct from other kinds of religious professionals in the country. For instance, while the position of professional meditator, or *yogi*, is admired in Myanmar, a follower of the *weizzā* and their paths is looked upon with suspicion, especially when some of their beliefs and practices take them "beyond the avenues to enlightenment chartered within the monastic and lay domains."[42]

Many of these *weizzā* and their cult disciples in Myanmar throughout the twentieth century were messianic and millenarian in nature.[43] They saw indications around them that times were changing and that they were potentially on the threshold of a new era, of either prosperity or suffering. Whichever the case, the outcome was directly linked to the survival of Buddhism in Myanmar, and the *weizzā* and their disciples saw it as their duty to guard the religion in these dark times.

BURMESE BUDDHIST RESPONSES TO THE *SĀSANA*'S DECLINE

The first half of the twentieth century was the high point for the formation of lay Buddhist associations whose primary aim was to strengthen the *sāsana* throughout the country.[44] Groups of *weizzā* devotees that had advanced to some degree of institutionalization were referred to as *gaing*, a word with a range of synonymous meanings that include community, congregation, and association.[45] They were often exclusive associations, organized around a set of tenets, headed by a charismatic leader, and with devotion centered upon one or more *weizzā* saints. Members were given esoteric teachings aimed at developing supernatural powers through the practices of meditation, alchemy, reciting mantras and magical incantations, ingesting sacred diagrams, and studying cabalistic squares.[46] Members came from a wide range of socioeconomic backgrounds. Merchants, office workers, taxi drivers, booksellers, housewives, and monastics all joined these *gaing* to varying degrees of involvement and engaged in activities that included pagoda construction, healing ceremonies, sermonizing, and general Buddhist missionary work throughout the country, all of which members understood to be part of strengthening the *sāsana*. Regardless of the *weizzā* affiliation of these associations and the activities they chose to focus on, they all had in common the aim to defend and propagate, at all costs, the Buddha *sāsana*.

Protecting and maintaining the *sāsana* was important because it represented the potential for people who came into contact with it to attain nirvana, i.e., escape from the rounds of perpetual rebirth. Of course, the number of Buddhists who were actually intent on achieving such a goal in the immediate future was small, but the belief that the Buddha *sāsana* was the means for such an ambition was "a powerful impetus for preserving it in the present."[47] If the *sāsana* was the only gateway to Buddhist salvation, then it was crucial for Buddhists to protect and propagate it.

For the vast majority of Buddhists who did not aspire to attain enlightenment in their current or proximate lifetimes (as is the case for many *weizzā* devotees), the *sāsana* offered a means for improving their lives as they traversed the cycle of rebirths. As Carbine rightly points out, in addition to enlightenment, the *sāsana* offered "various kinds of action conducive to better rebirth," which, in turn, would help to further sustain the *sāsana* because those beings reborn into better lives would be more likely to support and carry out activities related to the *sāsana*.[48]

Changes in society and in the *sāsana* inspired large numbers of people to take up the charge as vanguards of the *sāsana*. Historians of Burmese Buddhism have shown how both monastic and lay Buddhists found it increasingly difficult to sustain the *sāsana* during the unstable period of British colonial rule, especially after the British dissolved the monarchy in 1885. Kings in Myanmar and throughout South and Southeast Asia had long acted as promoters of the Buddhist faith in order to justify their rule.[49] In Burmese coronation ceremonies, for example, kings were asked whether they would protect Buddhism.[50] Carbine notes that with the British dissolution of the monarchy, legal authority of the state-supported head of the monastic community, and monastic-based educational system, among other things, Burmese Buddhists perceived the colonizers to be undermining "the stability of certain kinds of communal activity long connected to the persistence of the *sāsana*" and thus hastening its decline.[51]

The deposition of the Burmese Buddhist King Thibaw by the British in 1885 required Buddhists to quickly think of new and innovative ways to protect and promote the *sāsana*. One of the main efforts was to come together and take responsibility for the *sāsana* by forming Buddhist associations. These associations carried out programs for educational, moral, and religious reform with the idea that a renewed enthusiasm and devotion among Buddhists could counter the erosion of the *sāsana*. Turner proposes that "what drove the Buddhist enthusiasm of this period, however, was . . . a rhetoric of decline, an intuition that the state of Buddhism was deteriorating."[52] A strong awareness of social turmoil and the fragility of the *sāsana* mobilized the wider Buddhist public with much intensity. For instance, the sharp and terrifying rise in alcoholism and the damaging mental and physical illnesses that resulted from it were understood by the Burmese to be consequences resulting from the deterioration of the Buddha *sāsana* under colonial rule.[53] An increase in young peoples' involvement in gambling, the wearing of British-style clothing, growing lack of respect for Buddhism and the elderly, and other negative influences of British culture, were all perceived to have caused Burmese to turn away from, or lessen their preoccupation with Buddhism, which led to a decline in the *sāsana*'s vitality.[54] As historians of Buddhism in Myanmar have noted, large segments of the Buddhist population decided that the most efficient way of combating such societal ills was to band together and engage in activities and that would renew the power of the *sāsana*. Erik Braun has shown how the activities of the monk Ledi Sayadaw in the nineteenth and twentieth centuries spurred large numers of laypeople to engage in studying Buddhist philosophical systems and mass meditation practice—all to bolster the strength of the *sāsana*.[55] Turner, focusing especially on the lay Burmese Buddhist population, similarly shows how groups of religious lay organizations sprang up all across the country during the colonial era to participate in widespread Buddhist propagation activities to improve the population's moral discipline, which would lead to a stronger *sāsana*.[56] Bolstering the *sāsana* through Buddhist means, therefore, quickly became a rallying cause of solidarity, an organizing principle for Burmese

Buddhists across society to work together while challenging the colonial regime and its degenerative legacies.

For such Buddhist associations, the task of combating the erosion of traditional values and institutions became intimately tied with national individuality and cultural heritage.[57] While the initial focus was primarily on religious and cultural issues, by 1920 Buddhist groups such as the Young Men's Buddhist Association (YMBA) and the General Council of Burmese Associations (GCBA) made a deliberate move to orient themselves around issues of ethnicity and the nation.[58] Many young nationalists were drawn to the YMBA's message, "To be Burmese is to be Buddhist," for instance.

In the early parts of the twentieth century, then, with a new sense of participation, the weight of the responsibility for the *sāsana* shifted down the social hierarchy to the broad base of the Buddhist laity.[59] As individual Buddhists became united by their participation in this collective body responsible for the *sāsana*, they could take on new duties and modes of preserving the teachings, which in the absence of a king fell to the laity at large. Drawing upon long-standing projects, "guardian associations" (B. *gopaka ahpwe*) or lay voluntary institutions made up of members who had shared interests in "doing *sāsana* work" (B. *thathana aloke*) developed throughout the country as laypeople strove to reverse the supposed decay of the *sāsana*. This concern created waves of Buddhist publishing, preaching, and organizing, and led Buddhist laypeople in towns across the country to found hundreds of associations.

LAY *WEIZZĀ* ASSOCIATIONS: PRINT MEDIA AND LITHOGRAPHY

U Kyaw Hein, an eighty-eight-year-old man who had spent most of his life as a member of a *weizzā* association, made this clear when he told me that his association's activities really "had very little to do with the British. Although we weren't monks, we saw ourselves as taking part in guarding the *sāsana*, the way we saw monks carrying out this duty." "But," he continued, "our association lead-ers making it a priority to talk about 'protecting the *sāsana* from the evil British' was certainly effective in gaining members. That's why me and my friends joined!"[60] He went on to say that most of their day-to-day activities and larger events were centered around activities to bolster the *sāsana*.

Wizard-saint associations had their own means for adapting to the changes taking place around them. Whereas the YMBA and GCBA stressed more orthodox forms of Buddhist practice based on morality, meditation, and scriptural study, *weizzā* associations attempted to harness the powers of esoteric rituals, teachings, and spells to attain their political and religious goals. Such *weizzā* groups were a natural outgrowth of other lay Buddhist associations whose members, such as the well-known Saya San, belonged to. As an affiliate with the GCBA, Saya San chaired a commission in the 1920s that investigated peasant grievances against colonial tax collec-tors.[61] He eventually left the GCBA and began recruiting members for his own association, one that bore characteristics of the *gaing* congregations discussed above. Saya San issued membership cards, amulets, incantations, and tattoos and assured members that such objects would protect them from bullets and other forms of British aggression. Influenced by nationalist discourse and preaching man-uals of the time[62] and deeply troubled by the destruction of the Burmese economy, values, and institutions, Saya San and members of his congregation were convinced that expelling the British would restore the authority of the Burmese monarchy and revive the Bud-dhist religion, thus ensuring that the *sāsana* remained strong in Myanmar. In fact, during his trial by the British for sedition in 1931, Saya San stressed that his anticolonial mission was primarily for the "interest of the religion [*sāsana*] of Our Lord [the Buddha]."[63]

Small bands of diverse, loosely connected networks of *weizzā gaing* continued to form throughout the country in the 1930s and '40s, many of them professing anticolonial nationalist agendas similar to that of Saya San's group. None of these groups, however, was as systematically organized or influential as established lay

Buddhist associations like the YMBA and GCBA. This most likely had to do with the British criminalizing *gaing* by associating them with rebellious activities.[64] It is, therefore, not surprising that large-scale *weizzā* groups were systematized immediately after independence in 1948. What separated *weizzā* associations from other Buddhist associations, however, was the strong emphasis they placed on not only saving the *sāsana* but also saving all human beings around the world by exposing them to it. Because of the missionary zeal characteristic of so many of these *weizzā* associations, I have come to refer to them as "salvation armies."

I use this term for several reasons. First, on an organizational level, like the Protestant Christian Salvation Army or the Roman Catholic Militia Immaculatae, these religious associations were organized in hierarchical chains of command.[65] Just short of using military titles—although the *weizzā* associations did employ royal terminology and some of the associations' subcommittees referred to their members as "Buddha's soldiers" (B. *hpaya sittha*)—many of these associations printed command hierarchy charts, complete with profile pictures, indicating a senior member's station or rank, and inserted them into handbooks read by new recruits. Often the associations used the term "army" (B. *tap*) in their descriptions. While some endorsed and practiced actual physical paramilitary activities, these armies were not overtly militaristic, but acted more as reserve groups who united to carry out, with warlike zeal, the task of defending and propagating the *sāsana*.[66] Accordingly, they constituted an army seeking to conquer the entire world to bring it under the dominion of a Buddhist world emperor and Buddhist norms and values.[67] "Burma and the rest of the world is going through a time of great unrest. Many people are suffering. Everyone is hoping for peace," wrote the editor of a magazine published in 1948 by a *weizzā* association, before going on to condemn the use of weapons and violence: "We have seen many people suffer from the dangers of weapons. While nowadays it is trendy to talk about rebelling against the establishment and to use weapons to help usher in peace . . . this goes against Buddhism. One cannot be a Buddhist soldier using weapons for peace. Only through loving-kindness can we be free from dangers."[68] According to these critics, *weizzā* associations' battles against perceived threats to the *sāsana* were fought to save Buddhism from a feared extinction.

Like the Christian "armies" and "militias," the *weizzā* associations adapted Anglo-American temperance pledges.[69] Identical to the Salvation Army's opposition to alcohol and frequenting brothels, for instance, *weizzā* associations required all members to take an oath to refrain from drinking alcohol and engaging in sexual misconduct. As social and religious fraternal orders (like the Freemasons) expanded rapidly in Europe and North America during the nineteenth and twentieth centuries, so too did they take root in Myanmar as the number of colonial officials residing in the country grew.[70] Many of these orders were strong proponents of promoting temperance and other kinds of moralistic campaigns. With its establishment in Myanmar in 1915, the Salvation Army, as well as organizations like it, must have had at least nominal influence on Buddhist lay associations during this time.[71]

Lastly, I use the term "salvation army" because such associations were fully committed to protecting and propagating the *sāsana* for the literal collective salvation of all humanity. These Burmese religious groups saw it as their duty to spread the teaching of the Buddha as taught to them by the *weizzā* throughout the world. Manuals for associations like that of the Mano-maya-iddhi, as well as published books about the life and teachings of the *weizzā* Bo Min Gaung, all contain language about providing salvation for fellow humans who come into contact with the *sāsana*. Common words used throughout include *kay*, as in saving someone from danger, and *kay-tin*, as in saving a person from succumbing to immoral acts. Indeed, as Rozenberg writes in his book about a *weizzā* cult in Myanmar: "Rendered as the paradigmatic opposite of a sorcerer, a [*weizzā*] can be seen or rather can be imagined as the agent of salvation par excellence."[72]

Organizations such as the Pathamam Association adopted martial terminology and ways of structuring their ever-expanding networks of members.[73] In a 1948 issue of their monthly magazine, the editor explained that his association decided to embark on publishing a monthly journal of this sort because "the Buddha's *sāsana*, which nourishes followers with the medicine of the *dhamma*, has reached its halfway point" and needed protection at this crucial juncture.[74] Those entrusted with the protection and dissemination of the *sāsana* included "the *Weizzā* and Master Committee; Buddha King *Sāsana* Propagation Committee; and the Royal Emperor Committee." Together they formed the "Ultimate Army" (B. *Pathamam Tap Oo*), one of many "armies" of the period. Each of the association's subcommittees was charged with carrying out certain tasks: the *Weizzā* and Master Committee were in charge of management, the Buddha King Committee's role was propagation, while the Royal Emperor Committee was in charge of security. Together they wrote up a set of "*sāsana* regulations" that were rules for this particular association's dissemination of its message and activities not only in Myanmar but also around the world. The association dedicated itself to carrying out its mission until resurgence in the power of the Buddha *sāsana* and an overall interest in the *weizzā* path throughout the world occurred. The editor warned that members of the salvation army would be on the frontline in the battle to carry out *sāsana* propagation, and that to be "successful in our missions" they must be endowed with intelligence and kindness, as well as a strong resolve to do *sāsana* work and gain new members.[75]

Drawing upon techniques and technologies employed by Buddhist and non-Buddhist lay associations, *weizzā* associations incorporated print and pictorial media into their proselytizing missions.[76] During this period, magazines, books, and other forms of print media enabled the diffusion of their messages across the country and offered a new way for members and nonmembers to have access to teachings and practices centered around the *sāsana*. Many of these publications were produced on a monthly basis and were even mailed to members who purchased subscriptions. This enabled the swift spread of ideas to many parts of the country where *weizzā* associations may not have had local chapters established. In addition to bringing in revenue to the associations' operations and *sāsana* missionizing works, it helped to create a collective endeavor among *weizzā* devotees.

Just as effective as incorporating print media into their proselytizing missions was the *weizzā* associations' use of visual material, like chromolithographs and black-and-white photographs. Chromolithographs and photographs were, and remain to this day, the primary means for devotees to interact with the *weizzā* and other semidivine beings. Unlike in India, where "framing pictures," or chromolithograph prints on thin paper framed by local suppliers, were popular, Buddhist *weizzā* devotees in Myanmar preferred unframed paper prints, most of which were pinned or pasted to walls in homes, shops, and places of worship. Modern-day devotees prefer large, glossy prints (20 × 30 inches) or wallet-size prints (2.5 × 3.5 inches), laminated to protect them from bending, molding, and ripping. None of my interlocutors who used such images expressed any interest in the details of the artists or publishers that produced them, "even when such information was identifiable on the print, and understand with admirable clarity that these are commodities churned out by some industry somewhere."[77]

Along with chromolithography, photography played a key role in the ways *weizzā* associations spread their messages and how individual devotees first came to know about and intereact with the wizard-saints. Photography equipment was expensive and scarce during the colonial era, but this changed in the early 1950s when the price of cameras decreased and the "presence of Burmese-owned photographic businesses, technical importers, and suppliers grew."[78] *Weizzā* associations around this time increasingly began including photos in their monthly journals of newly erected pagodas and holy men associated with the *weizzā* path. Indeed, as Mandy Sadan notes, the popularity of many of these *weizzā* may be attributed to this new use of photographic media: "The latent challenge of Burma's many subsidiary religious figures on the populist edges of Buddhist orthodoxy was also potentially expanded through photographic media" and especially "through the circulation of photographic images of the *weikza* Bo Min Gaung in various embodied forms."[79] These religious figures and the images associated with them were (and continue to be) "connected to certain highly local agendas that operate independently of state control, manipulation, or support."[80]

One point that Sadan does not discuss but that I think helped photography become popular with *weizzā* associations and their devotees has to do with the Burmese word for "photograph": *dhat-pone*. Literally, "image or form of the essence," the word *dhat* is central to the *weizzā* and their devotees. *Dhat* derives from the Pāli *dhātu*, and carries similar meanings of element or essence, especially with regard to the elementary particles of a physical object, except that it also carries stronger connotations of power or force. The word *dhat* is used in *weizzā*-related terminology, like *dhat-khan* (shrine room), *dhat-si* and *dhat-win* (possession), *dhat-lone* (philosopher's stone), and *dhat-daw* (relics of a saint). Clearly, the term and its semantic layers would not have been lost on *weizzā* devotees at a time when photography was a means for interacting with one's chosen wizard-saint in place of, or in conjunction with, lithographs (see figs. 11–16).[81]

In addition to images of the *weizzā*, one image that helped to create new lineages and histories depicts a mystical meeting of the "Great *Weizzā* Committee on *Sāsana* Propagation" of 1888. These images were used not only to document and highlight events and people relevant to *weizzā* associations' missions but also, to quote Justin McDaniel, "in the social construction of reality—how they, in a sense, encourage certain behaviors . . . promote new developments in practice, create new lineages, and cultivate new histories."[82] This is perhaps most evident in a particular genre of images developed and circulated by *weizzā* associations that saw themselves as continuing to carry out the mission that the legendary, original "*weizzā* association" began in 1888. Referred to as the "Foremost *Sāsana* Propagation Committee" (B. *pathamam thathana-pyu ahpwe*) or the "Great *Weizzā* Committee on *Sāsana* Propagation" (B. *Thathana-pyu Weizzā-dho Ahpwe-gyi*), this association and the reasons for its development were described in oral accounts spreading across the country during the colonial era, along with various other stories and prophecies about supernatural figures helping to guard the *sāsana* while the country was under colonial rule. Perhaps the first written account of this association's gathering is to be found in a 1952 hagiographic account of the *weizzā* Bo Min Gaung. This best-selling book was widely circulated at the time and was still in print as of 2017. The author writes that after the annexation of Upper Burma in 1885, Bo Min Gaung "became alarmed that the Buddha's *sāsana* would vanish" and therefore organized a "Buddhist Missionary Wizard-Saint Committee," made up of the most powerful *weizzā* to devise a plan. Their goal was to defend and propagate the Buddha *sāsana* without using violence against the British occupiers through peaceful means in line with the Buddha's teachings.

One of the most popular ways of depicting the "historic" event of the meeting of the first *weizzā* council was through chromolithographs sold at pagoda stalls or shops selling religious accouterments. Related to both the meeting and this particular genre of its representation are pictures that do not directly portray the 1888 meeting but call to mind the event by including the full pantheon of *weizzā* belonging to the Supreme *Weizzā* Council (see figs. 17 and 18). The structures of these committees most likely reflected the organizational structure of lay Buddhist associations of the early 1900s, which was similar to the bureaucratic structure of colonial governmental and economic bodies of the time. Formal and rule-driven, these associations held frequent meetings and compiled detailed agendas.[83]

This secret, high-level meeting of *weizzā* saints continues to play an influential role in how Burmese *weizzā* devotees understand the *sāsana* to have fared in Myanmar and how they take part in maintaining it. David Morgan has argued that "religion happens materially in relationships prompted by encounters with images."[84] While researching the affective tones of "religion as relationship" in the lives of *weizzā* devotees, I have observed that this particular image, which can be found hung in homes and shrines, published in magazines, and sold at roadside stalls and bookstores, has helped to serve the specific function of making associations between individuals of different time periods and between persons that may never have even existed. Such groupings and legends create a new, imagined lineage to which the various, often competing *weizzā* associations can trace their own congregations. One of the strategies used by authors to establish their credibility and expertise in magic and healing practices was to trace their lineages through famous monks and other religious figures.[85] And borrowing ideas from Anne Blackburn's work on the vitalization of Buddhist space by linking it to Sakyamuni Buddha, we see *weizzā* congregations doing something similar by evoking their connections to religious virtuosi from various time periods and "imbuing new and restored environments with temporal depth and instinctive authority."[86] Such connections to idealized past models are crucial, as is clear from the elaborate detail with which *weizzā* saints and their devotees attempt to recount their karmic connections with one another and even with great kings, queens, and religious authorities of the past. These images also allow the viewer to join in the "physical creation of a collective or social body, the perceived or imagine community of believers" in the present.[87] Although my informants may not have thought of these connections in such terms (or in such reified discourse), if nothing else, these pictorial representations also help to portray a *weizzā* united front against any forces that pose a threat to the *sāsana* and the country and "share in one another's prestige and partially create it, each for the others."[88] Devotees enjoy imagining this group acting as a kind of security council or league of indigenous superheroes watching over those in need and intervening whenever the *sāsana*, country, or devotees are in trouble. This "council of *weizzā*," as many of my informants expressed it, are "guiding Myanmar to transform it into a peaceful and prosperous land where the teachings of the Buddha will shine throughout the country," one Bo Min Gaung devotee explained to me when he saw me observing such a laminated picture on his *weizzā* shrine.[89] A devotee of the *weizzā* Yatkansin Taung Sayadaw told me that "these members belong to what is called the 'Supreme Council of *Sāsana-pyu Weizzā*' who protect and promote the

Buddha's teachings not only in Burma but throughout the world."[90] Other devotees, such as the editors of the recently published journal *Weizzā Magazine,* who wrote an op-ed article on this supreme council, maintain that there is a core group of eight *weizzā* who form the "executive committee." This group, known as "The Eight Great Powerful Ones" (B. *maha-iddhi shit-ba*), are *weizzā* who "guard the *sāsana* by keeping people who are part of the Buddha *sāsana* away from dangers."[91] Other *sāsana* works done by this committee include "providing knowledge and wisdom to those meditators engaged in meditation so that they remain on the right track; making sure requisite donations arrive to those monks engaged in religious works; and helping pagodas and monasteries to be built."[92] We will return to how devotees believe these *weizzā* protect the country below.

THE "LIBERATION ERA" AND A NEW WORLD ORDER

As noted above, *weizzā* associations began to proliferate and increase their missionary activities immediately after independence in 1948, especially as British forces were no longer in authority to outlaw such groups and their practices. However, there was a different set of reasons these groups believed the *sāsana* to be in decline during the postcolonial era. With the British as the main threat being gone, members of *weizzā* associations looked to the current political and religious state of affairs and read into it, with the help of prophetic literature, information about what was to come and how to act. Books and magazine articles related to the *weizzā* that began appearing in 1948 contained little to no vitriolic rhetoric targeted at the British, nor any mention of exactly how colonization was thought to be directly hastening the *sāsana*'s demise. In place of the British, *weizzā* associations worried about other issues that could threaten an already weakened *sāsana*. The monk and *weizzā* devotee U Jotipala, for instance, complained about the proliferation of socialists and communists in the world and the suffering they caused the people of their respective countries because their ideologies were opposed to Buddhism.[93]

Other *weizzā*-related publications looked to the local newspapers for evidence of the world being in its final days. This period in Burmese history was a tumultuous one, marked by waves of insurgencies by communist factions, rebel army groups, and ethnic minorities.[94] A popular *weizzā* monograph focused on local newspaper reports of Kareni soldiers killing 900 people in the town of Pyin Oo Lwin, communist forces entering Mandalay,[95] the rise of violent crimes and debilitating poverty throughout the country,[96] rebels killing monks and laypeople on a daily basis;[97] and ethnic groups, like the Shan, Kachin, and Chin peoples, constantly quarreling due to their adherences to false and heretical ideologies.[98] All of this, coupled with similar political and societal unrest around the world, was evidence to *weizzā* association members that the *sāsana* had reached an all-time low. It was not all doom and gloom, however: these events were also taken as signs that Myanmar was on the threshold of a new and better future.

What exactly did *weizzā* associations envision this future to be? To answer this question, we must first understand the overarching narrative of *sāsana* decline that informed their present and future worldviews. The Buddhist temporal scheme for the life of the *sāsana* comprises cyclical progressions of eons of decline, destruction, and renewal. Some eons have buddhas while others do not, and for the former, this buddha puts forth teachings that will endure for a finite period of time before disappearing from the world, at which time a new eon will commence. These teachings, and the institutions and practices that support their flourishing, are what is meant by *sāsana*. For example, the period of time for the flourishing of the current buddha's *sāsana* (5,000 years) is the temporal scheme that has been informing Buddhists' conceptions of the duration of the *sāsana* and with it, the eon in which they live and into which they will be reborn.

Buddhist sources offer a variety of schemas for *sāsana* decline and disappearance, but the one proposed by the fifth-century Buddhist commentator Buddhaghosa became normative for Buddhists in Myanmar. Buddhaghosa details a fivefold sequence through which the *sāsana* will disappear over the course of a five-thousand-year period, beginning with the demise of Gotama Buddha. The following five components that contribute to the life of the *sāsana* will take place, each corresponding to a one-thousand-year time span: inability to attain insight, monks no longer living in accordance with monastic discipline, loss of textual knowledge, lack of adherence to the ascetic life, and finally the disappearance of the Buddha's relics.[99]

Jan Nattier has pointed out that Buddhist texts from both the Theravāda and Mahayana traditions say little about whether human intervention has an impact on the decline of the *sāsana*: "In a number of narrative texts where the effects of human actions are the center of attention, we find specific timetables for the duration of the Dharma. Yet the very existence of these timetables suggests that the lifespan of the Dharma is fixed, and thus not subject to human intervention."[100] Such ambivalence has allowed Burmese in the colonial and postcolonial eras to make diverse readings that were, as we now see, determined by the conditions of the time.[101]

One such reading was by *weizzā* association members in the mid-twentieth century. A popular belief that had spread through Myanmar was that as the halfway point of the Buddha's *sāsana* was approaching, the country would soon be entering what was to be known as the *Vimutti Yuga Khit*, or Liberation Era. This notion of a time of prosperity and relative ease in making progress along the Buddhist path to nirvana was widespread, most likely brought on by a powerful sense of optimism Burmese experienced in light of the country's newly gained independence, the proliferation of lay associations working to strengthen the *sāsana*, and Prime Minister U Nu's Buddhist revivalist plans.[102]

This view of a coming Liberation Era was part of a *sāsana* temporal scheme different from the one put forth by Buddhaghosa, that the *sāsana* would endure for five thousand years and its deterioration would take place in five one-thousand-year increments starting from the moment of the Buddha's death and continuing until it vanished completely from the world.[103] This theory had provided Burmese Buddhists with a basis for making sense of the fall of the monarchy and subsequent social ills brought by colonialism, but it was not adequate to explain for *weizzā* associations how the *sāsana* was to survive once the colonial power left and Myanmar was granted independence. However, an alternative chronological scheme addressed this.

With the colonial powers gone, *weizzā* associations could now focus on restoring the Buddha *sāsana* to its earlier, albeit imagined, splendor. Not on their watch was the *sāsana* to disappear from their country; with lots of hard work, they could counteract the negative effects that had been wrought on it, stabilize it, and then propel its power into the future, which *weizzā* association members believed would be a liberated one. Foxeus has brought our attention to the importance placed on notions of this Liberation Era among *weizzā* groups by showing how important the cyclical scheme of decline was to their mission.[104] As stated in the decline theory in the commentaries noted above, the waning of the *sāsana* was believed to take place in two 2,500-year phases. This theory differed in that instead of a long, sustained decline lasting 5,000 years, the *sāsana* would decline for 2,500 years, renew itself, then go through another decline until it disappeared. Foxeus explains this complex theory well: "The cyclical scheme comprised five stages as follows: 1) the Liberation Era, 2) the Era of Concentration Meditation, 3) the Era of *Suttas* [scriptures], 4) the Era of Buddhist Precepts, and 5) the Donation Era. After the Donation Era had reached its end, the Liberation Era would thus begin again."[105]

The *weizzā*-related source material, therefore, places the Donation Era during the years of colonial rule; at the point when that era reached its lowest, "the cycle would all of a sudden shift to the highest point of the first phase, the Liberation Era."[106] According to most sources, the Liberation Era would recommence sometime in the 1950s.[107]

There were prophecies of a messianic Buddhist king appearing in Myanmar during this exact time period. Two well-known

prophetic sayings were: "At the midway point of the *sāsana*, a virtu-
ous king will shine"[108] and "At the midway point of the *sāsana*, a vir-
tuous king will carry on [the *sāsana* into the new era]."[109] This, no
doubt, added a sense of urgency to *weizzā* associations' missions.
This period during the 1950s happened to coincide with a
historical moment characterized by millennial beliefs in the
Theravāda world about the approaching midpoint of the Buddhist
dispensation and the imminent arrival of a Universal Monarch
whose reign would bring prosperity. Such beliefs were linked to
notions of religious decline and revival by way of a messianic figure often associated with the buddha Metteyya, who was prophesied to appear in a future time and restore the Buddha's teachings
and monastic community.[110] One *weizzā* monograph even went so
far as to claim that this messianic figure was none other than
Hitler. Drawing from the widespread belief that a legendary
nineteenth-century *weizzā* named Bo Bo Aung would one day reap-
pear in the world as a universal monarch, the book *Bo Bo Aung and
Hitler* argued that Hitler was this savior and had appeared in Europe
to unite the world in peace (see fig. 19).[111] Members of some *weizzā*
associations believed that the royal savior would possess a powerful, supernatural wheeled weapon akin to a boomerang (something
I always imagined to resemble the magical, five-pointed throwing
weapon from the 1983 movie *Krull*).[112] The author of the book, a
Buddhist monk, posited that Hitler did indeed wield a version of this
weapon: the swastika. There was the obvious connection that the
swastika was a symbol of the Buddha, and segments of the Burmese population during the late 1930s and early 1940s believed
Hitler to be a saint due to his alleged vegetarianism and abstention
from alcohol, qualities often associated with Buddhist saints.[113]

Still other authors of *weizzā* publications proclaimed that the
country was on the threshold of a new era—an era governed by the
weizzā—and provided step-by-step instructions for what members
needed to accomplish so that a *weizzā* emperor could arise to unite
all the continents under Buddhist rule and "usher in an era of peace
and prosperity in the world."[114] "There are all sorts of news and

rumors going around these days about *weizzā* appearing soon to protect the *sāsana* and country," a leading figure from one of the *weizzā* associations of this period writes. "Some even believe that Bo Min Gaung is [this king] coming to protect the *sāsana* and country at the halfway point of the *sāsana*'s dispensation."[115]

Much of this activity and religious fervor was reflected in, and no doubt heightened by, the convening of the Sixth Buddhist Council and its preoccupation with how to protect, sustain, and propagate the *sāsana*. The Sixth Buddhist Council held in Yangon from 1954 to 1956, was, according to Jordt, "the most visible and renowned effort" of the government and ecclesiastical authorities to revitalize the *sāsana* in Myanmar and was "seen as marking off a new period in history in which the *sāsana* would be universalized."[116] The timing was significant, for it concluded in May 1956, which coincided with the 2,500th anniversary of Gotama Buddha's *parinibbāna* and thus the halfway point of the 5,000-year period thought to separate the historical Buddha from his successor, Metteyya Buddha. Similar to the councils held in the fifteenth century, the Sixth Council was embedded in millenarian thinking and Metteyyanic expectations.[117] Even the location chosen was linked with the *weizzā* when, in 1948, a "Holy Man, who was dressed in pure white clothes" presented a devout layman with a staff and urged that it be handed over to Prime Minister U Nu so that he would be convinced to erect a pagoda that would usher in an era of peace and prosperity across the world.[118] Many *weizzā* devotees believed that the Liberation Era was to commence in 1956 at the end of the council.[119] The dual cycle of *sāsana* decline of two 2,500-year periods favored by *weizzā* groups was even brought up at the council, but the more normative theory of a gradual decline over the course of five periods of 1,000 years was considered valid.[120] At least by the 1990s and probably as early as the 1980s, most *weizzā* devotees no longer adhered to the Liberation Era theory. No informants or sources I consulted from the 1990s onward referred to the cyclical schema of the *sāsana*'s decline that was popular in the middle of the twentieth century. It seemed that most Buddhists (*weizzā*-affiliated and otherwise) had settled upon the more traditional view. Many devotees believed that an era when *weizzā* ruled the country was about to arrive but that it still fit with the general theory of the gradual, 5,000-year decline of the *sāsana*. Most of the *weizzā* associations had disbanded or were absorbed into non-*weizzā* organizations during the 1980s. As a consequence of General Ne Win's purge of the religious landscape early in the decade, *weizzā* associations, especially those concerned with practices that could be interpreted as black magic or sorcery, were more closely monitored.[121] Immediately following independence in 1948, Burmese authorities were preoccupied with suppressing ethnic insurgencies and worrying about communism invading the country. By the late 1970s, when these issues were under control, Ne Win turned his attention to religion and undertook a mission to purge the *sāsana* of elements that he perceived as deviating from orthodox Buddhism. In a speech delivered in December 1979, he likened these *weizzā* associations to Jim Jones's Peoples Temple cult and warned that such groups only sought to exploit their members for their own self-interest.[122] A series of restrictions were then placed upon the *weizzā* associations, and those considered illegal, like the Shwe-yin-kyaw Association popular among soldiers and civil servants, were banned, while others, like the Mano-citta-pada Association, were heavily monitored.[123] During this period, Ne Win also banned magazines, printed books, and other forms of media created by *weizzā* associations and even had portrayals of *weizzā* and their supernatural powers censored from written works and films. Houtman noted that books on such topics were prohibited from being sold in bookshops during his years of fieldwork in the 1980s.[124]

When the associations dissolved, *weizzā* members did not simply stop their activities, however. A further trickle-down effect seems to have occurred: instead of being in the hands of larger organized *weizzā* groups, *sāsana* responsibility fell to individual *weizzā* devotees. The power and responsibility for the care of the *sāsana* diffused still further to a wider swath of individual Buddhists, both lay and monastic, who were sought out by the *weizzā* to carry out their *sāsana* propagation missions. Keiko Tosa discovered during her fieldwork in the late 1980s and early 1990s that although *weizzā* beliefs and practices were still very popular among individual devotees (and were becoming increasingly so in the years she was in Myanmar), no one was particularly interested in forming new associations or joining the few remaining ones. Instead, they were devoted to personal, direct relationships with *weizzā* and carrying out *sāsana* propagation activities as directed by their patron *weizzā*.[125]

The few *weizzā* associations that remain active, and especially a growing number of individual devotees, continue to see themselves as the principal vanguards of the *sāsana* in a time when its vitality is still under attack. Instead of fighting colonialism or societal unrest, however, present-day associations and their devotees consider the greatest threat against the *sāsana* to be Islam. Although in recent years there has been a dramatic increase in physical violence that Buddhists have inflicted upon Muslims in Myanmar, for at least the past decade, *weizzā* associations have been engaged in spiritual warfare with what they perceived to be the evil, anti-Buddhist forces of Islam—a war, Foxeus reminds us, "fought by members seated in a cross-legged position."[126] Believing that their meditation techniques of the mind can influence the physical world around them, members of some associations engage in rituals to create earthquakes, tidal waves, typhoons, and similar catastrophes that could be used as weapons against Muslims. One *weizzā* organization believed, proudly, that their ritual activity generated the tsunami that struck South and Southeast Asia in December 2004 and that they navigated it away from Myanmar and toward Muslim-dominated Indonesia.[127] In their view, if large numbers of Muslims could be weakened or killed outside of Myanmar, they would be less likely to invade Myanmar at a later date. At a *weizzā* association's ritual celebration in 2004, about a year after the Iraq War began, a member of the congregation leaned over to me and said, "President George Bush is a great man even though he isn't Buddhist." When I asked what he meant by this, he replied that the president was doing a great service to the world by waging war on Muslims and "it is karmic retribution for the Muslims destroying the great Buddhas in Afghanistan!"

(referring, of course, to the desecration of the Buddhas of Bamiyan by the Taliban in 2001). Rozenberg also noted anti-Muslim rhetoric in the *weizzā* groups he studied.[128]

The majority of *weizzā* associations and individual devotees eschew such violence and focus instead on promoting the longevity of the *sāsana* through obtaining prowess in particular meditation techniques and engaging in missionary work of conversion, preaching, and healing. Such efforts are not made by royalty or monastic authorities, but by Buddhists from all walks of life who take seriously their responsibility to ensure that the *sāsana* is protected for future generations, despite the inevitability that it will eventually disappear completely from this world. For such devotees, the actions of the *weizzā*, like the wizard-saint at the beginning of this chapter, offer models for how they should live and how the world should be governed. They continue to look to and emulate the many great *weizzā* of the past who protected the *sāsana* in dynamic and multivalent ways and vow to carry on the mission that the *weizzā* began.

2

THE BUDDHA'S CHIEF WIZARD

One day while Ma Than Sein was sitting doing breath meditation, a man approached her and touched her head with his forefinger. The next thing she remembers is passing out. When she came to, she found herself in a dreamlike state. Suddenly, her body split into two: one part was dead while the other was still alive. The man reappeared in her vision. He picked up the half of her body still living and ascended into the sky. They flew through the air until they reached the great wizard-saint Bo Min Gaung. Upon seeing them, Bo Min Gaung exclaimed, "Hey! I didn't call for you yet! Go back to where you came from!" Startled, she began descending downward until she found herself whole again, alert, and sitting right back in the same spot where she began her meditation. For her, this experience was so powerful, so profound, so real that she interpreted is as a sign from Bo Min Gaung to ordain as a nun and devote her life to the *weizzā*'s mission of propagating the Buddha *sāsana*. After ordaining under the name of Daw Sundari, she continued to relish the karmic connection she believes to have with Bo Min Gaung, who has promised to watch over her for the rest of her life.[1]

Bo Min Gaung is arguably the most popular and revered *weizzā* in contemporary Myanmar despite, as we will see below, a modest degree of controversy that surrounds him. He continually appears in the lives of men and women throughout this book as it deals with instances of possession and dream states and matters pertaining to protecting and propagating the *sāsana*. To devote an entire monograph to the *weizzā* phenomenon as it manifests in the lives of Burmese Buddhists without exploring the life and times of Bo Min Gaung and the ways devotees interact with him would be a disservice to the study of lived religion in Myanmar. As most of this book takes a horizontal approach in looking at the ways a wide range of devotees engage with a spectrum of *weizzā* phenomena and saints, choosing to concentrate on one *weizzā* in particular offers something of a vertical case study, a deep exploration of how the themes raised throughout the book appear in people's relationships with a single *weizzā*.

In this chapter I attempt to understand what it was (and still is) about this figure that inspired such faith and devotion among everyday Burmese, irrespective of socioeconomic and religious background. Drawing on hagiographies, both written and oral, and iconography, I analyze how this old man could have risen to the rank of "Chief Wizard," second only to the Buddha, in such a short period of time. First, I will discuss the biographical process through which the figure of Bo Min Gaung has been created for devotees in publicly circulating media and word of mouth. Next, I will show that Bo Min Gaung's devotees expand his biography through their own experiences of him, and in doing so, transform his life story into something very personalized with an expansive past, present, and future linked to their understanding of their own experiences, karmic biography, and aspirations. Finally, I will explain how the selective appropriation of visual images of Bo Min Gaung and physical engagement with these images reveals another dimension of this personalized relationship to the saint, as well as how Bo Min Gaung as icon becomes a powerful focus for personalized affect.

Over the past decade, I noticed what appeared to be an increase in the popularity of Bo Min Gaung and people who claimed to be his devotees. I say, "appeared to be," because I was unsure if the number of books, lithographs, statues, and stories of Bo Min Gaung was indeed increasing or if I was increasingly aware of things related to him, as he had recently become the focus of my research. But as I made a conscious effort to be attentive to the cult of Bo Min Gaung, I learned that my initial suspicions were correct. Attending four annual Bo Min Gaung anniversary celebrations at Mount Popa (the site of Bo Min Gaung's death) and witnessing the number of attendees grow significantly each year, for instance, I knew that his cult was on the rise. My assumptions were supported by longtime anthropologist of Burmese religions Brac de la Perrière when she recently observed that it is not that "weizzā related practices are new, but that devotion to the leaders of weizzā cults has known an increasing favour among the overall public. The weizzā phenomenon has gained in visibility through the significant increase of weizzā representations everywhere in Burma. At Mount Popa, it has resulted in the displacement of the December (natdaw) spirit festival with the September (tawthalin) [weizzā] celebration and the explosion of Bo Min Gaung's iconography."[2]

Surprisingly, very little is known about Bo Min Gaung.[3] He was a layman born in northern Myanmar around 1885 and spent the last years of his life in the small town of Kyaukpadaung, located about thirty miles southeast of Pagan, before passing away in 1952. Small cults already began to develop around Bo Min Gaung during his lifetime, and by the 1950s his prominence is reflected in Emanuel Sarkisyanz's ethnographic research, where he learned that Bo Min Gaung "ranked second only to Lord Buddha himself";[4] that caused Michael Mendelson to proclaim that his death was a "watershed for the formation of gaing [weizzā associations]."[5] This is still true today, and as scholar of religion Per-Arne Berglie recently pointed out from his fieldwork in Upper Myanmar, "the importance of Bo Min Gaung for Burmese contemporary popular religiosity cannot be overestimated."[6] If one were to enter any Buddhist holy site, for example, there would most likely be a statue or image of Bo Min Gaung somewhere on the premises, usually to the side of the main Buddha altar or in an area specifically reserved for *weizzā* devotional activities. Images of him can be purchased at most Buddhist shrines throughout the country and can now be found in the religious accoutrements sections of supermarkets and department stores.

In spite of his popularity and ubiquity, most devotees know little, if anything, about the circumstances of Bo Min Gaung's life. For them, the most important aspect revolves around his attainment of *weizzā*-hood in 1952. This is the date when he "exited dead" (B. *athey-twet*) and his spirit left his body to dwell with a retinue of other *weizzā* in another realm. It is from this abode and with his spirit that Bo Min Gaung continues to enter this world to interact with his devotees. As I traveled the country collecting stories about Bo Min Gaung, and the more I read about him in books, magazines, and websites, the more I found it difficult to understand how he could be an especially good figure for this kind of imaginative intervention. Mentally and emotionally unstable, he was prone to violent outbursts and periods of moody isolation. According to interviews with people who knew Bo Min Gaung when he was alive, he barely spoke, and if he did, it was often in gibberish or unclear statements that were later interpreted by his disciples. Soon after his arrival at Mount Popa Village, "many people came to see him," one lifelong resident recounted. "I did not like him. He did not behave well. Completely shameless, he did not care about anybody else as he urinated holding his anatomy before the people. He was also found cursing rudely to some people."[7] He often "sat carelessly exposing his genitals" even to women who came to show him reverence, reported another man who knew Bo Min Gaung when alive.[8] Others remember him "flinging his own feces at those who came to visit him."[9] These few, yet detailed interviews describe a man who appears to have suffered from significant psychological disorders. And yet in spite of his actions, the number of people who came to pay respects to him grew steadily from about 1947 until his death in 1952. Some have attributed his fame to his handlers, a husband and wife with whom he lived, who were cunning in the ways they created a cult around a man who had severe mental problems.[10]

In his incarnation as a modern Burmese saint, Bo Min Gaung first became well known during World War II, a time of great upheavals and changes for a country that had already known much chaos. Both he and his initial devotees were marked by the time, as many of the stories that are connected with his living years are related to the war in one way or another. One man remembers that during the Allied forces' bomb raids in the Mount Popa area, Bo Min Gaung fearlessly remained atop Mount Popa while the rest of the villagers scrambled into the jungle for cover.[11] He was even thought to possess the uncanny ability to foresee the bombings before they occurred. "When Bo Min Gaung stood atop a rock and flapped his arms, we all knew to hide. For soon, the bombs would fall," recalls one man.[12] When the war was over and communist rebels took control of the area, stories about Bo Min Gaung's defiance in the face of oppressive forces once again began circulating. A communist rebel stationed at Mount Popa in the early 1950s was ordered by his superiors to interrogate Bo Min Gaung. He later said in an interview that the interrogation group fired five rifle shots at the *weizzā* and missed him entirely. This young communist knew right away that he was no ordinary crazy old man.[13]

With Japanese, Allied, and communist forces wreaking havoc throughout the country, it is not difficult to imagine how heroic Bo Min Gaung appeared to the Burmese, especially when stories circulated about his disrespectful and astonishing actions toward the soldiers. Foxeus points out that this period (from the late 1940s onward) was a tumultuous one characterized by ethnic separatist insurgencies, communist rebellions, and communal tensions between Buddhists and Muslims, and sees it as "a breeding ground" for *weizzā* cults.[14] Bo Min Gaung most likely resembled other World War II–era heroes, real and imaginary. The hope that help would come from a hidden, unexpected source was shared in various quarters at the time of his cult's founding. For many people, the chaos that had descended upon the country and affected so many of their lives must have seemed foreseen or put into motion by hidden forces working from an otherworldly realm. For such devotees, the suffering was too great for the *weizzā* not to intervene unless, as many believed, this series of events was predestined and allowed to take place by the *weizzā* as a result of the negative collective karma of the Burmese people. (We will return to this topic in chapter 5.)

The many heroic accounts in written and oral forms that were produced in the years immediately preceding and following Bo Min Gaung's death did much to inspire people to become devout followers. As he was not widely known, however, his life, activities, and teachings were, in a sense, a blank slate to be filled by the imaginations of the new devotees. By looking at the kinds of stories his devotees chose to include in hagiographical accounts, we can see how Bo Min Gaung was a saint of his time whose miracles were reflections of that period. The most popular miracle he was thought to have accomplished, for example, was starting and driving a broken-down car that had been neglected for years. An elderly man living in Mount Popa Village at the time recalls that "the most wonderful [miracle Bo Min Gaung performed] involved the old car with a busted engine. He started it up all by himself and drove it down the road. It was really amazing!"[15] If asked to recount just one miracle of Bo Min Gaung, devotees will almost always tell this story, and it is given much attention in written hagiographies. Although devotees find nothing unusual about this miracle, it always struck me as odd that this, in addition to his other well-known miracle of magically placing a derailed train back on its tracks, is most associated with him, considered "King of the *Weizzā*." Upon further reflection, however, and following historian of religion Sophia Deboick's idea that saints can be seen as "hazy mirrors of their surrounding society," "invested with a range of social ideals by their devotees, and thus providing a reflection of the societies that venerate them,"[16] I wonder if these miracles reflect early devotees' fascination with technological advancements that were making inroads into Myanmar around this time. In the next two chapters we will see how devotees came to equate *weizzā* power with electricity, radio waves, and power lines, and special pagodas were erected that acted as antennae for intercepting the wavelengths of the *weizzā*. Historians of technology have recently shown how, beginning at the turn of the twentieth century, the success of urbanization in Southeast Asian countries and the pace with which technology made its way into the everyday lives of people, had a significant impact on the "inner histories and local narratives of these regions."[17]

Bo Min Gaung was a saint of modern times—able to foretell when bombs would fall, restart broken mechanical equipment, and protect Myanmar from catastrophic events.[18] He was (and continues to be) a modern-day superhero: although a distinctly Burmese Buddhist champion, he was also equated with the popular American superhero Superman. "As a boy I was fascinated by the movie *Superman*," writes Kyaw Myaing, a Bo Min Gaung devotee who runs a series of popular *weizzā*-related websites and chat groups. "One day my father told me, 'Do you know, my son, we also have superman in our culture and tradition?' . . . Bo Min Gaung is an extraordinary man."[19] Another devotee alive during Bo Min Gaung's time remembers that "one day while we were sipping tea together, a communist fired his gun at Bo Min Gaung. It failed. He pulled the trigger again, and it also failed." Like a superhero impervious to bullets, Bo Min Gaung said to the rebel, "You cannot kill me. Only I can kill myself."[20]

Although his cult began during his lifetime, the apotheosis of Bo Min Gaung began immediately after his death when admiring disciples expressed their adoration in writings and oral stories of the virtues and miraculous feats of their master. Unlike fairy tales of fictional people and places, there was a certain veracity to the legend of Bo Min Gaung, centered on a real personality from an actual geographical location and dealing with real facts. These facts, however, are embedded within a great deal of fabrication. Regardless, such accounts do more than merely entertain by exaggeration; they make serious arguments as well. These legends define a good part of what people understand to be the content of their devotional lives, specifically, and religious traditions, more generally.

Religious biographies are less concerned with presenting a chronologically accurate rendering of the subject's life than with paying special attention to the subject's supernatural attainments.[21] Bo Min Gaung's biographies are an excellent example of this. Making sure to emphasize the miraculous events that manifested in his life, his biographers move freely forward and backward through decades and even centuries, connecting Bo Min Gaung to events and people that help to highlight his status as a Buddhist saint. The episodes are "chronologically disjointed" in that he migrates from one time period to another.[22] Bo Min Gaung is thought to have been involved in carrying out Buddhist activities during periods stretching back five hundred years and is believed to do so continually now and into the future. An ongoing concern of biographers has been the writing of biographies of Bo Min Gaung dealing with successive rebirths.[23] There is a preoccupation with tracing his spiritual lineage back to several high-profile individuals who bear the same or a similar name. The purpose is to firmly establish the genuineness of his saintliness and royal prestige. Biographers count among his precursors such kings as Min Pyauk (r. 1352–1364), Min Gaung (r. 1401–1422), Dhammazedi Min Gaung (r. 1460–1491), and Min Gaung II (r. 1481–1502).[24]

Next, such biographies often "spiritualize" their subjects by purging any references to human weakness.[25] In biographies of Bo Min Gaung we find nothing, for example, of his emotions and thoughts and are presented with a person who is exalted in ways typical of Buddhist saints in general. He is called the "Master of Loving-Kindness" (B. *metta-shin*), "Master of Supernatural Powers" (B. *siddhi-shin*), and "Master of Virtue" (B. *pāramī-shin*). He is said to have lived as a hermit in the jungle practicing meditation and to have traveled the country erecting pagodas in non-Buddhist areas, converting Christians to Buddhism, and teaching villagers to observe precepts, offer donations, and develop compassion. The hagiographical tradition associated with Bo Min Gaung consists of the stories his contemporaries began telling about him and continues with the retelling of these and newer stories in various places by devotees whose imaginations are captured by this ambiguous and passionate holy figure. Already during his lifetime, and certainly in the years immediately following his death, his biographers were recasting Bo Min Gaung from a man who may very well have suffered from mental disorders into an enlightened being whose madness was merely a guise for imparting esoteric teachings that would bring about spiritual realization in those he encountered, testing the faithfulness of his disciples, and keeping unwelcome authority figures from bothering him.[26] One day while I was sitting in a teashop at the base of Mount Popa a homeless man, clearly dealing with some kind of mental affliction, was shouting at and harassing people in front of the shop. When I asked the shopkeeper if he did not find this man annoying, he said that he did but that "no one can tell for sure if he is Bo Min Gaung or not. He may be pretending to be crazy."[27] An elderly man who witnessed some of Bo Min Gaung's erratic behavior while he was alive argued that it was not to be taken at face value and instead needed to be interpreted, for it "offered secret information," sometimes about "impending danger." Providing an example, he recalled that "when six bombers emptied all their bombs over Mount Popa, we remembered Bo Min Gaung's behavior prior to this: he went out between the rocks, opened a packet of food, and swallowed it all down. So next time we saw him do this, we all hid in bomb shelters. And, sure enough, the bombers came as expected and showered bullets and bombs."[28]

For our purposes, I am not so much concerned with the biographer whose personal reasons for writing accounts of Bo Min Gaung we cannot clearly discern as with the biographical extension that I witness in the lives of weizzā devotees. This is particularly pertinent to the study of the religious lives of weizzā devotees because examining how and why the biographer's process of creating the religious biography, whether it be a formal publication, a story shared among devotees, or, as we will see below, the acquisition of an iconographic representation of Bo Min Gaung, allows us to see stages in the deepening of a devotee's engagement with the wizard-saint. Religious biographies are traditionally defined as stories about saints, but in the case of Bo Min Gaung they become stories about both the *weizzā* and the circumstances the devotees telling the stories found themselves in over the course of their relationships with him. Telling their stories about Bo Min Gaung is a narrative practice that first describes the personal problems of the biographer before describing how the *weizzā* intervened to help. The focus turns from the person and activities of Bo Min Gaung during his lifetime to the person and activities of Bo Min Gaung at definable moments in *their* lives, in which he intervened and will potentially intervene in the future. Most devotees do not particularly know or care a great deal about Bo Min Gaung's life before he "exited." For instance, most know little, if anything, but the year of his death and several well-known anecdotes about his life. "I think you are more of an expert on Bo Min Gaung's life than me," the owner and caretaker of a Bo Min Gaung shrine in Mandalay told me during one of our initial discussions. "I only decided to build this shrine after Bo Min Gaung appeared to me in a dream," he continued.[29] Such became the common refrain from most of my informants, even from mediums of Bo Min Gaung whom I questioned about his life during those moments when they were channeling the saint. Instead of focusing on the particulars of his life as a historical person, devotees delighted in regaling me with stories of Bo Min Gaung's supernatural interventions in their worlds. They would end their often long-winded accounts with a personal story of how Bo Min Gaung interceded in their lives or in the lives of friends and family, thereby adding a new thread to the hagiographical corpus.[30] What mattered most for them was that Bo Min Gaung appeared to them or intervened at an important point in their life—a point where, as Orsi beautifully phrases it, "the transcendent broke into time."[31] Orsi continues, "A saint's story was not exhausted by the details of his or her life on earth, just as stories about family members do not stop being told when they die. Hagiography is best understood as a creative process that goes on and on in the circumstances of everyday life, as people add their own experiences of a saint to his or her *vita* and contemporaries get woven into the lives of the saints. Such storytelling was one of the ways the communion of the saints became real in people's experiences and memories."[32]

Although the devout understand Bo Min Gaung to be an entirely autonomous being with his own will, his actions are nonetheless intimately related to the circumstances of devotees' own lives. They describe him as an active presence and frequently recount stories about his mystical activities, integrating their personal experiences with themes drawn from a larger mythical corpus. In addition to acting as an interpretive lens that orders and imparts coherence to the world, these stories also are employed to reimagine events over which their narrators have little control, disclosing a world of alternative possibilities and meanings (as we will see with the female *weizzā* mediums in the next chapter). Let us explore this theme further with particular emphasis on devotees' visual and physical engagements with Bo Min Gaung.

PRESENTLY POWERFUL

"Grandfather cured my heart condition over twenty years ago at this very spot," a middle-aged man told me at a *weizzā* shrine in Mandalay while holding the hand of a statue of Bo Min Gaung. His hand never left the statue as he went on with his story of how he was born with heart disease and endured a childhood of illnesses. During those parts of his life story that were particularly emotional, he would tenderly stroke the arm and caress the hand of his "grandfather." In fact, it was to such laying of hands upon the statue that he attributed his direct healing. Beaming with happiness, he confided that he did "not forget Grandpa, and Grandpa does not forget me."[33]

Tremendously powerful, Bo Min Gaung is not one to trifle with. Harsh, rude, and domineering on the outside, he has a tender side that his devout see. Affectionately referring to him as "Grandpa," his close devotees imagine him to be a gentle, yet stern and protective grandfatherly figure. He could and would (although seldom did) perform acts of kindness to his most faithful. However, the appellation of grandfather only began to be used within the past thirty years or so. During his lifetime and for years after, he was referred to as *bodaw* (religious mendicant) or by other, lofty-sounding names, like "Mahāgandhārī Vijjādhara Bodaw Aung Min Gaung,"[34] that, when translated to English, illustrates the way his early devotees viewed him: "religious master and powerful teacher who possessed wisdom of the secrets of attaining perfection."

More important, the way people began to interact with him after his bodily departure, that is, the tone of their relationships, took on a softer, gentler character. The Bo Min Gaung who began appearing to them aurally and visually was also much milder, speaking in soft words that were easily understandable instead of the incomprehensible jibberish that he spoke when alive. Although still retaining some sternness that was a mark of his power, and which invoked great reverence, he became more easily accessible, relatable, and thus more widespread and encompassing than he had been when alive. And perhaps like a grandfather who mellows out in his twilight years, Bo Min Gaung went from being remembered as a mad saint throwing fecal matter at those who came seeking his counsel to a protector saint who watched benevolently over his grandchildren. This widespread appeal helped his fame and influence to grow beyond the boundaries of the cults and made him a patron saint who transgressed social, geographic, institutional, and even religious boundaries.[35]

Not only do devotees see themselves as family, they also see themselves as karmically related to Bo Min Gaung. Regardless of the different ways various devotees see him, how they see themselves related to him is the same and is predicated on a karmic bond spanning lifetimes. Known as *patthan-set* (literally "connected by karmic rebirths"), this bond between the devotee and Bo Min Gaung has its genesis in a previous life encounter.[36] Because devotees consider themselves karmically bonded with Bo Min Gaung, they do not necessarily see that they have much of a choice about being part of this relationship for the time period Bo Min Gaung wishes to engage them. "Grandfather's voice is always in my head nudging me to do this or that," one devotee, a goldsmith, told me. "He's always right. When I don't do what he says, he doesn't punish me. The bad results of my actions are punishment enough!" He smiles as he goes on to tell me of a business deal that went sour when his partner, whom Bo Min Gaung had indicated was untrustworthy, left town with all his money.[37] Another devotee, who is currently living in Australia and offers advice to people through online messaging apps whenever he finds himself under the partial possession of Bo Min Gaung, told me that he has a "permanent connection" with the *weizzā* because he was "Bo Min Gaung's son for many lifetimes." He sounded rather frustrated when he went on to say that he "has no choice, really" and "doesn't want to be in this role" but after witnessing how everything "Grandpa" said came true, he became a firm believer in both Bo Min Gaung's power and his own power as a *weizzā* medium.[38]

Patthan-set with Bo Min Gaung is not restricted to adult devotees. Children too are known to possess strong karmic bonds with him, and some, under the direction of their parents, go on to be revered individuals in their small communities. One such child, an eight-year-old boy named Ye Kyaw Min, was thought to be the reincarnation of Bo Min Gaung who had returned to this world in 1987 to help sentient beings and propagate the *sāsana*.[39] He began to exhibit behavior similar to Bo Min Gaung from an early age, and his parents started dressing him like the saint. Within months, people from all around the area, including monks from Mount Popa, came to visit and pay respects to this young Bo Min Gaung. During his fieldwork, Foxeus came across a similar case of a young novice monk about six years old who had the ability to channel the spirit of Bo Min Gaung. This boy also exhibited adultlike behavior reminiscent of Bo Min Gaung and even possessed the power to predict winning lottery numbers.[40]

Whether Bo Min Gaung comes in a moment of crisis or a moment of ordinariness, the moment is charged and never forgotten. As we saw in previous chapters, and in my personal anecdote that began this book, one often experiences Bo Min Gaung entering their lives when they least expect it. While they are almost always unexpected, there is certainly nothing random about these encounters. They occur exactly when and how they are supposed to as a result of one's karmic bond with him. A *weizzā* who visits a devotee in physical form, through a medium, or in a dream or meditative vision is the result of the person's developed *pāramī* (acquired virtue).[41] In a sense, the devotee is elected or chosen by Bo Min Gaung, whether they wish it or not. Confident in being chosen by Bo Min Gaung after having an experience with the saint that confirms for them the idea of *patthan-set,* men and women devotees remain faithful to this relationship for years and devote much time, energy, and resources to it. Such a bond "is interpreted as a consequence and reactualization of a relationship in one or several previous lives," Rozenberg writes, and "to be called constitutes both the continuation and the crowning of this relationship."[42] Even for those devotees who never asked to be elected by Bo Min Gaung, after the initial shock of experiencing him come into their lives, they accept that to be selected is a great honor. Devotees say that they "are very lucky" to have Bo Min Gaung to "go to for help," "rely upon," and "be protected by."[43]

DYNAMIC VISUALITY

Influenced by David Morgan's work on visual and material objects in people's everyday lived religious experiences, much of my research on *weizzā* devotees' engagement with visual representations of Bo Min Gaung has been driven by the following questions: How do lithographs, photographs, and statues of Bo Min Gaung function in the practices that make up the devotees' religious lives? How do devotees use these objects to articulate their social experiences? How do objects help generate and maintain the narratives and rituals that make sense of a lifeworld?[44]

Making contact with Bo Min Gaung and maintaining a close relationship with him are central concerns of his devotees. Even those blessed with the ability to experience more visceral encounters with the *weizzā* through possession or dreams still use material objects, most often in the form of images, to commune with their "grandpa." Devotional images of this sort are "media of presence,"[45] not simply copies of the original but rather an ontological closeness with the original. Such media, which in the case of Bo Min Gaung include holy cards, photographs, lithographs, statues, prayer beads, pieces of cloth, and a variety of other objects, are thought to hold the power of the *weizzā* and to make it, and him, present. Such iconography is "thoroughly 'interested,' 'engaged,' functional and extrinsically purposive.' Media of presence are efficacious and they serve as points of encounter—between . . . humans and sacred figures."[46]

As we saw in the previous chapter, religious images are an essential part of Burmese Buddhism, and engaging with them is an important aspect of devotional activities. People engage Bo Min Gaung emotionally and imaginatively, bringing him into their lives. In this process of exchange, Bo Min Gaung acquires another set of meanings, qualities, and associations than those presented in published and oral biographies. Such is the process of improvisation by which the wizard-saint is imagined into being. The devout have strong opinions about which iconographic representations of Bo Min Gaung are more "correct" than others, and it has little to do with oral or textual biographical accounts of Bo Min Gaung. Direct experiences that a devotee, or a close friend or relative, has had with Bo Min Gaung are highly influencing factors that contribute to their preference. Usually, a devotee would decide to acquire a statue or a two-dimensional picture of Bo Min Gaung for themselves only after having some direct experience of him.

These representations can be purchased for moderate fees or are freely given at most of the larger pagoda complexes and specific places of pilgrimage associated with Bo Min Gaung and other *weizzā*. Besides public shrines, two- and three-dimensional images of Bo Min Gaung are common in home altars or shrine rooms alongside images of the Buddha; inside vehicles, wallets, and purses; and on walls of shops and restaurants. Just as Bo Min Gaung can potentially be everywhere, so too is his power accessible to ordinary people in their everyday lives. For the many devotees who maintain shrines in their homes, for instance, the images installed within are used for meditation, chanting, and homage, often several times a day. Images of *weizzā* are always placed in an area that is lower than the Buddha statues for, as I was often reminded, *weizzā* are not *arahant*s (enlightened beings), and placing them equal to the Buddha would be disrespectful. Many devout even place statues and images of *weizzā* saints on a separate altar altogether, albeit immediately alongside the statues of the Buddha and his disciples. Despite Bo Min Gaung reportedly having said, "Forget about my body. I will not use my body. I will use my *nāma* [spirit]," people all over Myanmar continue to create and interact with images of him.

During one of my daily trips to a pagoda in Yangon associated with the *weizzā*, I got to talking with one of the caretakers there about statues of Bo Min Gaung and indicated that I wished to buy one for myself. There were some small shops near the pagoda that sold statues of Bo Min Gaung, and when I showed him some of the ones I was thinking of purchasing (Bo Min Gaung sitting cross-legged, with short hair, and holding a teacup), he told me to hold off and return tomorrow, when he would give me a statue that he insisted represented the true nature of Bo Min Gaung. When I returned the next day, he gave me a statue of Bo Min Gaung similar to the others I was thinking of buying, except that it had long hair and a hand extended as if holding a cigarette. When I showed him actual photographs of Bo Min Gaung that were reproduced and published in several biographies and asked why the image he gave me was better than any of those from the books, he simply replied, "This is an image based on my aunt's vision of him who appeared to her in a dream."[47] Asking other devotees why they chose a particular image to acquire, despite it bearing little resemblance to any iconographic representation of Bo Min Gaung as he looked in photographs and drawings from the 1940s and '50s, I was told that their chosen images were "awe-inspiring," "unusual," or "strange," or that they were similar to the Bo Min Gaung they knew from dreams or visions.[48] "One day while repeatedly chanting a mantra in front of a Bo Min Gaung statue, I had a vision of Bo Min Gaung," one devotee wrote in a *weizzā* devotional tract. "He looked mostly how he does in photos except that there were some differences in his clothing . . . I tried hard to stare at his face, but it was blurry. Suddenly, he closed his eyes, and the *Buddhānusati Gāthā* came out of his mouth.[49] When finished chanting, he opened his eyes and disappeared. From that time onward, I've been searching for any photographic evidence of Bo Min Gaung looking like the image I saw in my vision."[50] I came to understand that the devout had their own, more personal, criteria for recognizing Bo Min Gaung. Before they determined to obtain a representation, they would already have had some direct experience of him; the acquisition of an image was a gesture of gratitude, generally undertaken after some significant life event had occurred or was taking place. Such an acquisition, could also be a gesture of anticipation; creating a connection with the saint and thus opening a channel for meaningful events to occur. Christopher Pinney's argument that religious devotees of saints are "not interested in what images 'look like,' but only in what they can 'do'" or are not interested in what "artists had put into the pictures, but in what they . . . could get out of the images" is not quite relevant here.[51] Devotees do indeed have a vested interest in what their images look like, as well as what they can do, and will go to great lengths to find their preferred image.

Even for those devout who may not care what the image looks like, there is certainly a longing to have the saint who acted for them at a crucial moment nearby in visible ways. When they describe how they imagine Bo Min Gaung to look, his devotees emphasize his face or bodily comportment, and when they pay homage to or request something from him, they search to see him either in the statues, photographs, or paintings before them or in their imaginations. With each new iconographic representation, devotees add new biographical material to the life of Bo Min Gaung, created out of an event related to their relationship with him or through a miraculous event that occurred in relation to a particular image. Circulating biographical accounts, both written and oral, as well as personal encounters with Bo Min Gaung before he "exited" in 1952 are important for informing people's perceptions of and relations with the saint. But looking at the stages of engagement with Bo Min Gaung throughout the devotee's life, we find that, while written and oral biographies can create certain conditions of expectation, it is individuals' experiences that are understood by them as transformative in relation to the saint. This is evident in the case of an elderly woman I spoke with in Yangon regarding her previous experiences with the saint. This woman had the chance to meet Bo Min Gaung in 1950 and told me that "he didn't say anything. He just sat there staring blankly and mumbling nonsense."[52] She was not impressed and left not believing him to possess special powers. But when she and her husband led me into their shrine room, which contained more than ten Bo Min Gaung statues, I was shocked. Seeing the confusion on my face, the husband told me that only after Bo Min Gaung passed away did they begin to believe in his powers. When they faced obstacles in their life with regard to health and finances, he appeared to them to help set things right. Since then, they have been devout followers and make the pilgrimage to Mount Popa every year to take part in the annual celebration of Bo Min Gaung's passing.

Despite the disparity in opinions of what constitutes an authentic Bo Min Gaung, such images hardly vary by more than four different iconographic representations of him, which suggests that there is an accepted set of iconographic blueprints for how Bo Min Gaung should be portrayed (figs. 20 and 21). There are no associations or textual sources that indicate to the public what are and are not acceptable images.[53] Rather, it is the devotees themselves who consider some images to be more acceptable than others, and unlike the iconographic imagery of Catholic saints, Thérèse of Lisieux and Francesca Cabrini, for example, whose photographs are thought to be the most accurate representation,[54] the ways devotees interact with the images of Bo Min Gaung, can be innovated more freely. Although an image maker may engage in some experimental creativity, he will generally keep in line with previous versions of Bo Min Gaung and familiar themes, yet all the while refining his creation in accordance with any personal experiences he or his customer may have of Bo Min Gaung.

Examining the ways devotees modify images of Bo Min Gaung, both in the figurative sense and in terms of retouching, cropping, and graphically editing, offers valuable insight into how the devout understand their relationship with the wizard-saint. Because Bo Min Gaung lived fairly recently and was considered important enough by his devotees to have his picture taken at a time when photography was still quite rare in the country, we have access to about eight photographs of him. These portray an elderly and frail man and often appear in published biographies and magazine articles. The images that devotees engage with, however, are usually doctored representations of a healthier, more robust Bo Min Gaung image (figs. 22 and 23). His stern disposition and rugged, muscular appearance in such images are important for how his devotees interact with him and indications of his virile supernatural powers.

Unlike the concept of saints of other religious traditions, however, the devout do not necessarily believe that images of Bo Min Gaung are alive, and unlike images of the Buddha, they are not ritually charged. Bo Min Gaung has shed his corporeal body and does his work through his *nāma* (spirit) by having it enter into the bodies/minds of others. This leaves open the possibility that his spirit can enter into two- and three-dimensional images to enact miracles before moving on, leaving behind an image that is ontologically more potent than before he had entered into it. *Weizzā* images display no outward signs of their potency. Statues of Bo Min Gaung do not cry blood or oil, for example; the power of an image is left to the discretion of the devotee. Oftentimes a devotee will feel a strong affinity to a specific image, regardless of its provenance. One man's faith in Bo Min Gaung increased significantly after a statue helped heal his daughter's skin condition. "My wife and I were distraught at how severe our daughter's eczema had become. It never got this bad before, and no doctor could help. I have several statues of Bo Min Gaung in my Buddha room, and one day while paying homage to him, my eyes fell upon one statue in particular," Nyaing Win told me. His eyes began to tear as he went on with the story. "I felt drawn to this statue and thought that perhaps Bo Min Gaung had come to visit me through this statue. I begged him to help cure my daughter. Suddenly, the hairs on the back of my neck stood on end, and a feeling of great coolness covered my body. I smiled, knowing that something special had happened. The next day we were amazed that my daughter's eczema was almost completely gone!" There was nothing extraordinary about the provenance of this particular image (he told me it had been purchased at a road-side shrine while on pilgrimage several years prior), but because of the intensity of the moment, this man formed an instantaneous bond with the statue, which has only grown stronger over the years as evidenced by the preferential treatment this devotee has shown. "I offer green tea and incense to Grandfather every morning," he told me, "and ever since that one day, my daughter's eczema has never gotten so bad as before."[55]

Over time, however, a common set of signs has become accepted by devotees as proof that Bo Min Gaung is acting through a particular image in some way. While the abatement of a skin ailment was a personal sign to the aforementioned devotee, other, externally identifiable signs are also sought out for proof of an image's potency. Magazines, devotional literature, and even online chat rooms and community groups are venues where the devout can share stories and even post images of the ways they believe Bo Min Gaung to be interacting with them through their two- and three-dimensional images. For example, photographs of cigarettes offered in which the burnt ash remains intact (figs. 24 and 25) are just one example of external signs of Bo Min Gaung's power.[56]

Such occurrences are catalysts for devotees to develop strong bonds with not only Bo Min Gaung but also the image itself. While it is much rarer for Bo Min Gaung to work through photographs and paintings, he has been thought to enter into two-dimensional images of himself. This is evidenced in an account provided by a photographer who took one of the few iconic photographs of Bo Min Gaung shortly before he died in 1952 (fig. 23). The photographer begins by saying that he had never experienced anything supernatural in all his life, but on the evening of December 25, 1993, at about ten o'clock, something very strange happened. While processing a role of black-and-white film, he saw that the water where he had placed the developing pictures began to bubble. "Like the sound of a scarab beetle, the water made a 'tichit, tichit' sound," he recounts. While looking in the water for the cause of this, he and his wife saw three Bo Min Gaung photos among the other photographs he was developing. "I immediately took out the three Bo Min Gaung pictures and the water went back to normal. When I placed one of the Bo Min Gaung pictures back into the water, it began to bubble again and make that sound. The sound became especially loud when my wife placed all three Bo Min Gaung photographs back with the remaining photographs. After we took the Bo Min Gaung photographs back out, the water went back to being calm."[57]

Amazed, he and his wife took this as a sign of something wonderful. He remembered taking this picture in the early 1950s only after Bo Min Gaung gave permission and was therefore convinced that the photo was, indeed, a *siddhi-win* picture (a picture into which supernatural power has entered). He went on to make nine thousand copies and distributed them to whoever wanted one.[58] Some of Bo Min Gaung's disciples drew lots to receive those photographs from an original set of twenty. As for the original photograph, however, the photographer pays homage to it daily, and according to him, "it still retains the power it exhibited on the first day." When the photographer had malaria and was in the hospital, he placed the picture on the wall next to his bed and gazed upon it until he got better.

Mass-produced religious objects without a context of ritual production, Walter Benjamin proposed, can be considered less potent and effective than, say, a sacred diagram, produced with magical spells. This is not the case with lithographs, photographs and statues of Bo Min Gaung, and as John Clark points out, "there is a kind of reversal in Benjamin's theory concerning the 'aura' of the image, where the image actually *gains* status with reproduction rather than *loses* it."[59] Take for instance the mass-produced edited images of Bo Min Gaung. When I visited the printing shop that produced it, I saw dozens of 1' × 2' printouts, each containing twenty wallet-sized copies of this image. Some images even retained the marginal marks left over from the printing process and had not been trimmed when laminated. The images did not need to be infused with any potency and were immediately disseminated to people who entered the shop.

I argue that the image's power derives from the affective tone it takes on when a devotee engages with it visually, physically, or imaginitively. "Charisma and aura find new ways to infuse themselves into mass-produced artifacts," Tarocco remarks, and this infusion takes place at the interface of the viewer and the image.[60] Unlike devotees of Hindu deities, whose relationship with the image is predicated on *darshan* or the "mutuality of 'seeing and being seen,'" *weizzā* devotees base their relationships more on feelings that arise when they interact with the *weizzā* image.[61] For both, however, the image's power is, as Pinney observed, "one that springs from a *corporeal* practice in which it is the devotee's visual and *bodily* performances that contribute crucially to the potential power—one might say completion—of the image."[62] In other words, the power stems from the personalized affective tone that the devotee experiences when viewing, touching, and imagining the image.

PERSONALIZED AFFECT

Statues and images are the preferred gateways for the devout to interact with Bo Min Gaung and to ask for his assistance. By touching, valuable qualities or powers are thought to pass from the image to a subject. The person making physical contact with the image intends, or more often hopes, to receive something: protection, health, good fortune, etc. And while it is not necessary to bring a body part into contact with the image to receive such beneficence, I came to see that such action works to seal the request made by the petitioner. As anthropologist of religion Anthony Wallace points out, it is as if "mere contact permitted its flow. . . . The fundamental principle is the universal law of power: to acquire a power, touch an object that contains that power."[63] Devotees engage in tactile interactions with images of Bo Min Gaung in the privacy of their homes or cars, or publicly at temple complexes or religious festivals. Touching his image, stroking it almost sensually, and whispering to it, the devout physically engage Bo Min Gaung.

Examining this practice is important for understanding the "felt life of religion."[64] This affective turn gives us insight into how it "feels" to be in relationship with a saint, and the recognition that that affect is often a religious goal in itself. A devotee's physical engagement with the image infuses it with a presence that is, in turn, felt in the body of the devotee. This creates an instant relationship between the devotee and the image. "So immediate" is this bond, Morgan writes, "that the image is experienced as more than a representation."[65] Such a relationship is not felt abstractly but rather in embodied and visceral ways.[66]

These kinds of interactions and relationships would be unthinkable with a statue or image of the Buddha, however. When I asked several devotees why, one told me that a statue of the Buddha is more like a monument that is erected to remember the deceased: "One pays homage to it, but since the Buddha attained enlightenment, he cannot help in this world any longer."[67] Another devotee admitted that a Buddha statue is alive and potent in the sense that it is infused with power after a monk consecrates it, but said, "I don't know, I just can't talk to it the way I can speak with Grandpa [Bo Min Gaung]." Perhaps concerned that I might think he was being disrespectful to the Buddha, he quickly added, "Know that the Buddha is all powerful [he chanted a portion of a Buddhist text that illustrates this] and can do what he wishes. But Grandpa is physically nearby, and I feel intimate with him."[68]

The difference in how the devout interact with representations of the Buddha and Bo Min Gaung further clarified this point. One rainy afternoon in Yangon, sitting in the corner of a shrine room dedicated to Bo Min Gaung located at a popular pagoda, I witnessed the tender affection the devout showed. One man, a taxi driver in his mid-thirties, after bowing to both the Buddha and Bo Min Gaung and offering incense to each, knelt down in front of the statue of Bo Min Gaung, lit a cigarette, and placed it in one of the statue's hands. He proceeded to stroke the statue, beginning with the head and working his way down to the feet, eventually resting his hands upon Bo Min Gaung's knees (fig. 26). In hushed tones, the man asked Bo Min Gaung to bestow some of his power to help him with his *adhiṭṭhāna* (religious vow). He then spent ten minutes speaking in a reverent, yet friendly, manner telling "Grandpa" about family problems and economic hardships he was facing. Initially, it was rather jarring to witness such intimacy being directed at such a revered figure, but the shock quickly turned to admiration as I continued to watch the warm and friendly bond that this devotee understood to have developed with the saint.

For the devout, the Buddha is someone they inherit. He and his representations are more static and less dynamic because there are prescribed ways to interact with the Buddha that are learned from multiple sources and inculcated from a young age. McDaniel talks about "protocols" that develop between devotee and object. These are "not orthodox prescriptions but certain expectations that the devotee understands regarding the proper body posture, the appropriate range of gifts, and the murmured and deferential voicing of both formal incantations and informal intentions."[69] Although Buddhists may have a preference for a particular image of the Buddha and direct their devotions to that, there is an approved way to interact with the Buddha that leaves little room for reinterpretation and divergence. With Bo Min Gaung, however, the devout, in one way or another, appropriate him for themselves, in their own idioms and styles, in their own spaces, and in response to their most pressing needs and experiences. *Weizzā*-related media do not create an orthopraxy but rather offer tools for personalized engagement. He is imagined into being and illustrates the religious lives of the devout in their forms of expression that are never static but vibrant and continuously transforming as individuals receive and adapt traditional knowledge and practices to specific circumstances. The saint to whom these devout directed their wishes is an in-between figure, made by the *weizzā* tradition's portrayal of him as the guardian of the *sāsana* and a wizard par excellence, but made as well from the intimate needs of the Burmese calling on him, and thus a private figure.

The ways *weizzā* devotees personalize their images tell us much about their religious lives. Instead of replacing their older images with newer or updated versions, *weizzā* devotees will often retain the old images, allowing their potency to grow with every touch, glance, or word. Even as the laminate encasing the lithograph or photograph begins to bubble from the heat or fades to a urine-yellow color from the sunlight, or the statue blackens and cracks from incense, candle, and cigarette burns, the devout will continue to interact with the images. For some, these marks or "traces" act as proof of the images' efficacy, as well as the strong bonds formed with the *weizzā*. Such images evoke emotion but also act as "bearers of affective memory," "archives of feeling," and "repositories of emotion" into which feelings and memories are encoded.[70] Memories, biographies, and emotions may be "materialized" in the image when sustained physical engagement imbues it with a personality and power that reflect the devotee's most pressing needs.

Devotees' practices are not static, but evolving, mercurial, and sometimes contradictory amalgams of rituals, practices, and beliefs. The visual dimension of *weizzā* practice, with its scope for interpretive adaptation by individual practitioners, is an arena for personalized affective focus, and for practitioners to independently confirm and authorize the powers of their *weizzā*. Like saints found in other religious traditions, Bo Min Gaung, as Kelly Hayes writes, "takes on the breath of life—that is, he exists and is meaningful—only at the permeable interface between an external, social environment and an internal world of personal experience."[71] Stories of and ways of engaging with Bo Min Gaung and other *weizzā* must also address issues or conflicts particular to the devotee in order to be considered potent.

Regardless of the gravity of a request, a devotee never forgets that Bo Min Gaung is a figure of power and must therefore be approached with a special kind of "devotional tact or courtesy that bespeaks an underlying reticence, or even caution."[72] This is not to say that the devout believe that Bo Min Gaung is going to act at once or give them what they desire. As when he was alive, Bo Min Gaung is unpredictable and uncontrollable. A devotee knows well that the result depends in large part on his or her thoughts and deeds. Bo Min Gaung has provided various meditation techniques, prayer bead practices, *mantra* and *yantra*, and precepts to follow so that wishes have a better chance of coming true. Entering into a vow or resolution (P: *adhiṭṭhāna*), for instance, before, after, or while petitioning Bo Min Gaung is thought to greatly increase the chance of a request coming to fruition.

Weizzā two- and three-dimensional images are objects "opulent with tomorrows,"[73] but when a devotee's wish does not come about, he only has him- or herself to blame for not having done the practices correctly, wavering from vows, or failing to keep a required set of moral precepts. Some devotees, however, eventually become exasperated or lose faith in the *weizzā* if their requests are not manifested. Such people seldom hold back in expressing their frustration. One man, annoyed that Bo Min Gaung repeatedly failed to make happen a series of requests, took all of his two-dimensional images of the *weizzā* and used them to wrap foodstuffs in his pantry.[74] In another instance, I accompanied a friend's father one afternoon to visit a Bo Min Gaung shrine located about thirty minutes outside Yangon. He told me that he wanted to pay homage to a particularly "potent" Bo Min Gaung figure in the hope that he could get the U.S. visa he so desperately wanted. Bowing to a standing figure of Bo Min Gaung, he proceeded to offer water and flowers and place lit cigarettes in the statue's hand, stroked its legs, and entreated Bo Min Gaung to make it possible for him to obtain the visa. I learned a week later that he did not get the visa; shortly afterward, he gave all of his *weizzā*-related paraphernalia to me. Houtman encountered dissatisfied devotees who enacted "drowning festivals" in which they placed statues and images of their *weizzā* onto a raft and sent it down the river.[75] Such "breakup" rituals and actions reflect the strong bonds and intimate relations devotees have with their *weizzā*. The offerings of food, incense, candles, flowers, cigarettes, etc. made to Bo Min Gaung are indeed meant as gifts, but also as part of a bargain made with him. And the devotees have their own established and evolving "set of affective postures" that go along with these offerings.[76] As Pinney points out: "The consumption of images by [devotees] needs to be understood in terms of these processes of bodily empowerment, which transform [objects and images] into powerful deities through the devotee's gaze, the proximity of his/her heart and a whole repertoire of bodily performances in front of the image."[77] The bowing, touching, whispering, and cries of joy and pain draw attention to this personal relationship between a wizard-saint and his devotees. The relationship, though, is a contingent, contractual association, dependent in no small part on the whims of the saint and how well a devotee maintains certain vows and practices. Devotees certainly fear that they may fall out of favor with Bo Min Gaung if they cease paying respects to him.

Nonetheless, devotees consider it a gift that Bo Min Gaung chose them to enter into a relationship—one that they cherish and continue to cultivate for years, if not for the rest of their lives. Given the profound social and psychological etiology of Bo Min Gaung's presence, he is not always a benign figure. Dealing with him may cause the most primitive fears to surface, such as dread of abandonment or rejection. Bo Min Gaung's "grandchildren" bring their most persevering needs to him, and there is always the risk that he will refuse or ignore them, or that they may fail to keep their side of the bargain. When a devotee believes that his or her well-being hinges on how, when, and even if Bo Min Gaung will intercede, it is no wonder that those places and moments of interaction with an image of him become emotional, psychological, and spiritual arenas where the most intimate needs and fears are put into play.

In addition to taking into account my interlocutors' claims that the material objects of Bo Min Gaung have inherent power or that their efficacy is bestowed by some form of *weizzā*-related consecration, we can also see their agency as relational. They are tokens of a connection, reminders of an adored grandfatherly figure whose presence was experienced in them. This governed how the devout used and interacted with these images, and this is why the interactions could happen—because the *weizzā* so present are enlightened beings charged with propagating the *sāsana* and protecting those in need. Just as Bo Min Gaung was animated by peoples' needs, desires, fantasies, so were these indications of his presence.

But what is presence? What accounts for Bo Min Gaung's "thereness"? One answer, of course, is that presence is a psychological effect. Bo Min Gaung exists in relationships: in the relationships of men, women, and even children with him, and in his involvement in complicated relational networks stretching between the *weizzā* realm and earth—between husbands and wives, for example, or parents and children, among members of Buddhist *weizzā* associations, between monastics and laity, between believers and nonbelievers. Bo Min Gaung is called upon to cure illnesses, to bring success in worldly and religious endeavors, and to listen to the most intimate sorrows and fears of his grandchildren. This is the interpersonal ground on which Bo Min Gaung arises, and this is what makes his presence real and emotionally resonant. In individuals' and communities' experiences of him, the *weizzā* saint draws deeply on the history of relationships, living and dead, present and absent. He borrows from and contributes to memories, needs, fantasies, hopes, and fears. Images of Bo Min Gaung are not simply copies of the original. As Donald Swearer eloquently put it, such representations are "in ontological communion with the original. Cognitively . . . presence may be expressed in ontological terms, but at the affective level it is simply felt. It is felt in our hearts and sinews as well as grasped by our minds."[78]

We see, then, that the efficacy of Bo Min Gaung images, and by extension all *weizzā* images, develops as a result of an "affective cognition of the ontological communion between sign and signified."[79] The stories shared by devotees about the supernatural attributes ascribed to certain two- and three-dimensional representations of Bo Min Gaung help to solidify the perceived potency of these images. Therefore, several factors must be present for an image to be considered effective: the devotee interacting with an image believes it to be both a representative of the original entity and an object that can have a positive impact on the devotee's life. Its power derives from the bond formed between the devotee and the chosen image of supplication.

1 Nineteenth-century mural painting that reads: "The Buddha entered *nibbāna* and his body was cremated. Monks, laypeople, Sakka, *devas, nagas, galons, weizzā,* and *zawgyi* came and paid homage." Photo courtesy Lilian Handlin

2 The four figures in the lower half of the *parabaik* represent four kinds of *weizzā*: Mercury *Weizzā*, Iron *Weizzā*, Medicine *Weizzā*, and Yantra *Weizzā*. Universities Central Library (Yangon) shelfmark 11180. Photo courtesy D. Christian Lammerts

3 Another nineteenth-century representation of the four *weizzā*. U Bho Thi Library, Thaton, white parabaik ms 1. Photo courtesy D. Christian Lammerts

4 Examples of Yantra *Weizzā* Ūh Ññāṇa. Vebhan-kyoṅh Charā. 1888. Mahesara bhesaya kyam·h (Buddhistische Mythologie)—BSB Cod. birm. 286

5 On this cover of a *weizzā* handbook (Mramma 'E'', Bhui'' to` 1962), from left to right, a *bodaw*, hermit, monk, and *zawgyi* (powerful sorcerer)

6 Shrine for the *weizzā* Yar-Kyaw Sayadaw

7 Statues of (left to right) an Iron *Weizzā*, Medicine *Weizzā*, Mercury *Weizzā*, and Yantra *Weizzā*

8 Image of a *zawgyi* from the cover of a book on the subject of *yantra*. Than' Po' n.d.

9 A hermit From M. Ferrars & B. Ferrars 1900

10 Hermit U Khanti

11 Laminated prayer card of the *weizzā* Bo Min Gaung

12 Laminated prayer card of the *weizzā* Yatkansin Taung Sayadaw

13 Laminated prayer card of the *weizzā* U Vijjādhara Bo Pauk Sein Sayadaw

14 Laminated prayer card of the *weizzā* Bo Bo Aung

15 Images of Bo Min Gaung and Indian saint Shirdi Sai Baba (d. 1918) professionally mounted and framed by a Burmese photo studio in Mandalay. Many devotees
believe that Shirdi Sai Baba sent his mind-spirit to enter into Bo Min Gaung. That
connection may have arisen from Indian diasporic communities, especially as
some of the wealthy donors who created some of the earliest shrines devoted to
the connection of Shirdi Sai Baba and Bo Min Gaung were Indian Burmese.

16 Images of Bo Min Gaung and Yatkansin Taung Sayadaw professionally
mounted and framed by a Burmese photo studio in Mandalay

17 One of the more popular pictorial representations of the *Weizzā* Committee

18 A computer-generated version that places the *weizzā* according to their importance. For example, according to the text below the image, Hermit U Khanti, Bo Min Gaung, Bo Bo Aung, and Yatkansin Taung Sayadaw are in the front row. An alchemical *dhat-lone*, or "philosopher's stone," hovers in the foreground. A separate photo of Bo Min Gaung is added to the right side.

19 Cover of the book *Bo Bo Aung and Hitler* Ñāṇa, Ū″ 1939

20 Painting of Bo Min Gaung sitting on a throne

21 Bo Min Gaung seated in three common poses

22 Doctored image of Bo Min Gaung

23 Famous photograph of Bo Min Gaung

24 The fingers and nose of this Bo Min Gaung statue are burned from cigarette offerings.

25 A cigarette offering to Bo Min Gaung in which the burnt ash remains intact

26 A devotee and Bo Min Gaung statue

27 and 28 A photograph of Ma Myin *dhāt-si*'ing Bo Min Gaung (pictured in fig. 28). The caption below Ma Myin points out that she is holding prayer beads in one hand and cigarettes in the other.

29 U Thilawunta (on the left) and the pagoda he erected in Allegany, New York. Photo dated 1958. Courtesy Dr. Steven Aung

30 An example of a "whole world long pillar of success pagoda" (B. *kambhalone aung-tan-kwan-taing zedi*) from the cover of a book about Bo Min Gaung (Jotipala, 1952)

31 An example of a "whole world pagoda"
(B. *kambha-lone zedi*)

32 Cartoon by U Ba Gyan about fake ascetics

33 A sample of the many notes strewn around a pagoda associated
with Bo Min Gaung

3
WOMEN OF THE WIZARD KING

In 1994, editors from a popular Burmese Buddhist magazine dispatched to Upper Myanmar one of their top investigative reporters, Aung Khain Lin, to look into the claims that a twenty-four-year-old woman named Ma Myin had the ability to heal people through power she received from a Buddhist *weizzā*. This kind of assignment was nothing new for Aung Khain. He had been investigating such events for many years now and had learned to take these claims with a grain of salt. "The number of strange and wonderful events like this has been on the rise all over Myanmar within the past fifty years," he reports, and "with this, comes an increase in the number of charlatans and fake stories."[1]

Taking an overnight bus from Yangon, Aung Khain arrived at the outskirts of the village at dawn. He wearily disembarked from the bus and hired a tri-shaw driver to take him to the young woman's home. Pedaling along the dusty backroads to the village center, the driver told Aung Khain, "There's been a rise in the number of these female faith healers in this area lately, and that makes us happy." When asked why, the driver smiled and replied, "More business for us tri-shaw drivers!"[2]

Aung Khain arrived at the home of the young woman, Ma Myin, at six o'clock in the morning and was surprised to see a large gathering of people already sitting out in front, apparently waiting to be healed.[3] "It's not easy getting the opportunity to see the young female master," remarked a passerby who saw the out-of-towner staring at the group. "Only when your name is called can you enter her house. I don't know where they get the names, but I know that not everyone who comes is allowed to see the female master, Ma Myin."[4]

Asking around where he might give his name to request an audience, Aung Khain was directed to a middle-aged man who turned out to be Ma Myin's uncle. Upon introducing himself as a journalist from a magazine and saying that he had come to do a story on Ma Myin, Aung Khain was told, "Only if she allows it will you be able to meet with her. Go inside and speak with her parents first."[5] Aung Khain entered the house and saw a group of monks and nuns all sitting in front of a Buddha altar using their prayer beads to chant Buddhist protective verses. After he exchanged introductions with Ma Myin's father and mother, they began to relate particular events in their daughter's life that illustrated her keen interest in religious activities from a very young age. They admitted that they were not an overtly religious family, but Ma Myin could always be found holding prayer beads and doing random acts of kindness. But it was not until she was a teenager that she was chosen by the *weizzā* to help those in need through the power of healing. Ma Myin's father recounted the following incident that marked this turning point in his daughter's life:

> When she was young, my daughter and I headed into the forest to collect wood and water for the day. When we took a break, a very old, yet distinguished man approached us and asked for some water to drink. But upon seeing that this old man had snotty, mucusy discharge coming from his eyes and nose, I did not want to offer him our water. The old man said that he had come to drink the water from my daughter because they had a karmic connection from a previous life. My

daughter took a cup of water and offered it to the old man, and asked, "Where did you come from? Have you eaten yet?" When the old man said that he hadn't and that he was vegetarian, she replied that she too was vegetarian and immediately offered him her food. As the old man ate the food, the discharge oozing from his face disappeared! The old man said that because of the little girl's goodwill, he would watch over and protect her during her entire life. Before leaving, he told Ma Myin to hold out her hand. When she did, the old man placed a sacred diagram into the palm of her hand,[6] and before walking away he said, "From this day onward, you must help and protect others and do religious works."[7]

The father went on to relate that when they returned home, Ma Myin fainted, and when she regained consciousness, she suddenly had the ability to foresee events before they occurred. When she was twenty years of age, she realized she had the ability to heal people. As word spread throughout the village about her healing powers, more and more people from all over the area began coming, seeking her help. Suddenly, as if anticipating Aung Khain's next question, her father made it clear that "all of this is done out of her own goodwill, mind you. No money is charged."[8]

While he was conversing with the parents, Ma Myin appeared in the doorway. When her father asked if she wished to speak with the reporter, without saying a word, Ma Myin turned around and left the room. "It is time to begin the healing," whispered her mother to Aung Khain.

Before long, Ma Myin re-entered the room dressed in a red shirt and skirt and immediately sat down in front of a Buddha altar to, according to her parents, develop concentration using her prayer beads. After a few moments, she donned a white shirt and placed a checkered longyi around her waist.[9] Noticing that the checkered pattern of the longyi was similar in style to that worn by the popular weizzā Bo Min Gaung, Aung realized which weizzā was possessing Ma Myin. His hunch was confirmed when he witnessed two men each light a Duya brand cigarette, very popular in Myanmar and supposedly Bo Min Gaung's favorite brand to smoke. They handed the cigarettes to Ma Myin, and she took a puff from each. She then ate an astonishing amount of rice, and her entire countenance suddenly changed from that of a gentle young woman to that of a gruff, older man. Her voice became deeper and louder. At this point, she was no longer Ma Myin. She was now Bo Min Gaung, or, as devotees know him, the "Wizard King."[10]

At this point Aung Khain also no longer addressed Ma Myin by her name, but instead as Abha, a word that means "grandfather." The following is the transcribed exchange that took place between Aung Khain and Ma Myin while the latter was possessed by Bo Min Gaung.

"Look at my granddaughter's arms and face," Bo Min Gaung began. "You will see knife wounds on her arms and face. See? These are from her previous life when she was murdered.

"Since my granddaughter cannot reject my working through her, I will always protect her. Don't think that my granddaughter is ridiculous. Don't think that what occurs here in this house is untrue. I only ask that you donate money to her and her family so that they can engage in religious activities.

"Wait a minute, won't you? I need to eat some medicine. Hey! Give me some medicine, man!" The male attendants near Ma Myin placed some tobacco in a large tobacco leaf which, to Aung Khain's amazement, she put completely into her mouth.

"Wow! If I were to put that in my mouth, I'd become dizzy!" Aung Khain remarked.

"But as I am Bo Min Gaung, I am able to do such things that regular people cannot. Is this not correct?" Bo Min Gaung asked. "Not everyone agrees with what goes on here, but for those who do, they donate as they like. But I don't cure for money. I cure for loving-kindness. You all work for money, but can you use it in the next life? Make sure you write this all down, okay?" Bo Min Gaung shouted at Aung Khain. "I've never allowed anyone to write about me before.

"Let me show you how Bo Min Gaung sits. He sits like this." Ma Myin crossed her legs in the same way Bo Min Gaung is often portrayed seated in iconographic representations and continued to puff on the cigarettes (see fig. 27).

"Many *weizzā* are here in the world helping the country. They are doing healings and *dhat-si'*ing."[11]

At this point, Ma Myin's uncle popped his head into the room to tell them that they had more patients than usual today. Bo Min Gaung told Aung Khain, "My granddaughter [Ma Myin] is exhausted. She worked the whole day yesterday without a break. But she happily healed everyone. You know, my granddaughter has been saying her prayer beads since she was three years old. Her entire family now does it as well. Tears come to her eyes when she does it.

"In the past my granddaughter's family was very unlucky and poor. It was also very noisy at her home. But she would continue her prayer beads, and eventually was able to gain deep concentration despite the racket. When I speak about my granddaughter, I feel bitterness in my heart. She did not have an easy life as a child. She had a bad life. But she had patience. Buddhism shines bright here in Myanmar, and I have come to keep it strong. But it is not easy.

"Please continue to write while I heal people. Write thoroughly and omit nothing so that your readers can learn. By the way, I wish to say something to those bad people in our country [who doubt me]. And despite what others may think, I don't do it as a means to make money. Sure, I may get 10,000 kyat one day, but absolutely nothing the following day. Some people don't want to see or hear the truth. They close their eyes and ears.

"Hey! Are you writing this all down accurately? If it is exaggerated or wrong, I'll be upset."

"Don't worry, sir. I am being true to your words," Aung Khain assured her.

"I will only remain with Ma Myin for a short time before moving on to another woman. My granddaughter never forgets to offer small donations to her parents and grandparents. And with this money, her family is able to do religious works because they don't have much income. My granddaughter only takes money that is offered to her out of faith from others. With that she can continue to engage in religious activities.

"People are always judging whether I am really Bo Min Gaung. They look to see if I do the things that he used to do. But I don't do those things. I only practice love and compassion."[12]

I began this chapter with the story of Ma Myin because it highlights central themes found in the relationships formed between Burmese Buddhist *weizzā* and their devotees. In this brief anecdote alone, we saw how issues of health, religious propagation, and gender roles, to name just a few, are found in the ways people see the *weizzā* working in their lives and how they, in turn, work in the lives of others around them through the power granted to them by the *weizzā*. This chapter specifically examines the linkage between people's religious practices and their practices for health and well-being, and explores how, perhaps more than any other factor, healing becomes the central element for devotees' bonds with the wizard-saints. *Weizzā* are thought to use their incredible power of healing to cure people and allow their devotees to live in more meaningful and dignified ways. Moreover, I will show how healing and maintaining health are often prominent parts of devotees' religion as practiced and examine instances of individuals' lived religion as it intersects with their healing experiences. That connection between religious practices and healing practices then serves as a springboard for interpreting an important feature of healing aspects of individuals' religion: psychological conflict and mental distress appear to be expressed in a specific system repertoire. This repertoire is not atemporally and stably cultural but rather produced through oral and textual fascinations with *weizzā* practice that have achieved a high level of diffusion in contemporary Myanmar, partly through print media.

Moreover, a general lack of access to and/or lack of confidence in allopathic medicine enhances the attractiveness of *weizzā* healing.

The remainder of this chapter will focus on those individuals who, due to their spiritual maturation along the *weizzā* path as a result of their present or previous lives' good karma, are privileged to experience powerful encounters with *weizzā*, either during periods of possession or in dreams.

RIDING THE MEDIUM; CHANNELING THE SAINT

The phenomenon that I refer to as "possession" is, in Burmese, *dhat-si*—a word that has no English equivalent. Broken down into parts, however, *dhat*, as we saw in chapter 1, derives from the Pāli, *dhātu*, and carries with it similar meanings of "element," especially with regard to the elementary particles of a physical object, except that it carries with it stronger connotations of power or force. *Si* can mean to ride, as in a vehicle, or flow, as in water or electricity.[13] The common interpretation is that the *dhat* of the *weizzā* rides, or flows through, the medium. A senior member of a *weizzā* association from Yangon explained to me that as *weizzā* are beings that live on a spiritual plane more refined than the human realm and have shed or transformed their physical bodies into immaterial ones, they essentially consist of only the air element (P. *vāyo dhatu*), which gives them the basic characteristic of motion. They act according to this nature by permeating the medium with their *dhāt* (energy) that is sent from their immaterial *nam* (mind substance).[14] "It's like they send their, how do you say in English, 'spiritual force field' into a practitioner who has done much practice on the *weizzā* path or who has good *pāramī*," he stressed, making the hand gesture of his fist hitting the palm of his other hand.[15] The development and accumulation of such energy is the result of years, if not lifetimes, of intense and disciplined spiritual practice that have granted the *weizzā* supernatural powers, with the ability to transform himself from a mere mortal to that of a semidivine being capable of operating in the human world in an immaterial way.

Although I use the expression "possession" to gloss this phenomenon, it is not exactly how practitioners themselves characterize their relationship with a guardian *weizzā*, for it carries certain connotations that may be misleading. In addition to the negative meaning that "possession" has in the context of Euro-America, as well as in most areas of contemporary Myanmar, the term also obscures the reciprocal nature of the relationship between saint and servant and the gradual, often rigorous, disciplined mental and physical training necessary for such temporary manifestations of the *weizzā* to take place.[16] The mediums describe this in relational terms: they "strive" (B. *a-toke*) to "receive" (B. *ya*) the *dhat* of a particular *weizzā*.[17] The word *dhat-si* is used in two different ways, each signifying the same phenomenon but placing agency in two different subjects. For example, while it is common to talk of a *weizzā* possessing or *dhat-si*-ing a human, it is just as common to talk of a devotee *dhat-si*-ing a *weizzā*. This is illustrated by the way the term is used in the following two ways: "the person who receives the '*dhat-si*' " (B. *dhat-si-khan-puggo*)[18] and "the female master who is channeling" (*dhat-si*-ing) (B. *dhat-si ne-de sayama*).[19] Both are used when referring to individuals who possess the power to act as mediums.

The two ways the term is used provide clues to how the process is believed to unfold. Devotees see the *weizzā* as the agent of action, that is, actively working through the medium, who is often portrayed as a vessel suitable for holding the *weizzā*'s energy. Not long after starting my research, however, I realized that the mediums play an active role as well. After learning that they have been chosen as medium for a particular wizard-saint, devotees gain the knowledge of channeling the *weizzā*, and their words and actions at the beginning stages of the possession period suggest that they have some control over when and how a *weizzā* possesses them. This is especially true when the *weizzā* seems to appear at the same time every day.[20] When a medium just prior to being possessed is chanting *gāthā* while fingering a Buddhist rosary, or using objects or wearing clothing similar to that which a particular *weizzā* is thought to possess, she is engaging in preliminary activities that she knows will bring the *weizzā*'s *dhat* to her. Eventually, there comes a moment when, like flipping a light switch, the person has channeled the *weizzā*, or, alternatively, the *weizzā* has possessed the medium. In the midst of the possession, when the medium is healing and preaching, acting and speaking like a *weizzā*, we no longer need to ask, "Is the *weizzā dhat-si*-ing the medium or is the medium *dhat-si*-ing the saint?" At this point it is irrelevant because they are two sides of the same coin. I belabor the point somewhat because it is important to establish the relational aspect of this phenomenon that places it in contradistinction to other forms of possession that exist in Myanmar.[21] It is also to show that these women, despite claims that they have no choice in being possessed, take on the role of medium and healer for very real, this-worldly reasons.

In most cases, individuals who are *dhat-si*'ed by the spirit of a *weizzā* cannot recall the events that occurred during their possessed states. However, after speaking with several of these mediums and reading dozens of reports about *dhat-si*, I have found common elements that appear in their accounts. While the medium is using her prayer beads, for example, the *weizzā* will send out his power *dhat* to her. When this powerful force makes contact with the body of the medium, she will feel a strong tingling sensation, and since the force entering her body is great, the medium will often feel that she is growing in size or expanding. As the *dhat* enters the body by way of the crown of the head, the medium will feel that her head is swelling. Within moments, this *dhat* descends to the rest of the body, going into the arms and hands, then down the spinal cord into the legs and feet. The first time this happened to Ko San Lwin, a young man who was attending a military college in Upper Myanmar, "my fingers began to twitch. I was scared at first, but then I remembered that sometimes when I am reciting a *gāthā*, like the *Itipiso*, there might be unseen beings sitting nearby listening to me reciting. I can feel their presence. I know they are there because I feel goose bumps all over my body."[22] An alumnus of Rangoon

Institute of Engineering had such an experience and shared it with his fellow alumni by publishing it in one of the school's annual newsletters. Reminding his readers that he is a man of science who is not supposed to believe in such things, he wrote that he was therefore shocked when a *weizzā* decided to use him to heal others: "Like I said, my whole body felt like I was fully charged with static electricity, and my hairs stood upright and my speech and my hand went into autopilot. Whatever I touched in the process became blessed with healing power."[23]

At one of the possession sessions I attended in Mandalay, a gentleman who had come to obtain holy water from the medium described this idea of "autopilot" in a different way. Sitting next to me while we watched a female medium undergo possession by the *weizzā* Bo Min Gaung, he interpreted what he understood to be happening. He said that the people being *dhat-si*'ed often feel as if they want to cough. This is the *weizzā* activating and taking control of the vocal chords (B. *hnoke-si*).[24] As we observed the medium gradually entering a state of possession, we noticed that her movements were more pronounced and "jerky," unlike the graceful and smooth movements she made when not possessed. The man told me that the *weizzā* had taken full control of the young lady's body and voice at this point, controlling all her strings (B. *kyo-sone*). Like a puppet master with his puppet, the *weizzā* was manipulating his medium to help heal the many people who had assembled there that afternoon.[25]

Among mediums and devotees, there seems to be agreement on what takes place physiologically when the *weizzā* makes contact with the person. As Brac de la Perrière's informants told her, "encountering the *weizzā* does not imply that they enter the body, but that their mind sends their energy to 'ride' the medium."[26] Celine Coderey, in her research among mediums in Rakhine State, Myanmar, made note of informants who told her that *weizzā* do not enter the bodies of mediums and that whoever insists they are possessed in such a way is lying.[27] I encountered similar explanations when I visited the healer-medium Ma Tin Tin at her home in Yangon on a day when she was to conduct a healing ritual for people who had gathered in front of her house. When I arrived, I noticed that there was an area cordoned off by rope where no one was allowed to enter. Ma Tin Tin was behind that line, and she began the ceremony by reciting: "All the *bodaw*, please watch over and protect me, your reverend daughter. Please know that my body is also your body, so please use it. My ten fingers are also your ten fingers." When I asked her later what she meant by this, she told me that a medium can be completely in a trance state or can be partly possessed while still retaining full consciousness. What sets such an experience apart from other types of possession, she told me, is that with *dhat-si* a *weizzā* will activate at least one of the following *dhat*: *a-kya dhat* (hearing), *amyin dhat* (seeing), and/or *mano dhat* (intuition).[28]

Possession by *weizzā* is quite different from possession by other beings in several ways. First, the terminology used to describe the phenomenon is different. Instead of *dhat-si,* the phrase *nat-win* is used. *Nat-win* refers to deities (B. *nat*) entering (B. *win*) the body/mind of an individual. Belonging to a group of deities called the "Thirty-seven Lords," these *nat* are trapped in the karmic cycle without any possibility of escaping by themselves and must therefore look for embodiment opportunities by grasping the soul (B. *leikpya*) of a living being.[29] Other lesser deities and spirits can also possess a person. When an individual is possessed by a demon, for example, he or she will usually exhibit characteristics commonly associated with demon possession in other parts of the world. Witches and sorcerers can also take possession of an individual through the use of spells.[30]

Initial experiences of possession are often met with fear and disbelief by the medium (as much as he or she is aware of what is happening, and even more so when they emerge from their trancelike state) and from those around them. Ma Myin's parents "were so worried the first time she went into a state of trance after saying her prayer beads. We cried because we saw that she was tired and could not get her to come out [of the trance]."[31] The father of another well-known medium, Ma Win Yee, was so afraid when his daughter awoke in the middle of the night the first time she came under the influence of the *weizzā* Bo Bo Aung's power that, even though she had reported seeing a white-clad *weizzā* figure sitting in her room two days prior, "I thought for sure that my daughter had fallen under an evil spell. . . . She began shouting, 'Father, wake up! Light some incense! It's done, man, it's accomplished! Your entire village will be peaceful. I am Bo Bo Aung, and I will give you my medicine!' "[32] Another father of a teenage girl capable of channeling the *weizzā* Bo Bo Aung had a similar reaction the night he first heard her frantically calling for him: "When I went over to her and asked what was wrong, she was shaking and was acting as if she had lost her mind. It seemed as if she was *dhat-si*'ing [because] . . . she said, 'I have succeeded, man. And because of my success, light some incense, won't you?! Light some incense!' "[33] Such fears of insanity or other illnesses befalling a medium are often allayed when someone from their community familiar with these kinds of experiences informs them that *weizzā* will not make contact with a human being unless there is a special need. Sometimes, a person might have been related to a *weizzā* in his past life as a son, daughter, or sibling.[34] In that case, the *weizzā* might try to establish contact and help that particular person when he or she is in trouble or has fallen into wrong ways. The *weizzā* cannot send his *dhat* to someone unless that person has fulfilled the basic conditions to be a recipient of such power. For example, the person has to, at the very least, keep the five Buddhist precepts and recite *gāthā* using prayer beads on a daily basis, for the *weizzā dhat* can be received only when the recipient is "pure at heart and when his mind is in deep concentration."[35] When the *weizzā* arrive, it is always for a noble purpose. They come when they want to give guidance in the personal spiritual development of a devotee, cure someone of an illness, or help a person successfully complete *sāsana* propagation work, such as building a pagoda or a meditation center.[36]

DREAM WEAVERS

Dreams are the other means by which the majority of my interlocutors experience *weizzā* coming into their lives. Unlike possession, however, these experiences are completely passive: although devotees can engage in preliminary religious rituals and exercises to increase the chances that a *weizzā* will visit them during their sleep, the will of the *weizzā* determines when and how such a visitation may occur. Those whose first contact with a *weizzā* is made during a dream frequently cite that initial experience as the most formative and influential in the bond they developed with the *weizzā* world. Dreams offer glimpses of devotees' connections to certain *weizzā*, which is important for providing confidence in their roles as healers or guardians of the Buddha's teachings. One female healer whose power stems from her relationship with the *weizzā* Bo Min Gaung traces her and her mother's healing powers to an instance in which her mother, when pregnant with her, had a dream in which she flew through the air with the help of the *weizzā*'s power.[37] Such dreams are often referred to whenever devotees share stories with one another and in devotional literature about how initial contacts with wizard-saints changed the way they saw the world around them and the spirit entities that inhabited it.

Articles about and interviews with *weizzā* devotees that have appeared in the popular *weizzā*-related magazines from the 1990s to the present consistently include content of individuals' dreams as they pertain to the ways the *weizzā* worked in their lives. The detail with which these dreams are recorded offers valuable insight into the recurring themes and elements considered important by devotees from a wide spectrum of socioeconomic and religious backgrounds. For my interlocutors, dreams are more than just visions created by the mind during sleep. They are windows into the *weizzā* world that offer ways of communicating with the wizard-saints that are otherwise not available during their waking states. There are aspects of the dream state that devotees believed to be just as real as what they would experience in their waking state and are understood as directly influencing, in tangible and concrete ways, experiences with the waking world. This will become clearer when we look at the ways *weizzā* appear in dreams for the sake of curing disease and providing information on how to build religious structures.

Although the content of such dreams and their interpretations fill the pages of popular magazines, there are no sophisticated sources of dream literature (oneirocritical works) as are found in other religious traditions, certainly not as sophisticated as what one finds in Islam, for example. As Jamal Elias shows in the context of Islam, dreams and their systematic collection and interpretation formed the basis for an oneirocritical tradition to develop and maintain a prominent position throughout the history of Islam. Accepted as authentic sources of knowledge, dreams and their connections to revelation and religious authority were clearly defined in *hadith* literature.[38] Because no such authoritative sources exist for dreams involving *weizzā*, devotees rely on an informal oral tradition of dream interpretation, unpublished manuals, articles in popular religious magazines, books on visions and prophecies, and a host of professional dream interpreters and fortune-tellers. However, as in Islam, dreams in the *weizzā* tradition remain important sources of revelation and moral lessons, and there is a "broader, less easily defined variety of literature in which dreams serve a variety of functions including conferring status, providing evidence, and symbolizing interpersonal relationships."[39]

PATTERNS OF HEALING

More than half of all narratives shared with me by my interlocutors and gleaned from magazines and devotional literature that pertained to people's relationships with the *weizzā* had to do with being healed from illness or being given the power to heal others' suffering or sickness, physical and mental. These narratives were split roughly equally between healing by a medium who is possessed by a *weizzā* and healing directly through dreams. Stories of *weizzā* possession and dream accounts are popular material for articles.[40] Stories like Ma Myin's possession by Bo Min Gaung, as well as pitches for traditional medicine healers, clinics, and medicine and, for a brief period of time, advertisements for healers who could supposedly cure HIV-AIDS appeared in popular Buddhist magazines.[41] Although the number of articles pertaining to *weizzā* had decreased through the 2000s due to stricter government control over all media, these magazines are still full of various spiritual remedies for ailments afflicting many Burmese.

I have determined that sickness and relief are felt and conveyed in terms of, and with reference to, culturally available idioms. Two such idioms are perceptions of the modern medical landscape of Myanmar and the ways devotees make sense of and interpret the diseases that they experience. How *weizzā* devotees become ill and are made well can be better understood in relation to these two culturally specific expressions. Despite an increase in public medical knowledge and access to healing techniques and drugs in Myanmar, the *weizzā* continue to play important roles. Local medical healers' power and prestige are intact, all the more so if they can trace their powers to a specific wizard-saint or specific practices.[42] Therapeutic powers that are understood to come from the *weizzā* are thought to be of a higher order than even modern medicine and indigenous healing methods. Supernatural in nature and stemming from the power of the Buddha, curative forces wielded by the *weizzā* can eradicate a wide spectrum of illnesses ranging from physiological ailments recognized in the modern medical world to afflictions thought to have developed as a result of ill luck, planetary misalignment, or witchcraft.

The healing powers of the *weizzā* are not only found in the homes and private clinics of mediums and indigenous medical specialists, however. With the growth of hospitals came an increase in the presence of *weizzā* at these facilities. *Weizzā* figure prominently in hospitalized devotees' accounts of being healed. Placed at bedsides, hung on walls, or carried in pockets, images of these wizard-saints accompany the patients throughout their illness. When visiting hours are over and family and friends return home, patients look to the saints for worship, guidance, assistance, or to express their thoughts and emotions. Devotional literature and reports from patients contain vivid accounts of *weizzā* visiting them at night in dreams and providing miraculous cures.

One twenty-nine-year-old female patient, who was not a follower of any particular *weizzā* and had no interest in such things at her time of illness, was admitted to the hospital with a loose bowel disease that left her weak, malnourished, and unable to move. The doctors and her family all thought that she was to die soon and left her alone in the room while they discussed the formalities of how to deal with her final hours. "While I was lying there in bed all alone and with doctors, nurses, and family all down the hall," she reported, "a large man appeared in the doorway. As he stared at me, he gradually approached. I could tell that his body was strong and full of vigor, yet there was still some harshness to his demeanor." At first she thought that it was just a hospital orderly come to check on her. But she was shaken when he pointed his finger at her and said, "If you want to take a shit, go ahead and go. If you want to take a piss, go ahead. You don't have any disease. Everything is all right." After saying this, he left the room. She had no idea who this person was but had an instinctual feeling that he was extraordinary. "I needed to know who this person was and immediately called out to my family," she continued, "but when I asked about that man, they responded that they did not see anyone. Thinking I was hallucinating, they had the doctors give me some sleeping pills."[43]

She spent the remainder of the night in and out of sleep. But at one point when she thought she was awake, she saw a *weizzā*. She tried hard to reach out and touch him but became so fatigued that she could not help but fall back to sleep. "When I awoke the next morning I found that I was completely changed. My entire body was free from sharp pains. Starting from that day, I no longer had loose bowel movements," she said, then stressed that "I continue to hear the voice of that man in my head, and I shall never forget him." She has accepted that Bo Min Gaung and "other persons not seen with the naked eye are important to my life and continue to protect me."[44]

Such accounts of hospital patients who have *weizzā* experiences at critical points in their illness, usually just prior to surgery or when they are expected not to recover, are quite common. Indeed, the majority of ailments reported are stomach illnesses, which is not surprising, as gastrointestinal problems are common in Myanmar where sanitary conditions are poor.[45] In my early days of fieldwork, I came across so many reports of *weizzā* healing people of incontinence, gas, ulcers, food poisoning, constipation, hemorrhoids, and fissures that I thought for sure *weizzā* must be the patron saints of gastrointestinal disorders. Patients reported suffering from such sharp pains that doctors on duty thought they would need surgery. An elderly hermitess recounted a time when she was forty years old and was admitted to a hospital to have surgery to alleviate intense pain she was experiencing in her abdomen. She recalls that at exactly one o'clock in the afternoon she was visited by an old *weizzā* who appeared to be dressed as a monk: "He told me, 'Now is the time. Will you follow?' " When she asked where he wanted her to go, he instructed her to enter the forest and devote her life to meditation. "From these good deeds," he told her, "you will live to be an old woman."[46] After she agreed to his request, the *weizzā* took out a knife and cut open her stomach, removing that which was making her ill. He then stitched her up, laid his hands upon her abdomen, and disappeared. Trying to describe the texture of the experience, the hermitess recalls that it "had a dreamlike quality to it, but I was fully aware." Anticipating that some readers may doubt the validity of her story and say that the figure she encountered were most likely a surgeon whom she, in her anesthetized, intoxicated state, mistook for a divine being, she stressed that no medical staff were in her room until the next morning, when it was time to operate. She remembers that after she was prepped for the procedure, the electricity suddenly went out. "When the electricity came back on, the radiologist used the machine to x-ray my stomach and was amazed to find that whatever it was that was causing the illness had gone!

The doctors and nurses were also very amazed and did not have to operate."[47]

What struck me about these experiences and did not escape the attention of my informants as well is that none of these patients requested intervention. This is typical for the devotional healing stories, especially those that take place within a dream: Not being a follower of a *weizzā* or the *weizzā* path, I was suffering from a debilitating illness that required surgery or was considered by medical experts to be incurable, and a *weizzā* intervened to heal me, whereupon I decided to become a devotee of this wizard-saint. The *weizzā* appeared of their own volition to provide healing to someone they deemed worthy of such divine intervention. Sharing these stories with me, my interlocutors always expressed in excited, out-of-breath tones, "You never know when they will appear . . . for they only come when they think you are ready, when your *pāramī* is good."[48]

The logic of devotion would assume that, having some foreknowl-edge of these wizard-saints, the devotees would call upon them during their times of need. Instead, however, the *weizzā* insert them-selves into the lives of these people during crucial moments of sick-ness and despair, whether they are entreated or not. Many times a person would not even recognize the saint who had visited them until later—either realizing the identity of the *weizzā* themselves or having it revealed to them by someone else.

Buddhists are not the only ones to be the recipients of *weizzās'* power. Adherents of other religious traditions are also visited by *weizzā*, and it is these reports that Buddhist *weizzā* devotees espe-cially delight in sharing. Devotional literature and informant accounts are full of stories of sick Christians and Muslims being healed by *weizzā* who appeared to them in dreams during periods of illness. A well-known account from the early twentieth century, told to me by many informants and included in a recent magazine article, tells a seventeen-year-old Christian woman dying of polio in a Yangon hospital.[49] At one point, as the young woman later told her story, she felt as if she had died. Lying there in the hospital bed and unable to move her body, she was approached by an elderly man dressed in white robes. She did not know who he was at the time but later discerned him to be a *weizzā*. He gave her three medicine pills to take. Other figures soon surrounded her and presented her with more pills. "After I ingested the pills, my senses returned. My soul became so light that it left my body and floated upward to the sky. When it arrived in the sky, I witnessed a monk sitting in a forest below. I also saw a hermit sitting in meditation and realized that the monk was teaching the hermit how to gain the power of flight. Eventually, my soul descended back into my body and I found myself back in bed. After recovering, I converted to Buddhism."[50]

Muslims too were also granted the beneficent grace of the *weizzā*'s interventions. During one period of my fieldwork in Myanmar, I would spend days at the famous Shwedagon Pagoda, sitting on a raised platform in a shady corner of the compound watching the day's events unfold. I would always see the same middle-aged woman arrive around lunchtime and leave three hours later. After several days, she offered me some tea, and we got to talking. She was dressed all in brown like a Buddhist yogi or hermit, and on her shirt was pinned a small plastic amulet of the *weizzā* Bo Min Gaung. When I casually remarked on her pin, she immediately made it known to me that she was not a Buddhist, but a Muslim whose son was very ill. She had had a dream in which "Bo Min Gaung came and said that if I were to make a vow to come to Shwedagon every day for three months, my son would be healed."[51] The way she told me this, I could tell that she was still beside herself that she would have had such an experience as a Muslim. She went on to tell me that she came daily to the pagoda to chant Buddhist verses using her prayer beads for three hours and had so much respect for Bo Min Gaung that she wore his picture on her shirt for the entire period of her vow. "Bo Min Gaung does not belong to any particular religion. He helps everyone, even foreigners," she said, smiling. We enjoyed daily tea together for another two days, but unfortunately, I never saw her again after that. Perhaps she had completed her three-month resolution; if so, one can only hope that Bo Min Gaung kept his end of the bargain by healing her son.

What should we make of the surprising number of similarities and common themes in these dreams that reflect the ways the devout understand the *weizzā* to be acting? How can one undertake a scholarly examination of healing experiences without trivializing religious practices and beliefs when reducing religion to nonreligious terms? One way of skillfully navigating between these two extremes is by looking at healing phenomena and imagination in an ongoing, dynamic relationship with the realities and structures of everyday life in particular times and places (insofar as these are both the framework of interpretation for locals and something the locals reconstruct in their lives). As Robert Orsi reminds us, people in these situations do not simply act; "they attempt to understand and narrative themselves as actors," and the stories they narrate and interpret are part of the "ideas, gestures, and imaginings, all as media of engagement with the world . . . [for] it is pointless to study particular beliefs and practices apart from the people who use these ideas in the definite circumstances of their lives."[52] In other words, the religious lives of *weizzā* devotees do not exist in a vacuum or a separate section of their lives. When examining the stories shared by my interlocutors, we must take into account the circumstances of their experiences and the cultural structures and conditions from which these stories emerge.

A useful heuristic for such an endeavor can be found in the notion of cultural repertoires. Such "repertoires," as Justin McDaniel puts it, "do not pre-define how a person embedded in a certain culture will act but shape the way she or he interprets, recounts, and manipulates the events they take part in in creating, as well as shaping the way new information is processed and articulated."[53] Stories of *weizzā* healing, by circulating through networks of family and friends as well as through a wide range of popular media, have become, for the time being, solidified and perpetuated as Burmese culture's "symptom repertoire," that is, a range of physical symptoms available to the conscious and unconscious mind for the physical expression of psychological conflict.[54] Medical historian Edward Shorter points out that "in some epochs, convulsions, the sudden inability to speak or terrible leg pain may loom prominently in the repertoire. In other epochs patients may draw chiefly upon such symptoms as abdominal pain, false estimates of body weight and enervating weakness as metaphors for conveying psychic stress."[55] Keeping in mind that "culture shapes the way general psychopathology is going to be translated partially or completely into specific psychopathology" can provide us with a deep understanding of how the expectations and beliefs of the sufferer shape their suffering.[56] This is similar to the findings of Burmese anthropologist Soe Thein, who in the 1970s did fieldwork among devotees who were believed to have been healed by *weizzā* from a variety of ailments, many of them gastrointestinal. His informants would complain about headaches, giddiness, weakness of voluntary movements, and abdominal pain and connected them to aggravation brought upon by domestic problems, business breakdown, bad marital relations, and so on.[57] *Weizzā* devotees' bodies, to use the words of affect theorist Supp-Montgomerie, "bear affect as a sort of 'memory without content,' accumulating and activating a store of nonrepresentational 'perspectives of the flesh' " where their "affective autonomic activity flouts the illusions of mind over matter and pushes the body to the foreground."[58]

The development and dispersion of such repertoires are often expressed through dreams and possessions. Stories shared among family and friends, magazines dedicated to *weizzā* devotees' reports, and books in the popular genre of occult Burmese literature focus on accounts of people's dreams and possessions by *weizzā* and the extraordinary events that occurred as a result.[59] Perhaps most striking about these stories is the appearance in them of the figure explicitly excluded by the Burmese Buddhist environment that has been so heavily dominated by the exploits of monks and government-sanctioned religious virtuosi. Instead of popular *vipassanā* (insight meditation) monks or revered *arahants* (fully enlightened beings), we encounter individuals that the authorities have attempted to marginalize. Moreover, these stories give voice to men and women (but especially women) from all socioeconomic backgrounds:

uneducated cleaners, women who left their families to become nuns or wandering hermits, well-to-do jewelers, etc. These are strong-voiced women who give sermons, heal large numbers of patients, have cult followings, and raise large sums of money to do Buddhist propagation.

The *weizzā* are sought out for their abilities to cure a wide gamut of ailments, and humans are not disembodied entities. Individuals' religious expressions are linked to their material bodies and become manifest where the senses (both physical and social) move through space and time. As we will see in the next section, devotees' lived religious expressions develop out of a set of embodied practices.[60]

ABHA'S GRANDDAUGHTERS: EMBODIED CONSTELLATIONS OF BEHAVIOR

The distinction between the *weizzā*'s intercessionary healing power and the mediums' own roles in the healing process is not absolute. Although these mediums would never claim to be directly respon-sible for the healings that take place under their auspices, as we have seen in their accounts and in the popular devotional literature, the intensity with which they understand the *weizzā* to be working through them and the importance of their job as healer allow for a blurring of the lines. Returning to the report of possession that appeared at the beginning of this chapter, Ma Myin continued in her role as healer even after the spirit of Bo Min Gaung had left her for the day. Attending to the many patients she allowed to stay at her home, Ma Myin said that she worked most days morning till evening, treating dozens of people even when she was not under the influence of Bo Min Gaung. Part of her success as a healer no doubt stemmed from her pleasant disposition and compassionate way of interacting with her patients, all of whom were allowed to rest and recuperate until they were able to return to their homes. She made rounds, visiting with each patient and reassuring them that they would get better because Ma Myin, speaking as herself and not Bo Min Gaung, had taken the illness from their bodies: "Go ahead, now. Give me all your illness. Give to me your ailments. Only then will you get well," and "Starting from today your illness is no more. I've taken it all. You're cured."[61] It appeared that she understood herself as having an active role in the healing process. Asked how taking on all this illness made her feel, visibly exhausted, she said that she often felt the same ailments as her patients, but that she had the ability to take them all in.[62]

Having gotten to know some of these devotees whose lives have been changed by their interactions with the *weizzā*, we cannot help but seriously examine what their lives are like now. What do they understand their role to be in their communities? How has being contacted by these wizard-saints affected their lives and relationships with others? When the *weizzā* have left for the day and the female mediums are back to their "regular" selves, how do they feel?

The majority of my accounts in this chapter come from or deal with female devotees. This is partly intentional. First, over half of the accounts found in popular literature and provided by my informants that deal with healing through possession and dreams came from or were about women. Poring over thousands of pages of literature on the *weizzā*, I was taken aback at encountering so many female voices. A cursory examination of the subject would give the impression that only male actors are involved. While it is certainly true that only men have attained to the state of *weizzā* and are the authors of books, leaders of congregations, and preachers to disciples, examining the variety of source material shows that it is women who act as the cornerstones of this phenomenon. Such women are part of the *weizzā* world through their positions as healers, clairvoyants, meditation masters, hermitesses, and, although rarely, *weizzā* association leaders. It would be wrong to declare that this is a female-oriented phenomenon; I simply encountered a larger number of instances of female possession and dream visitations than of male experiences.[63] However, the *weizzā* do not discriminate based on gender, and men with the ability to channel *weizzā* are known and appear in other works.[64] I intentionally chose to focus solely on female mediums, and in large part how female devotees are healed through dreams, for a couple of reasons. First, I wanted to heed the call by Steven Collins that more "work is necessary on the terminology—and hence the imagined phenomenology—of *weizzā* possession. This is an area also . . . where further differentiation and nuance in the involvement of women in the *weizzā* phenomenon might be possible."[65] Second, I wished to examine social aspects of female *weizzā* mediumship, in particular, that directly affects the women involved and how they relate to members of their community.

Being visited by a *weizzā* and carrying out the wizard-saint's bidding can be seen as a creative yet culturally sanctioned response to restrictive gender roles, a means for expressing otherwise illicit thoughts or feelings, and an economic strategy for women who have few options beyond traditional wife or daughter roles. Juliane Schober makes a similar point when writing that "*weizzā* knowledge may also appeal to those who are displaced at the social margins of a field of merit and who suffer a lack of power that is manifest in social or physical injury or other forms of ill fate."[66] In this sense, channeling *weizzā* provides a set of symbolic resources and ritual strategies by which these women are empowered to work on themselves and the world around them. Daw Vaṇṇathingagī used to be a Buddhist nun but found the life and its rules too strict and not conducive to helping people with the powers bestowed upon her by the *weizzā* Bo Min Gaung. She found it best to disrobe and, instead of returning to lay life, re-ordain as a hermitess. Daw Vaṇṇathingagī moved to a small hut on the outskirts of Yangon. Living as a hermitess afforded her the luxury of devoting all her time and energy to spiritual pursuits without the responsibilities of a nun or female householder, many of which involve domestic duties catering to monks or male members of one's family. The eldest of nine siblings, she recalls the evening when she was first visited by a *weizzā*. She had a dream "that seemed so real," she remembers. "A voice said, 'Awake, my child.' When I sat up and looked around the room, I saw an old man dressed in white standing there."

The *weizzā* (she believed it to be Bo Min Gaung) entreated her to enter into a prolonged period of meditation in a forested area far from her home.

She replied, "Grandfather, I have never been to this area. I don't even know where it is. Please let me practice meditation at the local temple."

Bo Min Gaung reassured her, "Child, you have a connection with this area and it is there you must go."

"Grandfather, I am a single woman and must get permission from my parents," she continued. "Moreover, it will be difficult to sustain myself in the forest."

"You will get their permission. And as for surviving up there, you will succeed," Bo Min Gaung said before disappearing.[67]

Daw Vaṇṇathingagī was fortunate to have been able to make the transition from lay life to that of a renunciate with ease. She obtained permission from her parents to ordain first as a nun and then as a hermitess. Being the eldest unmarried child, she would have been expected to remain with her aging parents to care for them until their deaths. Most women face similar significant obstacles in their desires to live a life centered around religious activities. However, not every woman wants, or even has the chance, to enter the renunciate life. It is not as easy as leaving home, finding a community of hermits, and requesting permission to ordain. If the woman is single, she must still get permission from her parents or, if they are no longer alive, the next eldest male member of her family. And if she is married, her husband must consent to her request. Although the image of a female renunciate in Myanmar is changing, the role is still considered by many people, monastic and lay, as the domain of spinsters, widows, and brokenhearted girls. Families are therefore cautious about granting permission to their daughters or sisters to enter the renunciate life because of such preconceptions or fear of such attitudes in others. This is made all too clear in the following account of Daw Sumangala, a hermitess who was forced to endure years of suffering until she was able to freely live out her days as a renunciate. "When I was twelve years old I had the desire to ordain as a nun, but my parents did not agree," she recalled. "At age eighteen I was told to marry, but I did not want to. Without any interest [in marriage], though, I was eventually wed anyways at age twenty-two. I cried so much that blood, not tears, poured from my eyes. But the doctor found nothing wrong. I finally decided to leave home at forty-one years of age to become a hermitess, but my family came looking for me and when they tried to forcibly drag me home, I ran away to another temple." She has not seen her family since.[68]

The scenario of leaving home only to be forced back by family was common in many female *weizzā* devotees' accounts. Another hermitess, Daw Vimala Candārī, remembers her early days of trying desperately to avoid being married so as to devote her life to religious works as directed by the *weizzā* who appeared in her dreams. Continually being brought back home by members of her family after each attempt to leave, she was finally successful one evening when she "left home quietly so that no one would know and went to Shwedagon Pagoda. I ate only a little fruit, bread, and water. I didn't shower, and so that no one would see me at night, I hid and practiced meditation without going anywhere." After some time, her family came looking for her one last time. She was still legally married and needed to return home to dissolve the marriage. She went back just long enough to give her husband permission to marry another woman before leaving for a pilgrimage to visit *weizzā* holy sites all around the country.[69]

Other female *weizzā* followers who have families of their own feel particularly strong obligations to take care of husbands, children, and extended family members, and are thus hesitant to leave home. "I want to devote my time to religious activities, but many people depend on me at home," one woman told me; another confided that "even though my husband is a drunkard, he still needs me to take care of him. He's not such a bad man."[70] Burmese norms expect women to be wives and mothers whose activities are restricted to the domestic arena, where their reputations are based on the successful management of the home and financial resources. As much as they would like to go off and use the powers given to them by *weizzā* to help others, it is not a realistic way of life for most. "Although women in Burma had for a long time an influential presence in the economic sphere, as in other premodern Southeast Asian societies," historian of gender in Myanmar Chie Ikeya writes, "the active role of women as economic agents—the very attribute that gave women their autonomy and power—subordinated them to men socially, spiritually, and politically."[71] Even if women do get the chance to leave home to follow a religious life, any number of circumstances, such as family illness or economic hardship, would require them to rejoin their families to help deal with the problems.

The allure of *weizzā* mediumship and similarly related healing vocations is that women who believe they have been granted power by *weizzā* acquire a similar degree of power, status, and influence in their communities and families as that of a renunciate, without having to leave the home. Living this way while also engaging with the dissatisfactions that result from the limitations of a householder is a culturally sanctioned way for working through frustrations of restrictive gender roles, prohibited thoughts or feelings, and economic instability. Being a *weizzā* medium is not gender neutral.[72] The young women who channel the male *weizzā* undergo sex changes of sorts by wearing men's clothing, smoking cigarettes, and speaking in deep, forceful tones. These can be seen as transgressive actions, taking a cultural repertoire and putting their own spin on it, which supports McGuire's claim that "the religious meanings attached to gendered bodies are likewise socially defined, contested, and changeable."[73]

Observing closely and getting to know some of these women over the course of my several years of fieldwork, I have learned that bonds with *weizzā* have been positively life-changing experiences for most.[74] I met one young woman, Ma Aye Aye, who had just recently before my arrival to Mandalay come into her own as a medium of the *weizzā* Bo Min Gaung. I was able to observe the early changes in her life that occurred as a result of her powers of healing. Ma Aye Aye was of a very shy disposition, but with her newfound abilities and confidence in the *weizzā*'s power, she suddenly became a self-assured, strong-willed woman, especially during periods of possession, fond of barking orders at her family, most notably her husband and mother-in-law. Always modest, she did admit to me that although being a medium and healer was "physically and mentally exhausting," she delighted in the respect shown to her by members of her family. "At first they thought I was crazy, but when they saw me heal people who came to our home, they were amazed," she said with a smile before lowering her eyes and sighing. "But you have no idea how mean by mother-in-law was to me over the years. She struck me whenever I made mistakes with cooking and cleaning, and even when she saw me crying, she wouldn't stop. Always yelling at me." Ma Aye Aye's smile returned to her face, though, when she said with a giggle, "Now my mother-in-law is scared of me! She doesn't dare do such things to me now that I am Abha's granddaughter."[75] We see, then, that entering into relationships with, and identifying themselves with fiercely powerful otherworldly beings allows these women, to borrow Daniel Gold's words, "alternative models of being religiously powerful in the world."[76]

At times while observing possession sessions, I could not help but be impressed with the power and influence that these young women exerted over their communities. Arriving early to a medium's home in Mandalay one morning, greeted at the door by Ma Soe, a twenty-nine-year-old female medium, I was immediately struck by her countenance: smiling, radiant, and with an unassuming charisma, she invited me inside to have tea with her parents while she got ready for her healing session. When the moment arrived for channeling Bo Bo Aung, the transformation was striking. Her presence became immense, seemingly encompassing the space of the large room filled with more than fifty kneeling guests whose palms were raised in respect. Thunderously chanting Buddhist verses of protection at the front of the room near the Buddha altar while grasping rosary beads, I felt the hairs on the back of my neck stand up. Men and women around me were weeping, and the little girl next to me suffering from first-degree burns was quivering. I found myself swept up in the waves of emotions that seemed to be washing over the audience.

At the beginning of my research, my attitude was somewhat critical of these healing activities. I approached them with the same skepticism I felt toward healers from certain Christian groups who are often accused of taking advantage of people for the sake of money. As I observed and interacted with Burmese people involved with *weizzā* mediums and healings, I soon came to see that the relationships, roles, and motivations of the agents involved were much more complicated and nuanced than I had initially imagined. People's suffering was being allayed. Women were gaining a voice in their families and communities. Religious and public works were being completed with donated money.[77] These vocations as faith healers, hermits, and clairvoyants provide women avenues of employment, power, and self-esteem not easily found in other parts of Burmese society. They are often sought out for help even during those times when they are not possessed by a *weizzā*. And not only the women who hold such positions but also the women who come to seek their help benefit. "I feel shy going to a monk to tell him about my problems," one woman told me. "There are certain things we can only share with other women," giggled another, while her friend added, "Family issues, female only problems, and" smiling shyly, "relations with one's husband."[78] Indeed, the hermitess Daw Vaṇṇathingagī and others like her say that most of their clients are women who come seeking her advice on marital, money, and job problems.[79]

For the *weizzā* devotees in this chapter, the wizard-saints are mediating entities in more ways than one. First, the appearance of and healing by the *weizzā*, through either dreams or visions, appease physical maladies that manifest in forms of culturally specific repertoires. Second, the *weizzā* act as supports for their (mostly female) devotees against communities that challenge the devotees' hopes and aspirations. My findings fit with well-established analyses of similar spirit possession phenomena throughout the world as forms of "conflict management that disguise and yet resolve social tensions."[80] Certain ways of conceptualizing problems that devotees might be dealing with, as well as understandings of healing power, are dispersed, internalized, and propagated throughout the country through various media, which helps people to experience their material bodies as closely linked with their religion as lived. Common themes that continually appear in interviews and literature include poverty, physical or mental trauma, domestic problems, desire for freedom from their current lot in life, and the sudden increase in social and economic prestige as a result of their power.[81] In the process of telling their stories, devotees move from being casualties of karmic circumstances to the narrators of them.

4

PAGODAS OF POWER

I n May 1958, a Burmese Buddhist monk by the name of U
Thilawunta arrived in the small town of Allegany, New
York. He was the first Burmese monk to ever set foot on
U.S. soil. He had been invited by an American businessman named
Gus Rogers after the two men struck up a friendship during Rogers's
travels in Myanmar several years earlier. U Thilawunta departed
from Rangoon in March 1958, making ports of call at Sri Lanka and
London before stopping in New York City. U Thilawunta eventually
made his way to Rogers's small farm in Allegany and immediately
began to erect a pagoda on the farmland (see fig. 29).[1] This was
significant for two reasons. First, it was to be the very first Burmese-
style pagoda, and most likely the very first Theravada pagoda, to
be built in the United States.[2] Second, U Thilawunta built this at
the request of his teacher, the famous wizard-saint Bo Min Gaung.
What's more, this was a specific type of pagoda that, as we will see
in this chapter, contains incredible protective power derived
from the *weizzā*.

CHANGING VIEW OF *SĀSANA-PYU*

In chapter 1, I showed how *weizzā* networks engaged in *sāsana* work in order to defend and bolster the Buddha *sāsana* in Myanmar during and immediately following British colonization. Context-specific anxieties that arose among *weizzā* devotees in response to vicissitudes of the period they lived in influenced the ways they understood and made manifest *sāsana-pyu*. Literally meaning "to do religion," *sāsana-pyu* is understood to simultaneously encompass meanings of propagate, spread, develop, or missionize the *sāsana* and guard the Buddha's teachings.[3] Devotees in different time periods and places have placed more emphasis on one or the other of the various denotations, depending on the current circumstances. For instance, Buddhists were in such a panic over the potential threat to and loss of the *sāsana* during and immediately following the colonial era that they developed a number of associations with the purpose of keeping the perceived degenerative forces at bay and launching a spiritual offensive to strengthen and spread the *sāsana* throughout the country. In the decades following liberation, however, there was a general acceptance of the stability of the *sāsana*, and Buddhists became less concerned with keeping the *sāsana* from disappearing and more with strengthening it at home and spreading it to other parts of the world for the benefit of humanity.

During this time (the second half of the twentieth century), there was a subtle change in the way the term *sāsana-pyu* was understood. In earlier decades, especially during and immediately after colonization, *sāsana-pyu* referred to those activities that defended or rejuvenated a *sāsana* that had deteriorated during the period of British rule. In the years following independence, when a large number of *weizzā* and non-*weizzā* Buddhist associations were active, the emphasis was more on sustaining a *sāsana* that had begun to regain some of its initial splendor during the so-called Liberation Era. From the 1980s onward, after the containment and rejuvenation of the *sāsana* had been accomplished, efforts were made to energetically push out, or propagate, the healthy *sāsana* into farther reaches of the country and eventually the world. A strong impetus for this latter change can be attributed to the *sangha* reforms of the 1980s and the national monastic organizations that were formed as a result of the government's interventions in attempting to legitimate its power after the 1988 antigovernment uprising. This shift in state religious policy was a result of the government's "Buddhicization" scheme whereby the Buddhist population was subsumed into the state's agenda promoting the Buddhist polity for purposes of nation-building. There was always some unease, however, in the way my informants looked upon the current state of the *sāsana* in Myanmar. On one hand, they were happy to see that the *sāsana* was now firmly established in the country and even in other nations thanks in large part to the government's *sāsana-pyu* missionary activities that, according to the national newspapers, seemed to be taking place at an unprecedented rate. On the other hand, Burmese Buddhists were uneasy that the government was the entity that seemed to have uplifted the *sāsana* to a strength not seen since the days before British rule. There was always skepticism that the government was doing this for other, more nefarious reasons, such as validating its ill-gotten authority or trying to overcome the negative collective karma created over the years.

A wave of *sāsana-pyu* projects, such as building and refurbishing pagodas, undertaken by the military government throughout the 1990s was so widespread that the designs of such works came to be known, as Brac de la Perrière notes, as "SLORC style," following the acronym for the junta that ruled Burma from 1988 to 1997, the State Law and Order Restoration Council.[4]

MAGIC NUMBER NINE PAGODAS

From the 1940s onward, *weizzā* devotees took as their model the *sāsana*-related activities carried out by the chief wizard himself, Bo Min Gaung. Hagiographical accounts report that Bo Min Gaung traveled around Asia propagating the *sāsana* by converting people to Buddhism through the display of his supernormal powers and by establishing power places (B. *dhat-pannek*) in the towns he traveled through.[5] After permanently settling in the village located at the base of Mount Popa, he is said to have sent out "those of his disciples who were capable of attaining *nibbāna* and requested that they set up *dhat-pannek* in each and every place in Myanmar."[6] These power places were almost always pagodas, but could also "include *weizzā* altars, original images conceived to be objects of veneration by the specialists or the donors, and sometimes even a kind of religious museum housing objects related to a particular *weizzā*."[7]

Some of the earliest models of the kinds of pagodas built could be found in *Pathamam Taya Magazine*. Beginning in 1948, the magazine began to publish drawings and photographs of these pagoda power places and entreated readers to replicate the design throughout Myanmar. Articles reported that these were the types of pagodas that Bo Min Gaung and other *weizzā* had made known to their devotees through dreams, visions, and states of possession. The editors explained that such *weizzā* knew the way to bring peace and prosperity through Buddhist means and that it was important to erect pagodas all over the country so that the *weizzās'* power-energy, or *dhat,* could reach all people and influence them to live in accord with the Buddha *sāsana*.[8] Among the various duties *weizzā* devotees were expected to carry out to bring everlasting peace, the most crucial was to erect pagodas and congregate at these power places.[9]

These pagodas can differ quite radically from the more traditional models found ubiquitously throughout Myanmar.[10] As anyone who has spent time in the country or looked through picture books on pagodas knows, the typical style, like the Shwedagon, is similar to an upside-down bell with only slight stylistic variations. Pagodas that trace their provenance to directives provided by the *weizzā,* however, deviate substantially in that they exhibit variations in shapes and configurations seldom found in more traditional pagodas. One of the more widely recognizable styles is known as the *kona-win,* or nine cubit, pagoda. Almost always associated with the *weizzā* Bo Min Gaung, this kind of pagoda was thought to be that which he ordered his disciples to build while he was still alive and teaching at Mount Popa.[11] Roughly nine feet high, these pagodas can be of various architectural styles. Many a *weizzā* association's goal was to erect a nine cubit pagoda in each city and town throughout Myanmar in order to, as a writer for *Pathamam Taya Magazine* put it, "keep the areas free from danger, increase the power of the *sāsana* and its supporters . . . and prevent uprisings and revolts."[12] In an article called "Erecting Pagodas and the *Weizzā* Path," the author explained that devotees were so preoccupied with building pagodas around the country because they wanted to "cleanse the world" through the power of the pagodas. Specifically, such pagodas protected the country, strengthened the *sāsana*, brought peace to the country by purifying it of non-Buddhist ideologies, and provided strength to those individuals following the *weizzā* path.[13]

These nine cubit pagodas can be seen all over Myanmar today: on hills and mountaintops, in many villages, on roadsides, and along riverbanks. Although this style of pagoda did not originate with Bo Min Gaung, he and his devotees helped popularize it, making this the representative type of *weizzā*-inspired pagoda. It was in this style that U Thilawunta erected the *ko-na-win* pagoda in Allegany, New York. The term *ko-na-win* encompasses a range of esoteric meanings. For example, it can refer to the standard list of "Nine Qualities of the Buddha" found in the *Itipiso gāthā*. More likely, however, it refers to the seemingly mystic quality of the number 9 that displays what appear to be magical mathematical properties. For example, when you multiply any number by 9, then add the resulting digits and reduce them to a single digit, it is always 9. Any number, no matter how large, multiplied by 9 reduces to 9. From a numerological perspective, the 9 simply dominates. No other number has this superiority. This makes the number 9 an integral element of pagoda-building projects, Buddhist sacred diagrams, and magical spells, associated with various other rituals of "success."[14]

The dictionary defines "cubit" as "an ancient measure of length, approximately equal to the length of a forearm. It was typically about 18 inches."[15] Pagoda builders consider it an auspicious measurement because of its connection with the powerful number 9: $1 + 8 = 9$. *Konawin* pagodas, therefore, do not necessarily have a specific architectural style, but more a measurement that is thought to have magical properties related to accomplishment, success, and perfection. Such pagodas are often erected in cubit factors of 9: 9 feet; 18 feet; 27 feet, etc. Photographs of these pagodas can be found in various issues of *Pathamam Taya Magazine* dating back to 1948.[16] Even during Bo Min Gaung's lifetime, devotees began building these pagodas, referred to mainly as "Bo Min Gaung pagodas."[17] Others call them *dhat i khain zedi* (power rod pagoda); *dhat-khyo-khain zedi* (electric power pillar pagoda);[18] *phyi-daw-win aung zedi* (success for the country pagoda);[19] and *18 taung zedi* (18 cubit pagoda). A second pagoda style associated with Bo Min Gaung is the whole world long pillar of success pagoda (B. *kambha-lone aung tan-kwan-taing zedi*) or whole world pagoda (B. *kambha-lone zedi*) with a distinctive large globe with an obelisk or pillar jutting out from the top (see fig. 29).[20] Many of these pagodas, built before the end of the colonial era, were erected on the orders of Bo Min Gaung so that the Burmese would be free from "colonial life."[21] First appearing in the 1940s, this style of pagoda, as explained by a *weizzā* devotee who was part of my Bo Min Gaung pilgrimage group, "signifies that Bo Min Gaung prophesied that the Buddha *sāsana* will eventually cover the entire world."[22] The author of a popular hagiography of Bo Min Gaung suggests that "these magic pillars were installed as a measure to drive away the British rulers from Burmese soil" and even may have been influenced by a popular children's song of the time:

> A ball of cake, on a piece of paper.
> Put on a tray with a stem,
> Decorated with lotus petals.
> Placed on the throne and offered to Buddha.
> Little monkey ran down from the throne.
> (Miss) Ja-aye was beaten by her mother
> So sitting in one corner, she sobbed.

Through an opening in the bamboo wall
A young man pulled out Ja-aye's leg.
The leg was left dangling out,
Rumbling thunder from the south
A ball of cake, on a piece of paper.[23]

And so it continues from the beginning, and the song repeats again and again. Bo Min Gaung's biographer took this song to be a prophecy that held a secret message. He interpreted the ball of cake to be a globe representing the Earth, while the stem stood for the magic pillar that was installed on the globe. It was believed that this magic design would scare away all the evil from the country and would especially hasten the departure of the monkey (i.e., those forces posing a threat to the *sāsana*). According to the biographer, such events came to pass: "In 1885, when the king was taken away, the British came. The monkey [British] had come upon the throne. In 1942, with the approach of the Second World War, the monkey [British] had run away from the throne."[24]

Related to these pagodas are ones with names like: the "world peace pagoda" (B. *kambha-nyein-kyan-aye zedi*), "entire country peace pagoda" (B. *pyi-lone-aye zedi*), "epoch-protection pagoda" (B. *kap-ka zedi*), and the curiously named "gourd pagoda that overcomes the three catastrophes" (B. *kap-kyaw-bhu zedi*) (see fig. 30).[25] Reports from devotees and popular religious magazines say that such pagodas, like the ones erected in the country during Bo Min Gaung's wanderings during the 1930s and '40s, were built by him or, like the several erected in southern Myanmar between 1948 and 1949, by his close disciples according to specifications he provided.[26] Serving as protective devices whose powers would spread across the land and guard the country from calamities, as well as power conduits that housed and ejected the powers of the *weizzā* to influence people to propagate the *sāsana*, they are also places of potency that continue to attract devotees seeking to advance along their own paths to enlightenment or *weizzā*-hood. They are still important sites for those wishing to do *sāsana-pyu* because devotees believe that the power of the *weizzā* resides within such structures and can be obtained if one enters into prolonged periods of meditation practice in their vicinities. As Tosa observed in her fieldwork related to pagoda construction, "large numbers of people believe that the supernatural power of the pagoda is boosted by association with these prominent figures. Embodied in the space of the pagoda, it can be said that *weizzā* knowledge and practice are also presented to laypersons."[27] Indeed, anyone wishing to accomplish their goals is urged to meditate, recite Buddhist scripture, or make an offering at the base of such a pagoda. The person will be infused with the supernatural power of success (B. *aung-dhat*) simply by being in the pagoda's field of influence.[28]

The Pathamam *Gaing*, an association devoted to the teachings and life of Bo Min Gaung, engaged in extensive and aggressive pagoda-building drives as early as 1948. The editors of their monthly magazine extolled the benefits of pagoda building and urged their followers to erect them in towns across the country or donate money for the building projects. In their words, the pagodas were meant to do three things: 1) make Myanmar a great Buddhist nation; 2) help Bo Min Gaung's *sāsana* propagation work succeed; and 3) allow the power of the *dhamma* and supernatural powers to grow. Other articles from this publication argue that the country has been filled with the power of wrong views since the fall of the monarchy in 1885 and the *sāsana* has descended into disorder. This can be reversed by building such pagodas around the country.[29] Moore also points out that the demise of the monarchy was "buoyed by continued lay donations and repairs to pagodas in Upper and Lower Myanmar throughout this era, from the Shwedagon in Yangon to small *zedi* throughout the country."[30] These "small *zedi*" include these nine-cubit pagodas.

Perhaps more than in any other Theravada Buddhist country, building, donating, and commissioning the construction or repair of pagodas has held a prominent role in Buddhist life in Myanmar. To this day, popular Buddhist magazines are full of articles and photographs of pagodas from all over Myanmar documenting their sizes, shapes, donors, and any unusual or supernatural occurrences associated with them. And as Tosa points out, since the country's independence:

> Heads of powerful families and government leaders have paid much attention to pagoda building. This is evidenced in the World Peace Pagoda at Kaba Aye, built in 1952 by then-Prime Minister U Nu, and the Maha Wizaya Pagoda, built in 1986 by then-chairman of the Burma Socialist Programme Party (1962–88), U Ne Win. The State Law and Order Restoration Council (SLORC, established in 1988 and reconstituted currently as the State Peace and Development Council) also set up, under the Building Act, a Committee of Pagoda-Building and Repairing and has encouraged the building and repair of pagodas.[31]

Pāli scripture indicates that there are four distinct types of pagoda: *dhātu*, in which bodily relics of the Buddha are installed; *paribhoga*, which contain the accouterments of a buddha, such as robes and bowl; *uddhissa*, in which an image, such as a statue, drawing, or painting, is placed; and *dhamma*, which contains Buddhist scriptures.[32] What distinguishes the *weizzā* pagodas from these four is the inclusion of the supernatural power of success (B. *aung-dhat*) that is associated with the great wizards. A pagoda may very well contain any of the four above-mentioned sacred objects, but it is not considered a *ko-na-win* or any other kind of *weizzā*-related pagoda if it is not instilled with the *aung-dhat*.[33] Such conferring of power is done by ritual specialists who are associated in some way with the wizard-saints, often as devotees or aspiring *weizzā* themselves. In fact, almost all pagoda contruction in Myanmar, *weizzā*-inspired and otherwise, is assisted by ritual specialists knowledgeable in *weizzā* lore, especially sacred diagrams, protective incantations, and astrological calculations used to ensure that the construction process is accomplished successfully.[34]

Included in popular wizard-saint magazines, as well as in similar literature from this period up to the present, are articles explaining why these sites are referred to as places of power. The special pagodas are designed to act like electrical conductors for the *weizzā* power-energy—likened to electricity—to run through. My interlocutors also explained these power places in terms of electricity. In the previous chapters we saw that the *weizzā*'s power is likened to radio waves. This, however, usually only refers to messages received from *weizzā* via dreams, messages, and possession. Pagodas, however, are physical structures built in various places throughout the country to act as conduits of a kind of energy that can conveniently be described in terms of electricity—an invisible, physical, fundamental form of energy—spreading out across the land. Indeed, as Rozenberg concluded from his observations of a *weizzā* association, being a devotee "amounts to plugging oneself into the energy grid of which they are the source. Just as customers of an electric grid receive a current that they are incapable of producing themselves and that they pay for, so the disciples receive the *weizzā*'s energy of success, which they pay for, one might say, with their gifts and their contributions."[35] The names given to these pagodas invoke the connection to electricity. At times, the word *dhat-taing* (electric post) or *dhat-kyo* (electric wires) is used when referring to these edifices. The fact that *dhat* is also used in the words for alchemy (B. *dhat-lone*) and buddha relics (B. *dhat-daw*) is not lost on the followers. Such pagodas are believed to act like antennae, converting the *weizzā*'s supernatural powers into frequencies that are disseminated across the world and intercepted by devotees. My interlocutors often brought up the analogy of a wi-fi hotspot, in the sense that, like physical locations where people can access the internet with their computers or mobile phones, these pagodas are created so that people who enter their fields of transmission are able to obtain access to a higher level of knowledge and power.

Conversely, my informants have explained these structures to me as having magnetic properties that draw people in like a whirlpool. "These pagodas harness the forces of the universe and of all the buddhas to create something like a vortex," the elderly female devotee Daw Tin Tin explained. "It's kind of like setting up a power plant that radiates energy, in this case spiritual energy, while simultaneously attracting people karmically connected to one another and the *weizzā* to assemble at that spot."[36]

I came across a slightly different explanation of the power of these pagodas when, during my research among hermit communities in lower Myanmar, I made a pilgrimage with two female hermits to Hermit Hill, near the famous pilgrimage spot Kyaiktiyo. Climbing to the top of the hill, we were allowed an audience with the head monk who oversaw the pilgrimage area. "Where you are standing is the very center of the Buddha *sāsana* in Myanmar," he told me while smacking his walking staff into the damp earth. "My master, the great *Sāsana-pyu* Hermit, Bo Vannasippalankāra, had a dream where a *weizzā* appeared and ordered him to erect a pagoda on each of the four hills surrounding this one, for this would surely help make the Buddha *sāsana* shine forth throughout the land."[37] As if anticipating my next question, the monk explained how erecting pagodas can accomplish this awesome feat. In typical, long-winded Burmese style, his explanation lasted the better part of an hour, but essentially he said: When a pagoda is erected, the sacred power that it holds spreads out in every direction. Its radius is not unlimited, however, and cannot therefore spread continuously to cover the entire country, let alone the world. But wherever such a pagoda is built, it creates a force field or dome of sorts that protects the area from evil influences while also infusing it with a power generated from the glory of the Buddha *sāsana,* thus fertilizing the location so that positive things occur.[38]

If we view affect through the theoretical lens of "vital materialism" to include the capacity of any body to affect or be affected, then even inanimate items, nonorganic bodies, and cultural objects are affective "actants." Political theorist Jane Bennett, who coined the term "vital materialism," explains that "an actant is a source of action that can be either human or nonhuman; it is that which has efficacy, can do things, has sufficient coherence to make a difference, produce effects, alter the course of events."[39] Affect, then, takes place not just between sentient beings but between any two or more bodies. For devotees, these pagodas are material manifestations of, and alive with, the power of the wizard-saints. The pagodas "are subject-actors" that possess, in the words of Hughes, one of the few scholars applying vital materialism to the study of religion, "an agentic potency to effect social relations, behaviors, and outcomes."[40] While the devout would not attribute animus to the pagodas in the sense that they would be considered alive, as if somehow transmutated into the semidivine being of the *weizzā* himself, they would acknowledge that the pagodas are alive because of their potential to affect the world, to have effects, and to shape the network of interrelationships of which they are a part. At the same time, the pagodas are not mere representations of the *weizzā* and their powers but the very places where the *weizzā* and their powers are made manifest on Earth.

PHANTASMAGORICAL PAGODAS

Devotees rely on dreams, visions, and meditative experiences of *weizzā* to gain instructions and inspiration for their pagoda-building projects, and just as with the creative innovation of Bo Min Gaung images, devotees create pagodas in some truly unique styles. And similar to the men and women who have visions and dreams of wizard-saints, devotees believe that the *weizzā* appear to them in these ways, providing instructions on how and where to carry out their *sāsana-pyu* work. These dreams are almost always unexpected, and at times experienced by Burmese who have little knowledge of or faith in the *weizzā*. When asked to explain how exactly devotees are drawn to the mission of preserving the *sāsana*, a well-known female *weizzā* hermitess, Daw Tin Tin, told me that "as it is the mission of the *weizzā* to be custodians of the *sāsana*, followers will be psychically pulled back to the *weizzā* through dreams, visions, or possession, regardless of where they are in the world."[41]

Perhaps more than with any other activity, devotees dedicate extensive amounts of time, energy, and especially money to erecting pagodas in various parts of the country and, as the Burmese diasporic communities continue to grow, the world. "Bo Min Gaung usually appears to me in dreams, visions, and through mediums," Daw May, a senior member of the Ministry of Health, admitted to me one afternoon after locking her office door.[42] Wealthy and well educated, Daw May said that she was never very interested in *sāsana-pyu* activities until one night she had a dream where she "saw a large man, who looked like Bo Min Gaung, riding a horse on a cold, misty morning." She could not make out the details of the man's appearance because of the fog, but the rider told her "that the next few years will be filled with natural and political catastrophes all around the world" and that she must erect a specific kind of pagoda in order to keep such catastrophes from taking place in Myanmar. She did not attach any importance to the dream until several years later, in 1994, when she had another dream of Bo Min Gaung while working in Shan State along the Thai border.[43] "Bo Min Gaung told me to erect a pagoda in this area using donations from Shan and Thai people and to make sure to invite them to the pagoda finial topping ceremony," Daw May continued. "He even gave me a vision of what the pagoda should look like." When she described it to the abbot whom she wanted to invite to preside over the pagoda conse-cration ritual after it was completed, he informed her that this was one of Bo Min Gaung's trademark pagoda structures. That is the moment she knew she had a karmic connection to Bo Min Gaung, and although she "was a scientist who never believed in such super-stitions," as she put it, she could no longer ignore the dreams and took them as a sign that Bo Min Gaung had chosen her to carry out *sāsana-pyu* activities "for the sake of the country and to usher in a new era of political stability and freedom." Using her considerable wealth and abundant social connections, both domestic and inter-nationally, Daw May began her *sāsana-pyu* projects of erecting Bo Min Gaung-related pagodas in earnest, mostly in remote areas of the country. "Pagoda donation is an altogether different phenom-enon from ordinary donation," as Tosa notes, and pagoda build-ers often explain that they have been chosen by supernatural beings, especially Bo Min Gaung.[44] Others insist that wizard-saints seek them out to undertake these building projects because of previous life connections.

My ethnographic work has shown me how intensely invested *weizzā* devotees are in the project of defining how their religious activities and practices operate in the propagation of the *sāsana* and in carrying out wizard-saints' mission of protecting human beings. Female hermit Daw Khin Hla clearly remembers the dream she had back in 1984 that sparked her interest in *sāsana-pyu* activities for the remaining years of her life. In this dream, the *weizzā* "Bo Bo Aung came to me riding an owl," she recounts in an interview that appeared in a popular religious magazine. "He landed on the Buddha altar, and while paying my respects, I begged him: 'Please don't leave me. Stay here with me!' But he simply smiled and bestowed upon me me the power to heal people from various illnesses." After having this dream, Daw Khin Hla decided to accompany a revered monk, Kalay-wa Sayadaw, well known for his *sāsana* activities, around the country on a "*sāsana-pyu* trip."[45] After seeing the monk offer donations at a pagoda for the benefit of the *sāsana*, she decided to do her part by playing the lottery in order to win money to be used for further *sāsana*-related activities on the trip. She won a considerable amount of money and donated it all for the building of a monastery.[46]

Such experiences, which often recur for extended periods of a devotee's life, act as catalysts for them to engage in a life-changing act.[47] An elderly female hermit named Daw Vimala recalls such a dream. Forty years old and working as a fishmonger, she had a "dreamlike vision" where a "*weizzā*—bearded with long sideburns, like an Indian—as well as an old hermit appeared and carried me off to hell. When I saw all the beings suffering in hell, I became very scared and asked the two men to bring me back home. They told me that if I continued to sell fish for a living, I would end up in hell after I died. Suddenly, a light atop a hill was calling out to me. When I followed it and arrived at the top of the hill, the pagodas and rest houses made me feel so peaceful. I knew I had arrived at Mount Popa." The dream had such a profound impact on her that very soon after, she ceased working as a fishmonger and became a member of a *weizzā* association, where she learned various techniques and meditation methods for following the *weizzā* path. With the knowledge gained from being a member of this association for many years, she now teaches others and "orders them to protect the Buddha *sāsana*"; any money she receives in donations is used for *sāsana*-related works.[48]

Some devotees interpret these dreams as a rallying call to aggressively proselytize to non-Buddhists through the construction of pagodas. A prominent and politically powerful monk, Myaing Gyi Ngu Sayadaw, had a pagoda built inside a church compound in Kayin State in April 2016. This was the second pagoda the Sayadaw had commissioned within a church compound. The previous year, he had instructed his followers to build one on the grounds of a church in Mezaing Village, Hpa-an Township. His disciples have since moved on to build a pagoda near a mosque in a Muslim-majority village in the same township of Hlaingbwe. The monk began these projects after experiencing a series of dreams where religious mendicants instructed him to build pagodas on parcels of land that, they said, once belonged to ancient Buddhists.[49] A member of the Anglican Christian community who was unsuccessful in convincing the monk to cease constructing these dream-inspired structures on private land said in exasperation, "Whenever he gets a dream to build pagodas in any place, he accomplishes it. And all the places he has dreamed of are in Christian church compounds. We pray that he doesn't dream anymore of building more pagodas on our Christian properties!"[50]

After the terrorist attacks in the United States on September 11, 2001, a Burmese woman and *weizzā* devotee living in California asked the wizard-saint Shwe Baw Gyun Sayadaw if she would still be safe living there. The *weizzā* told her that she would be safe in areas where there were Buddhists. When she asked him how it was that only Buddhists were protected, he replied: "America is not our land and it has its own spiritual guardians. We cannot intervene unless we are asked to do so. All we can do is protect those who consciously ask protection from us, meaning those who take refuge in the Triple Gem: the Buddha, Dhamma, and Sangha."[51] Taking this to heart, she set out on an ambitious pagoda-building project on a plot of land she purchased in Sebastapol, California, to help spread the teachings of the Buddha and wizard-saints to non-Burmese people in the United States. Ten years later, in 2011, she commissioned twenty-eight konawin (nine cubit) pagodas to be erected on her property "to avert natural catastrophes in this area of California."[52]

It was in a similar vein, and at the behest of a similar wizard-saint, that U Thilawunta created his Allegany, New York pagoda.[53] As mentioned at the start of the chapter, Bo Min Gaung himself instructed U Thilawunta to undertake a mission of constructing pagodas throughout Myanmar and eventually the world. The two men met at Bo Min Gaung's village in 1948, and U Thilawunta said that "this meeting brought about a radical change in his understanding" and that he came away with a new "vision and mission in life," to construct pagodas.[54] He immediately established a large Bo Min Gaung compound in Yangon replete with weizzā-style pagodas and went on to construct similar pagodas throughout the country. Shortly thereafter, U Thilawunta embarked on an ambitious international pagoda-building tour that spanned nearly five decades and saw the creation of nine cubit pagodas in New York; Iowa; Alberta, Canada; Ontario, Canada; Wangapeka, New Zealand; and Barrydale, South Africa, among other places.

Devotees' undertakings of weizzā-inspired pagoda-building projects outside of Myanmar are driven by similar concerns as those in the country: the desire to protect, propagate, and perpetuate the sāsana; the longing to safeguard themselves, other devotees, and potential converts to Buddhism from natural and man-made catastrophes; and as an outgrowth of some direct experience they had with a wizard-saint at some point in their lives. To appeal to non-Burmese, non-weizzā followers, and non-Buddhists, however, devotees have had to alter the ways they promote these projects abroad, especially when seeking monetary donations from the public and dealing with city zoning boards. Therefore, these devout *weizzā* devotees have couched their mission in terms of promoting international harmony, universal healing, and world peace. While other associations and individual Buddhists may focus on promoting the longevity of the *sāsana* through scriptural study, meditation, reforming the Sangha, or revering the Buddha's relics, *weizzā* devotees focus on sustaining the *sāsana* through pagoda-building projects and by using them as a means to engage in missionary work of conversion.

5
WIZARDS IN THE SHADOWS

Throughout my years of fieldwork on the *weizzā* and their devotees, Myanmar Buddhists would often entreat me to include a final chapter in my book making a disclaimer to my foreign readers that the Buddhism I portray is not, in fact, Buddhist, and does not fall within the parameters of what they consider to be "authentic Buddhism" (B. *buddha-batha asit*). I did not take such statements very seriously the first couple of times I heard them, but as they came with increasingly regularity I started to inquire into what exactly my interlocutors meant by this. Non-*weizzā* devotees would reply by saying things like, "What you are writing your book on is not found in the Buddhist scriptures"; "These are practices of black magic groups"; "The people you study are charlatans out to cheat people of their money." I was counseled instead to turn my attention to such topics as *vipassanā* (insight) meditation, monastic lineages, famous monks, or sacred pagodas. My interlocutors considered these topics to be part of an authentic and pure Buddhism, whose lineages could be traced back to the Buddha himself and were thus worthy of serious study. The characteristics these people associated with *weizzā* saints, activities, and practices contained a cluster of related notions: duplicity, corruption, the cultivation of supernatural powers for selfish and destructive purposes, an engagement with dark forces and malevolent entities, and most commonly, charlatanism. Such accusations of illegitimacy have at times been so prevalent that *weizzā* associations and individual devotees were subject to various forms of social control intended to censor, police, and eliminate the alleged deviance that made such beliefs and practices "not Buddhist."

After deciding to concentrate my research on the *weizzā* and their various channels, I unwittingly found myself on the underside of a rift that, while unclear to me, seemed obvious to many of my Burmese colleagues and friends. Our discussions about the legitimacy of the *weizzā* could get quite passionate, especially when I would point out parts of the Buddhist scriptures that acknowledged the beliefs and practices held true by *weizzā* devotees, or when I asked why they should appoint themselves arbiters of what constituted "true" Buddhism. Usually, in order to keep some decorum and maintain our friendships, we would "agree to disagree," and I would promise to take their concerns into account when writing my book.

You can imagine my surprise, then, when *weizzā* devotees themselves began asking me to downplay the prominence of the *weizzā* phenomenon in contemporary Myanmar in favor of other representations of religion and Buddhism. At first, the devotees had problems with the terminology I used. Observing that *weizzā*-related written sources from the 1940s to the 1970s that I read before doing fieldwork frequently used terms like *gaing* when referring to associations, *bodaw* when discussing revered and powerful religious figures, and *weizzā* to describe those saintly figures who have been so prominent in this book, I incorporated these terms into my daily conversations with my interlocutors. At first, such terms were met with uncomfortable laughter from *weizzā* devotees and eye rolling and dismissal from non-*weizzā* followers. As my research intensified, however, my interlocutors involved in the *weizzā* path politely, patiently, and subtly suggested that the terms *ahpwe* (organization), *yogi* (meditator), and *twet-yap-pauk puggo* (person who has "exited") be used in place of *gaing*, *bodaw*, and *weizzā*, respectively. Although I did not fully comprehend it at the time, the older terms that I was using in the twenty-first-century context mustered a whole host of imaginative associations in the minds of many Myanmar people: a world of clandestine rituals, meditation practices that could have damaging effects on one's mental health, black magic sorcery, and antigovernment ideologies. The terminology that has come to replace these and other problematic words carries with it an air of respectability. They are words that, like *twet-yap-pauk puggo*, invoke the image of a dignified saintly figure, similar to an *arahant*, as opposed to a madcap holy figure (even if they do refer to the same individual). Moreover, words like *ahpwe* and *yogi* are widely used in contemporary Myanmar to refer to Buddhist organizations (B. *ahpwe*) and *vipassanā* meditators (B. *yogi*).

More often, however, my *weizzā* interlocutors were afraid that my portrayal of Burmese Buddhism might give foreign readers the impression that the Buddhism of Myanmar is more concerned with superstitious activities involving placating supernatural beings than with striving for nirvana. "Although *weizzā* are popular here in Myanmar, please also tell your readers that Buddhists here mostly study the *abhidhamma* (abstract philosophical works) and do *vipassanā* meditation," a *weizzā* devotee requested. When I pressed him and others to explain more about why they wanted me to emphasize this or why they felt uncomfortable with me providing a non-Burmese audience with a sustained examination of the *weizzā* phenomenon, most assured me that *weizzā*-related beliefs and practices are "in accordance with" (B. *taik-hsain*) Buddhism or "genuine Buddhism" (B. *buddha-batha asit*). But they were concerned that my readers might think less of them and their country, that the practices they engage in might clash with more refined notions of Buddhism most foreigners bring with them when visiting Myanmar.[1]

What is it about the *weizzā* path that causes so much unease, even among those who subscribe to the beliefs and practices of the path? Or, as Kate Crosby asks, "Why the embarrassment, why the silence?"[2] I have found that a number of intersecting factors are at play. First, there have been long-standing and at times bitter discourses involving practices of *samatha* (concentration) meditation (favored by *weizzā* path practitioners and devotees) and *vipassanā* (insight) meditation. For example, governmental and ecclesiastical authorities fear the power of *samatha* meditation as a threat to their power, and there is widespread suspicion that organizations dedicated to the practice and propagation of *weizzā* beliefs and activities and *samatha* meditation engage in nefarious activities. Second, many of the practices of *weizzā* path practitioners, such as alchemy and the manipulation of sacred diagrams, are not thought to constitute Theravada Buddhism. A third factor is that most leaders of *weizzā* organizations, as well as independent *weizzā* healers, mediums, and practitioners, are viewed by large segments of the Burmese population as con artists.

SAMATHA CULTS AND BLACK MAGIC PRACTITIONERS

Samatha meditation (the practice of calming the mind through methods of one-pointed concentration) has been historically used, or at least viewed by authorities, as a mechanism for generating spiritual power that could be harnessed for rebellions, revolutions, or conquests.[3] Discourse surrounding *samatha* highlights the quest for supernatural powers and "is implicated in vernacular concepts of law, medicine, alchemy and magic [as well as] . . . revolutionary and anti-colonial discourse."[4] Such controversial figures as Saya San, leader of the 1930 peasant rebellion; Thakhin Kodaw Hmaing, grandfather of Burmese nationalism; and even Prime Minister U Nu were committed practitioners of *samatha* meditation techniques.[5] Such views have led governmental authorities over the past several decades to greatly discourage the widespread practice of *samatha* meditation for fear that, should people develop supernatural abilities that are by-products of *samatha* meditation, they could use this power against those in control.[6] Even the famous proponent of *vipassanā* meditation Ledi Sayadaw expressed as much when he wrote in 1910 that because *samatha* meditation allows for the development of supernatural powers, "rulers prohibit these occult practices, fearing lest they might give rise to violent commotions in the country."[7] During my time as a monk in Myanmar I shared a dormitory with several other monks who were disciples of Pa-auk Sayadaw, a famous meditation monk who specializes in *samatha* meditation techniques. They believed that the monk and his activities were under government surveillance because the government feared that, should large numbers of his disciples gain supernatural powers, they could use them against the government. I have been unable to confirm this, but Ingrid Jordt notes that, during her visit to Pa-Auk Sayadaw's monastery in 1995, five of his books on meditation were still awaiting approval for publication from the Government Scrutiny Board because it was feared that his claims of spiritual attainment included therein might count as a breach of monastic rules.[8] Houtman points out that, although some high-ranking government officials supported Pa-Auk Sayadaw, The Ministry of Religious Affairs refused to allow publication of his books because they feared that his views on meditation might cause discord within the Buddhist monastic order, as they were quite out of line with the more popular meditation methods of the time.[9]

Vipassanā, on the other hand, eschews supernatural powers and places strong emphasis on realizing the impermanent nature of all phenomena. Patronized by King Mindon (1853–1878) and practiced by such luminaries as UN General Secretary U Thant, Prime Minister U Nu (after shunning *samatha* meditation), and Aung San Suu Kyi, the *vipassanā* meditation tradition had become, even before independence in 1948, "thoroughly institutionalized and integrated into the orthodox Theravada establishment."[10] The *vipassanā* movement swept through Myanmar and into neighboring countries, where thousands of *vipassanā* meditation centers were established that continue to thrive today. "By all measures," Pranke writes, "the popularization of *vipassanā* was one of the most significant transformations in Burmese Buddhism in the modern era."[11] *Vipassanā* has even been

Myanmar's greatest export service industry internationally over the past six decades.[12]

But perhaps more problematic than the practice of *samatha* meditation and its stress on developing supernatural powers was the organizational structure and perceived secrecy of groups espousing *samatha*-related practices. Unlike those who joined the popular *vipassanā* movement that was accessible to anyone at any one of the hundreds of meditation centers throughout the country, *samatha* practitioners often assembled into semisecretive, hierarchical, and initiatory groups or sects (again using the Burmese term *gaing*) who engaged in *samatha* meditation techniques related to the *weizzā* path.[13] Such groups were not averse to giving off an air of esotericism, and this exclusivity and secrecy quickly made them the targets of criticism from the government and the general population. In chapter 1 we saw how Ne Win likened such groups to the Jim Jones cult and even went so far as to launch a campaign to ban any media that portrayed supernatural powers resulting from *samatha* meditation.[14] While Ne Win tolerated, and subsequent military regimes promulgated, *vipassanā* meditation, government attitudes toward *samatha* sects were harsh. Subjected to surveillance, many of these groups disbanded, went underground, or attempted to rebrand their image.[15] Many laypeople and monastics belonging to these groups were arrested or were accused of embezzling funds and/or sexually abusing female members.[16]

In addition to worries over threats to their power, government authorities became increasingly concerned about the large sums of money pouring into these associations. The members were from a range of socioeconomic backgrounds, but those associations led by charismatic religious figures claiming supernatural powers contained a disproportionate number of rich, urban clients, and even some from government power structures. The increased popularity of these associations and the large donations being made to the charismatic religious figures who often led them did much to, in the words of Burmese scholar Tin Maung Maung Than, "reinforce the sense of foreboding among the conservative clergy as well as the state authorities who probably viewed the increase of cult leaders as a challenge to state power and the maintenance of regime stability."[17] Religious reforms enacted in the 1970s and '80s were no doubt an attempt by the government and ecclesiastical authorities to neutralize these groups and their leaders in order to gain control over the influx of financial support and redirect it to government-sanctioned religious avenues.[18]

Although the Burmese government monitored the activities of *weizzā* associations and was swift in denouncing groups and individuals (both monastic and lay) they deemed to be straying from their notion of what constitutes orthodox Theravada Buddhism, this did not stop the same government officials from supporting the very segments of the Buddhist population they tried hard to condemn and censor. Ne Win, for example, the mastermind behind the suppression of *weizzā* associations in the 1970s and '80s, was widely thought to be an adherent to such ideologies and even publicly attributed his recovery from illness while in a Singapore hospital to the intervention of a *bodaw* (religious mendicant associated with the *weizzā* path) who was at the time in Myanmar.[19] And in the 1980s, on the advice of another *bodaw*, Ne Win changed the currency denominations that were divisible by the magic number 9, which included 45 kyat and 90 kyat notes. Many times during my years of fieldwork I witnessed government officials of high military rank at *weizzā*-related ceremonies. At a ceremony for the installation of a new Bo Min Gaung statue at a shrine outside of Mandalay, the son of one of the government officials who had donated money to have the statue made told me, "My dad is donating a gold statue of Bo Min Gaung to help protect the country. He's a big believer in Bo Min Gaung and has statues of him all over his Buddha altar at home."[20] At a pagoda consecration ceremony at a *weizzā* association compound outside of Bago, the aunt of another government official shared with me that her nephew "donated much money for this so-called *weizzā* to build this pagoda."[21] General Than Shwe (Myanmar head of state from 1992 to 2011) donated a statue of the *weizzā* Yarkyaw Sayadaw at a place in Yangon associated with hermits and *weizzā*.[22] So Buddhists are quite capable of claiming orthodoxy while "directly contradicting orthodoxy by their actions and statements."[23] While members of the regime's elite were turning to *samatha*-related practices and teachers for their own worldly gains,[24] members of the armed forces were believed to have carried, or even inserted under their skin, protective amulets associated with *samatha*-related practices.[25] In an ironic twist of fate (my interlocutors would say karmic retribution or even *weizzā* intervention), General Ne Win's son-in-law and three of his grandsons were arrested in 2002 on suspicion that they were actively trying to stage a coup by enlisting the power of a *bodaw* who was an expert in *samatha* and black magic.[26]

Members from all strata of the Burmese population are just as critical of the *weizzā* and associated beliefs and practices, but for different reasons. Their concerns revolve around beliefs that the teachings and practices put forth by members of these groups are not in accord with what they consider to be pure, Theravada Buddhism (B. *therawada buddha-batha asit*) or part of the *sāsana* path (B. *thathana line*). Large segments of the general population, especially lay practitioners of *vipassanā* meditation, claim that the *weizzā* path is not really Buddhist or is at best a form of Buddhism influenced by Mahayana doctrines. Devotees' beliefs in saints who have prolonged their lives through various alchemical and meditation techniques deviate from the Buddha's teachings on impermanence and no-self, they argue. Accused of being selfish and deluded, adherents to the *weizzā* path are thought to be preoccupied with goals that improve their current lot in life, such as gaining near immortality, supernatural powers, riches, or love. As a result, critics refer to the *weizzā* path pejoratively as "mundane" (P. *lokiya*), in contrast to a "supramundane" (P. *lokuttara*) path that, in their eyes, is most in line with the Buddha's teachings that aim at attaining enlightenment and escaping of the rounds of rebirth.

Weizzā devotees' attitudes toward their critics, and especially to the modern *vipassanā* movement, range from angry defense to "polite reservation."[27] They readily concede that developing supernatural powers and engaging in *samatha*-related practices do not lead to enlightenment; only *vipassanā* meditation can achieve that. But they are also quick to point out that their path offers an alternative method of salvation (albeit a more circuitous, and possibly longer, one) that still falls within the boundaries of Theravada orthodoxy. Freely admitting that *vipassanā* is a more direct and quicker route for attaining nirvana, *weizzā* practitioners maintain that it is a matter of personal preference to devote their energies to *samatha* meditation. Sayadaw U Uttamasara (d. 1995), considered by many to be a modern-day *weizzā*, when asked why he preferred *samatha* meditation, wrote: "I have heard some criticize [*samatha*'s] value contemptuously. The Buddhas-to-be have all fulfilled the ten kinds of *pāramī* (perfections) by means of practicing *samatha* meditation in their past lives. Passing through the earth and flying in space, and some different kinds of miraculous powers are the outcomes of practicing *samatha* meditation. Therefore, you should regard it as vitally important, and should not look down upon it."[28] Indeed, in the case of hermitess Daw Tin Tin, the *weizzā* path can also be referred to as the "*samatha weizzā*" path, whose saints are known as "*samatha weizzā*." "I had never attempted to practice *samatha* in this lifetime. In fact, I was fully involved in *vipassanā*," Daw Tin Tin wrote. "A whole new world opened up and the *Weizzā* Path was revealed to me . . . and the incredible mission of the *Samatha Weizzā* Masters."[29]

As other scholars on this subject have rightly observed, *weizzā* practitioners themselves, when providing information on their practices and doctrines, attempt to couch them within normative Theravada Buddhism.[30] The most common way of doing this is to reference the first chapter of the late nineteenth-century *Vijjāmaggadīpanī* (Manual on the path of wisdom [*weizzā*]) written by the famous *vipassanā* meditation master Ledi Sayadaw. In the first nine pages, Ledi Sayadaw lays out in detail the various kinds of *weizzā* knowledge and paths popular within Myanmar at the time. And although he goes on in the remainder of the book to show how these *weizzā* are inferior to the foremost *weizzā*, namely the "*ariya weizzā*" (referring to the path that leads to full enlightenment, or *arahant* status), he has nonetheless provided generations of *weizzā* path apologists with "an authoritative vocabulary and theoretical structure with which to articulate their system and defend it against criticism."[31]

Reference is also made to the classical Buddhist text *Visuddhimagga* and its descriptions of *weizzā* and their supernatural powers: "With regard to the case of the *weizzā* flying in the air through the power of the esoteric sciences, it is said: 'What is power through the sciences? *Weizzā*, having uttered their magic spells, travel through the air, and they show an elephant in space, in the air; a horse in space, in the air; a chariot in space, in the air; a soldier in space, in the air; a manifold military infantry.'"[32] *Weizzā* practitioners maintain that since such a prestigious, respected, and foundational text in no way disparages these powers or the *weizzā* who wield them, they must be considered central to the Buddhist path. Likewise, *weizzā* advocates specifically like to point out that one of the most revered Buddhist monks in contemporary Myanmar, the doyen of *vipassanā* meditation, Mahasi Sayadaw, makes positive references to *weizzā* and their supernatural powers in his Burmese translation of the *Visuddhimagga*. The monk offers copious commentarial notes, and in the section just quoted above, as well as throughout the text when referencing supernatural power, he provides the reader with a detailed description of the kinds of *weizzā* found in the Burmese religious landscape at the time.[33]

The commentary on the biography of Pilindavaccha Thera is another oft-cited reference to canonically sanctioned examples of the categories of *Cūḷa* (Small) and *Mahā* (Great) *Gandhāri Weizzā*. The commentary says that Pilindavaccha was a wandering ascetic who "had himself accomplished in such an applied-knowledge (*vijjā*) known as *cūḷa gandhāra*, become a sky wanderer as well as knower of thoughts of others."[34] One day when Pilindavaccha and the Buddha were in the same vicinity, Pilindavaccha found that his magical powers no longer worked. He thought, "I have heard, however, indeed, this being said by succession of teachers thus: 'Where the applied knowledge (*vijjā*) of *mahā gandhāra* prevails, the applied knowledge of small *gandhāra* [*cūḷagandhāravijjā*] becomes futile; beginning from the time the monk Gotama had come (here) this applied knowledge of mine has not worked well; undoubtedly the monk Gotama knows the applied knowledge (*vijjā*) of great *gandhāra*; it would be better should I serve him all round and learn that applied knowledge [*mahāgandhāravijjā*] in his presence." Realizing himself to be merely a *"Cūḷa Gandhārī Weizzā,"* Pilindavaccha entreated the Buddha to teach him the ways of the *"Mahā Gandhārī Weizzā,"* to which the Buddha replied, "Well then, you should become a monk." The Buddha then proceeded to teach Pilindavaccha the *vijjā* that leads to awakening, thus fitting the notion discussed above of a *Mahā Gandhārī* or *ariya weizzā* as someone who has achieved nirvana.

Then there is the commentary on the biography of Mahākaccāna Thera who, having been a *vijjādhara* in his previous life during the dispensation of Sumedha Buddha, used his supernatural powers to fly through the air and offer flowers to Sumedha.[35] In another account from the commentary on the biography of Uttaratthera, this monk was a *"vijjādhara* at the time of the Blessed One Sumedha, and wandered about in the sky. On that occasion, the Master, for the purpose of uplifting him, sat down at the foot of a certain tree inside a forest releasing His six-colored radiant rays of Buddha. On going through the sky, he saw the Blessed One, became pious-minded, descended from the sky and made his offering of bountiful excellently pure Kanikāra flowers to the Blessed One."[36] *Weizzā* practitioners are quick to point out that their practices are in line with those found in the Buddhist scriptures and advocated by ecclesiastical authorities. Similar to the argument made by Uttamasara Sayadaw about the centrality of *samatha*-based meditation practices to the Buddha's own path to enlightenment, *weizzā* path practitioners stress that practices such as the repetitive chanting of central Buddhist verses (like the popular *Itipiso Gāthā*) in various configurations and for extended periods of time, visualizing pagodas or the Buddha while doing breath meditation, practicing loving-kindness meditation, sharing the results of one's good deeds with all sentient beings, and/or practicing using any one of the forty *samatha* meditation objects prescribed by the Buddha are all considered methods sanctioned by the Buddha, scriptures, and eminent monks.[37]

Weizzā practitioners assert that they ultimately strive for nirvana but are not averse to taking a less direct route to get there. In fact, many would say that their practices might even offer a greater chance of achieving that goal than *vipassanā* methods. Adhering to the Buddhist temporal scheme that Buddha Metteyya will arrive in this world in the far distant future, many devotees are convinced that if they can prolong their lives through *samatha*-based techniques in order to be around when Metteyya appears, they will be able to gain enlightenment under his guidance.[38] For them, engaging in lifetimes of *vipassanā* meditation is too risky, especially as they may miss the opportunity to be reborn at the exact period of time when Metteyya will be here on Earth. Moreover, as we saw in previous chapters, a central duty of *weizzā* practitioners is to defend the Buddha *sāsana* and protect Buddhists from threatening forces. Such a longevity mission, advocates maintain, is inherently meritorious because they use their knowledge and supernatural powers to protect and propagate the *sāsana*.

Complicating people's perceptions of the *weizzā* even more is that people and groups whose aims are more nefarious (those participating in black magic, putting curses on people, etc.) engage in similar practices of alchemy, *samatha* meditation, and sacred diagram construction and manipulation as those who follow the *weizzā* path. Such individulas and groups may even associate themselves with a particular *weizzā* group or wizard-saint. As a result, critics often conflate these two groups and make sweeping generalizations about the nature of the *weizzā* path. In addition, *weizzā*-related healers are often looked upon with suspicion and perceived as ambiguous figures because they deal with occult forces and use mundane and esoteric techniques that become beneficial or harmful according to the intention of the user and the being invoked. Indeed, masters of the non-*weizzā* lower path (B. *auk-lam*) are said to use the same techniques as masters of the *weizzā* upper path (B. *ahtet-lam*).[39] One reason one of my interloctors gave for the *weizzā* path being looked down upon is, again, linked to *samatha* practice: many non-*weizzā* healers and black magicians often pick a specific *samatha* meditation technique or object and work with it until they have developed some kind of supernatural power. They also believe that the *samatha* practice increases the potency of their spells, curses, remedies, etc. Once they achieve this power, the person can use it for good or evil ends. "This scares the people," he said. "People who do *vipassanā* are thought to be 'safer' because advancement along the *vipassanā* path is contingent on the purity of one's morals."[40]

In spite of all this, *weizzā* devotees are still somewhat cautious about disclosing their associations with the *weizzā* path and its wizard-saints. I often asked devotees if they were embarrassed by their beliefs, and their responses can be summed up best by what one devotee, U Maung, told me: "Of course not! But even we have to admit that these things aren't easily believed by even people here in Myanmar. Those who are interested will learn a lot from your book and can explore more if they wish. But we want your readers to know that Myanmar is a developed country with people who don't live their lives according to superstition, which they may mistake our beliefs as."[41] This brings us full circle to the advice cited at the beginning of this chapter: many of my Burmese inter-locutors told me that the *weizzā* path was not a worthy subject of study. They repeatedly tried to convince me that the only authentic form of religious practice was the Buddhism found in monasteries and *vipassanā* centers. This was what I should focus my research on, I was told. When talking with *weizzā* path practitioners, however, I often asked them if *weizzā* cults can be seen as remaining within the orthodox Theravada fold and if attempting to demarcate layers or levels of orthodoxy only distorts our data by conceptualizing them as such, especially if these layers are indistinguishable to the practitioner. In their replies, my informants sometimes became agitated while trying to figure out what I was getting at, or they gave me an answer they thought I was looking for. Many admitted that they do not see their *weizzā* beliefs and practices as being in disharmony with Theravada Buddhism.

This self-consciousness can be traced back, as we saw at the beginning of this chapter, to the central role *vipassanā* meditation has played in Myanmar since the beginning of the twentieth century. Erik Braun has shown how attempts were made by religious leaders, most notably Ledi Sayadaw, to teach *vipassanā*-style meditation to Europeans as early as 1917.[42] Since then, as the *vipassanā* phenomenon increased in popularity throughout the world, *vipassanā* was pursued by non-Buddhists and convert Buddhists, and psychologized and incorporated into Western medical science.[43] It continued to be a source of national pride, while the *weizzā* phenomenom, as Crosby writes, was "still 'not for export,' an embarrassment to the Buddhism promulgated as a scientific method superior to everything and open to all."[44]

REAL VERSUS FAKE BUDDHISM

Many of these concerns, as we have seen above and throughout this book, are bound up with issues of power. *Weizzā* beliefs and practices subvert the cautiously circumscribed and contained notions of Theravada Buddhism created, in large part, by the government and ecclesiastical authorities via diverse channels that include laws, religious literature, sermons, and popular media, as well as by discourses with non-Burmese proponents of *vipassanā*. They are even seen by many Burmese as harmful to the embedded reputation of Myanmar as a stronghold of a pure form of Theravada Buddhism centered around *vipassanā* meditation and Buddhist philosophy.[45] With its reasons for monitoring, suppressing, and outright banning *weizzā* associations and the media produced by them, the government has had a vested interest in making such delineations. In May 1980, for instance, the government established a Committee of the Great Assembly of Monks (B. *Sangha Mahanayaka Ahpwe*), made up of the highest-ranking monks in the country, to oversee and regulate all monastic activities in Myanmar.[46] During the four-day meeting, the committee refused to

recognize the *weizzā*, their devotees and practices, or their associations as government- and ecclesiastically sanctioned avenues of
religious activity and devotion. This only further solidified the
public perception that such channels were outside the parameters of what was considered normative Buddhism.[47]

Many Burmese Buddhists from outside the various *weizzā* congregations do not identify what they see or hear as belonging to the
Buddhist tradition and take it upon themselves to delineate what
beliefs and practices can be sanctioned as "Buddhist," thus creating standards against which to measure authenticity and decide
who is and who is not allowed affiliation with Burmese Buddhism.
They stipulate what the majority of Burmese Buddhists are willing
to tolerate and not tolerate, which activities are socially acceptable
and which are offensive, and so on. Religious idioms like those associated with the *weizzā* have been designated superstitious, overly
materialistic, and manipulative.

Throughout the course of my fieldwork, hardly anyone I spoke
with doubted the power of the *weizzā*, but they worried that a
medium and her/his family, for instance, might have nefarious reasons for making such claims. Swindling people out of their money
was the most frequent complaint I encountered from interlocutors
(both believers and nonbelievers) and in literature. Words like
"charlatan" (B. *hsaya-yaun*) and "faker" (B. *lu-lein*) appeared repeatedly in reference to those individuals who were supposedly possessed by *weizzā*. A popular saying by interlocutors and in print
media was that "for every one authentic [person], there are one
thousand imitators and ten thousand impostors."[48] Brac de la Perrière put it well: "in a context in which civilians are the target of all
sorts of predations, [*weizzā*] play on the over-sensitivity about the
potential greediness of all kinds of ritual specialists. They make
an advantage of their avoidance of ritual procedures such as interactions involving monetary exchange in the ceremonies. . . . They
particularly insist on the fact that they do not trade protection
against monetary offerings."[49] The famous cartoonist and social

critic U Ba Gyan illustrated this predatory fear amusingly with a 1940s cartoon (see fig. 32).

Two sham ascetics tell their guests that the man wearing the turban is the teacher of the famous *weizzā* Bo Bo Aung and Bo Min Gaung; that he abstains from eating and drinking and only smokes cigarettes; and that his *weizzā* congregation is much greater than others. When the donation that one of the guests left for the two ascetics goes missing, the bald ascetic immediately accuses his hermit companion of taking it. Cursing at him and grabbing his throat, the bald ascetic causes a 100 kyat note to pop out of the hermit's mouth where he had it hidden. When a female devotee rushes over to see what the scuffle is about, the bald ascetic quickly tells her that whenever anyone wrings his hermit friend's neck, money will pop out of his mouth. The female devotee tells her friend that the hermit is "Very powerful, for whenever one chokes him, a 100 kyat note will appear from his mouth!"

WIZARD ILLUMINATI

During the second half of the twentieth century and the first decade of the twenty-first, all forms of media dealing with *weizzā*-related subject matter were prohibited by the government. Houtman noted that books on such topics were prohibited from being sold in bookshops during his years of fieldwork in the 1980s. And during my years of fieldwork, most *weizzā*-related publications were banned, although several magazines were allowed to be published so long as stories of *weizzā* and their supernatural abilities were omitted or couched in fictional accounts.[50] For some reason, the early 1990s saw a very large number of *weizzā*-related articles printed in magazines, but by the late 1990s, the national censor board (Press Scrutiny Board) prohibited such stories from being published, and words such as *weizzā* and *bodaw* could not be printed. One of the rare instances where such words were permitted to be printed was in an article written by an author who was hostile to the *weizzā* and who referred to me by name as a foreigner who had come to Myanmar to study such subjects.[51]

This has all changed with the recent political developments in Myanmar. Within weeks of the government abolishing the Press Scrutiny Board in February 2013, publishers began putting *weizzā* books back into circulation. At least twenty new books on Bo Min Gaung were published in the following four years alone.[52] Publications, general news stories, and now websites about Bo Min Gaung and other *weizzā* increasingly manifest and circulate *weizzā* cultural forms that extend beyond the semisecret associations, previously hard-to-find wizard-saint publications, and the country of Myanmar iself, to reach a much wider public sphere. Whereas previously there was only a handful of government approved monographs dedicated to the *weizzā*, the past couple of years has witnessed an explosion of *weizzā*-related publications, articles on devotees' experiences featured in long-running popular religious magazines, and even YouTube videos. Coupled with this are newly established daily journals and online video news clips that carry stories about the *weizzā*. One online Burmese socialite journal even filmed famous Burmese movie stars taking part in an annual Bo Min Gaung festival at Mount Popa.[53] The wizard-saints have, indeed, become chic!

This is all going according to the *weizzā*'s master plan, say devotees. The Supreme *Weizzā* Council, introduced in chapter 1, are "guiding Myanmar to transform it into a peaceful and prosperous land where the teachings of the Buddha will shine throughout the country," as one of my interlocutors expressed it.[54] Another devotee who told me back in 2007 that the *weizzā* were "pulling the strings" in order to usher in a new period of peace and prosperity "sometime around 2010" was overjoyed to see her prognostications come true. When we met for coffee in 2015, she exclaimed: "See! I told you the *weizzā* were working in the shadows. They are now invisible participants of the new government!"[55]

Perhaps the most detailed explanation of the *weizzā*'s supposed manipulation of current events comes from the personal diary of a devotee of a *weizzā* who died in 1997. According to the diary, this *weizzā* told his followers in 1990 that Aung San Suu Kyi's party would win the election of that year but that the army would not hand over power because the people of Myanmar have accrued, for whatever reason, a large amount of negative collective karma that would require another nineteen years to dissolve.[56] He went on to say that the Council of *Weizzā*, headed by Bo Min Gaung, held a meeting at this time to discuss how, and if, they should intervene on behalf of the people of Myanmar. The council was split on what was to be done. Both sides agreed that the nineteen years of negative karma needed to run its course, but one group wanted to let the people have a period of respite after which they could expiate the negative karma, while the other wanted the people to endure the remaining years of suffering, after which they would have reaped the fruit of their collective karma and could be completely free. Since they could not come to a consensus, they took a vote, and the side that advocated for the continuation of the negative karma until it runs out won. That was why, according to the devotees, there was another two decades of military rule.[57] But, according to my interlocutor, the *weizzā* still had one trick up their sleeves.

According to this devotee's personal diary, the *weizzā* told his followers that Ne Win said in a 1981 speech that he would be stepping down from power and eventually allow elections and multiparty democracy because the *Weizzā* Council used their supernatural powers to put those words in his mouth. The military government was therefore compelled to hold an election in 1990. Although Aung San Suu Kyi's National League for Democracy won, the military government refused to cede power. This too was all according to the Council of *Weizzā*'s plan, said the devotee. In addition to the people of Myanmar needing to endure the remaining years of their negative collective karma, the *weizzā* needed to make Aung San Suu Kyi a global icon for freedom and put Myanmar on the world stage so that the country's transformation could take place naturally and when there was real reconciliation between Aung San Suu Kyi and the military government.[58]

With the country's democratization, the liberalization of the media, and increased commercialization of the wizard-saint phenomenon, a new public sphere is emerging in which *weizzā* are shifting from being thought of as "forces operating in secret, below and behind the surface of appearance, to becoming subject to vision and visibility."[59] The demographics of *weizzā* devotees are changing. Within the country, monastics who may have been reticent to publicly declare their interest in or devotion to the wizard-saints are now writing books and magazine articles related to *weizzā*, constructing *weizzā*-inspired pagodas, and installing Bo Min Gaung statues in their monastic compounds. I have witnessed an increase in Muslim devotees of Bo Min Gaung, many of whom donate large sums of money to organizers of *weizzā* ceremonies and festivals. Most notable, though, has been the increased interest in the *weizzā* by people from mainland China, Thailand, Taiwan, Malaysia, the United States, and parts of Europe—many of whom are wealthy and donate large amounts of money to individuals thought to be living wizard-saints. One of my most surreal memories of doing fieldwork includes trekking through a malaria- and bandit-infested forest to finally track down a supposed living *weizzā*, only to find a tour bus full of wealthy Chinese businessmen already there unloading sofas, television sets, and generators to donate to the *weizzā*.

CONCLUSION

Affectual Relationships

Trying to account for the increase in the number of individuals who are drawn to the wizard-saints, journalist U Aung Kyaw explained in a magazine article that with the waning of the Buddha *sāsana*, the *weizzā* have also arrived to take responsibility for protecting it. At this time, the head *weizzā*, most notably Bo Min Gaung, will become increasingly involved in such affairs. "It is evident in the number of people who believe in, have broad knowledge of, and place pictures and statues of them in their homes," he wrote. "And as more and more people enter into relationships with them, the more incidents of possession we see occurring throughout the country."[1] U Aung Kyaw interviewed a twenty-two-year-old woman named Ma Khin Khin who, like the young women in chapter 3, has the ability to *dhat-si* Bo Min Gaung. U Aung Kyaw had the opportunity to talk with Ma Khin Khin as she was possessed by Bo Min Gaung and provided a word-for-word transcription. When he arrived, the young woman (as Bo Min Gaung) asked in a dismissive voice, "Huh? Why have you come to see me, man?"

U AUNG KYAW: I am a writer. I have come because I write about *weizzā* who guard the *sāsana* and do propagation works, Reverend Sir. There is still something I want to know from your lips, Sir.

MA KHIN KHIN: Eh?. . . Good, man, good! There are many people in this world who have converted to Buddhism. But they are still full of greed, hatred, and delusion. They are more like ogres than humans. People lie, cheat, kill and because of that, they struggle in life. They work and have no time for giving attention to the Three Gems: Buddha, Dharma, and Sangha. . . . Yet, still in their minds, they know that they cannot do religious activities because of their [impure] state. It's just like this, man. They are like fish that are stuck in a net. They cannot save themselves and just sink deeper and deeper. I have a request for you now. Do you know what it is? Please spread throughout the country and have others pass on what we *weizzā* have taught.

UAK: Yes, I agree that we must do *sāsana-pyu* works throughout the country.

MKK: Good, good. What else do you wish to know?

UAK: Please tell me more about what business you *weizzā* have with entering into people.

MKK: Ahh . . . The Buddha *sāsana* has reached the 2,500-year halfway point. The time has come where we must accept the responsibility of working together to protect the Buddha *sāsana*. Therefore, we must make connections with people everywhere.[2]

The wizards may, indeed, be in the shadows when it comes to major political power plays, but such exchanges highlight the intimacy and immediacy of devotees' personal relationships with the wizard-saints. Far from being confined to darkened corners of their lives, these *weizzā* and the roles they play are out in the open. For individuals who have had astonishing encounters with *weizzā*, there may have been some initial uncertainty about which particular saint had come to visit, but there was never any doubt about the kind of being it was. Although the medium might have been encountering a *weizzā* for the first time, the wizard-saint was familiar, and they knew immediately that it was a special being bearing an important message. The devout themselves explicitly made the connection between a particular event in their life and the timing of the *weizzā*'s appearance, and there was almost always the feeling that the *weizzā* acted as something akin to an invisible guide helping the devotee through life. As I have shown throughout, such experiences are, to borrow Robert Orsi's terminology, "abundant events."[3] In other words, even though Myanmar Buddhist culture primes a person for an encounter with a wizard-saint, the person considers it highly out of the ordinary. Second, those having such experiences are certain that they are not delusions or hallucinations. Evens when the *weizzā* appear in dreams, devotees consider them real. Third, such events do not take place in a vacuum. They "arise at the intersection of past/present/future (as these really are or as they are dreaded or feared or hoped for). At the moment of such an event we have a new experience of the past while at the same time the horizon of the future is fundamentally altered."[4] The wizard-saints often enter people's lives when they least expect it: through visionary apparitions, auditory voices, dreams, spirit mediums, flesh-and-blood persons, and two- and three-dimensional images and objects. These encounters have such significant effects on the person that he or she often wishes to deepen the bonds with the *weizzā*. In essence, such encounters are so significant as to have a long-lasting, and predominantly beneficial, impact on the person's life. The encounter with a simple photograph of Bo Min Gaung was enough, for example, to motivate me to research wizard-saints for many years and eventually write this book.

Throughout this book I have attended to affect in order to highlight the fluid and variegated social lives of the *weizzā* devotees, as well as what matters to them in the context of their relationships and practices with the wizard-saints. Foregrounding affect, or the flow of forces through bodies, brings such phenomena into view and renders them explicable. Affect theory can explain "how discourses attach to bodies and get them to move" and is not "baffled" when "bodies sincerely 'believe' one thing and do another."[5] I have attempted to examine the religious lives of such individuals and the experiences they considered central along with the varied rituals and practices that make up their personal religious expressions. I considered religion at the level of the individual and took seriously their fluid, variegated, and at times, contradictory, beliefs and practices, to learn how my interlocutors actually did and imagined religion in the circumstances of their everyday lives. This approach has revealed aspects of Burmese religious life from the perspectives of those whose experiences are often misrepresented or ignored entirely, not only in Western academic works on religion but also in Burmese historical monographs and other written sources. In addition to increasing our understanding of the lived religious experiences and practices of the *weizzā* devotees, this method has also enriched our investigation of the complex interrelationship between these experiences and practices and the wider social world in which they are enacted.

The charged emotional experiences devotees have with the *weizzā* are not simply the spontaneous expressions of shared religious enthusiasm brought on by the charisma of a given wizard-saint, but rather "the circulation of particular, culturally validated forms of enthusiasm . . . [where] the sociality of affect pushes us to consider the interactive process through which certain embodied feelings and particular religious subjects were validated, discounted, and disciplined."[6] Indeed, they are "embodied performances fueled by excitation of matter."[7] Such devotees have ongoing phantasmagorical experiences: sequences of imaginary images, like that seen in a dream, of wizards appearing to them to convey new teachings, meditation practices, magical spells, iconography, and, in some cases, supernatural powers. These images are very real to the devotees experiencing them. As this book has shown, what develops at the intersection of imagination and revelation stems from a specific set of social and practical engagements and draws upon particular cultural repertoires. Moreover, the *weizzā* devotees' visionary and emotionally charged experiences that occur at the interfaces of their relationships with the wizard-saints show how both the felt anomalous nature of such experiences and the attribution processes through which these experiences are considered special are shaped into religious ideas and stable teachings and institutions in contemporary Myanmar. The religious worlds of the *weizzā* are intensely affective, especially in terms of the material and visual aspects of religion. Attending to such aspects conveys the "sensuous life of a religion, shaping, coloring, and organizing" *weizzā* devotees' relations with fellow devotees and with the *weizzā* themselves.[8] Such objects have moral efficacy and can mediate both efficacy and emotion.

Without understanding contemporary patterns of religiosity in the lives of Burmese *weizzā* devotees, one cannot understand Buddhist practice in contemporary Myanmar more generally. It is my hope that readers will realize that the phenomena described in this book are not at all exotic and esoteric. Those unfamiliar with the *weizzā* phenomenon tend to characterize it as occult, otherworldly, esoteric, and even bizarre.[9] But investigation shows that the people involved lead quite ordinary lives. They go to work in the morning, return home, and perhaps attend *weizzā* activities in the evening or on the weekend, or simply incorporate their practices into their daily devotions. This form of lived religion is commonplace in contemporary Myanmar. A select few members of secret societies may be concerned with obtaining supernatural powers, but the vast majority of *weizzā* devotees follow practices and beliefs associated with the *weizzā* path in everyday life. Their religion has gone mainstream, in a sense, with YouTube videos and Facebook postings, as well as Myanmar newspapers and online journals carrying stories on the growing cult of Bo Min Gaung. Even the international press has become interested in the *weizzā*, as evidenced by recent BBC and AFP news articles.[10]

This book began with an account of my initial contact with the world of wizard-saints, and of the "Chief Wizard," Bo Min Gaung. I would like to end with an anecdote of my final encounter with the wizard-saint while writing this book. The experience made clear to me what Christopher Pinney meant when he wrote that people's engagements with religious images act as "sources of future interventions, rather than as embodiments of past intentionalities."[11]

One afternoon, I witnessed a man in his forties bring lunch and share it with Bo Min Gaung. Laying out dishes of meat, vegetables, and rice at the base of the statue, the man lit a cigarette. "These are Grandpa's favorite cigarettes," the man looked over at me and said with a wink, as he placed them in one of Bo Min Gaung's hands. He proceeded to sit cross-legged, using his prayer beads to chant the *Itipiso Gāthā*, for almost forty-five minutes while periodically lightly touching the knee of Bo Min Gaung or placing another lit cigarette in the statue's hand. When he had completed his devotional activities, the man was covered in sweat, and black flies had begun feasting on the offerings of food. He gently swished them away with a hand-held fan and invited me over to share in his meal. I politely declined, saying I was too hot to eat, but went on to strike up a conversation with him about his relationship with Bo Min Gaung. When I asked him if these actions were part of a larger body of practices to help him along the *weizzā* path, he laughed heartily and said, "You certainly think highly of me! While I am indeed interested in *weizzā*-related matters, I am here today to ask Grandpa's help in passing an exam at my job as an income tax official. I will get promoted if I do well on it." He later pointed at a woman on the other side of the shrine room. "See that woman? She comes every day to ask Grandpa to help her daughter pass an upcoming matriculation exam." As we were about to leave, he guided me to the back of the room and pointed out a life-sized statue of Bo Min Gaung sitting in front of a pagoda surrounded by a metal fence covered with dozens of sheets of notebook paper and official-looking documents. "These are all requests people made to Grandpa." As this was the time of the year when high school students take their final exams, most of these notes were from students asking Bo Min Gaung for help. The rest dealt mostly with matters involving health, love, and money. "Dear Grandfather," one note read. "Please cure my arthritis. The medicine the doctors gave me doesn't help." "Grandfather, I really love this girl. I want to marry her. Let her also love me so we can marry and be happy," read another. My guide suggested I write a note to Bo Min Gaung as well. I did: "Dear Grandpa, Please help me finish this book successfully!"

NOTES

INTRODUCTION

1. Orsi 2005: 62.
2. I use the terms "wizard-saint" and "*weizzā*" interchangeably throughout. Burmese words have generally been transcribed according to the "standard conventional transcription system" recommended by John Okell (1971). An exception to this is *weizzā*. While scholars have traditionally transliterated it as *weikza*, I follow Foxeus (2011) in transliterating it as *weizzā*, which more accurately captures the Burmese pronunciation of the Pāli word *vijjā*, from which it derives.
3. I thank Anne Hansen for pointing this out to me.
4. Seigworth and Gregg 2010: 1–2. Italics in original.
5. Schaefer 2015: 3.
6. As there is no agreed-upon definition of "affect" among scholars of affect theory, some theorists prefer to think of affect as distinct from emotion. Supp-Montgomerie, for instance, argues that "unlike emotion (affection), affect is not the state of a body but the waves of energy that move through and among bodies in constant ebb and flow" (2015: 337). See Best (2011: 5–6) and Hicky-Moody and Malins (2007) for a more thorough discussion of emotion and affect. I treat emotion as a central component of affect theory.
7. Schaefer 2015: 221, n. 26.
8. Hughes 2016: 59.
9. Other scholars who have applied affect theory to their studies on religion, although on a smaller scale, include Ahmed (2004a; 2004b; 2004c), Sedgwick (2003), and McDaniel (2016).

10. Schaefer 2015: 3.
11. Van der Linden 2014: 430.
12. Schaefer 2015: 9.
13. Schaefer 2015: 8–9. Quoting affect theorist and anthropologist Kathleen Stewart, Schaefer proposes that power, "as a 'thing of the senses' feels before it thinks."
14. McDaniel 2011: 162.
15. Morgan and Promey 2001: 16.
16. In many ways, this is my attempt to rectify the claim made by John Kieschnick that study "of the role of the material culture of religion in emotional experience does not yet exist" (Kieschnick 2008: 234).
17. Hughes 2012: 20.
18. Lauren Berlant, quoted in Figlerowicz 2012: 13.
19. Taves 2012: 72.
20. Taves 2009: 58.
21. Taves 2009: 163, quoted in Schaefer 2015: 212.
22. Hughes 2010: x.
23. Hughes 2010: x.

1. VANGUARDS OF THE *SĀSANA*

1. "An den Ecken des überdeckten Steinsitzes (Teahosin oder Kanzel) für predigende Pungyi's, der von Löwen getragen wird, finden sich placirt, als Zuhörer, ein Naga (Schlange), ein Kalon (Drache), ein Witya (Weiser oder Zauberer) und König Koyopa-iningyi" (1866: 75).
2. Scott 1896: 409–10.
3. Orwell (1974 [1934]: 9): "The so-called weiksa, who is no other than a circus conjurer and the minion of U Po Kyin, have vanished for parts unknown, but six rebels have been caught" (20); and "During all this time, unknown to anyone of importance, further sedition was afoot. The 'weiksa' (now far away, peddling the philosopher's stone to innocent villagers in Martaban) had perhaps done his job a little better than he intended" (20).
4. The *Dhammapada Aṭṭhakathā* text in question is 33 C, "Story of the Present: The Elder Jatila." In his study of *paritta* in South and Southeast Asia, Jaini points out that the term *vijjādhara* only appears in commentarial and paraconanical literature and is used when referencing a class of practitioners, similar to what he sees with the *siddha* of the Tantric texts (Jaini 1965: 77).
5. See Strong (1992: 180–81) and Stadtner (2008: 35) for more detailed accounts of this chronicle.
6. Lammerts 2010a: 22.
7. For more on the *Kappālaṅkāra*, see Lammerts 2010b: 14.
8. I thank Lilian Handlin for bringing this mural to my attention.
9. See Green (2005: 45) for more on this mural.

10. There is a vast amount of Burmese-language sources that provide detailed explanations and analyses of the *weizzā* figure. See, for instance, Bhuṃ" Teja 2013.
11. Orsi 1996: 105.
12. Interview, DM-F-55.
13. Females do have the potential to become *weizzā*, however.
14. CP-55-M.
15. Interview, ZMO-31-M. Collins (2014: 225) sees the metaphor of radio waves and antennae as evidence that, regardless of its historical antecedents, the *weizzā* phenomenon is "now a fact of modernity." Spiro (1982: 177) makes note of a "tall brick tower" that was used as a station to receive messages transmitted by the *weizzā*.
16. Interview, DTP-65-F.
17. Pers. comm., KYH-75-M.
18. Spiro (1982: 178) makes brief mention of a *weizzā* devotee who claimed to have slept in the same bed with Bo Min Gaung after the *weizzā* had materialized in physical form.
19. Statues, lithographs, and photographs of famous *weizzā*, prayer beads, gongs, assortments of *yantra* designs, and so on, clutter these shrine rooms.
20. This is not only done in *weizzā* temples. Similar rooms or beds are maintained in temples that have no association whatsoever with the *weizzā* but whose abbot passed away, as something of a shrine to remember the deceased monk. That of the late Mahagandayon Sayadaw of Amarapura is an example. People can come and visit the bedroom to see how it looked just before the abbot passed away. What is different with the *weizzā* shrines is that the residents believe that their *weizzā* visits from time to time.
21. A Burmese teacher of *weizzā* practices based in California told me, "Yes, there is the tradition of keeping beds for the *weizzā*. At my center here I do keep chairs for them but not beds. I don't want to freak out my American students." Pers. comm., DTT-70?-F
22. Dickens 2000 [1861]: 48. It was not unlike what Pip must have experienced when first entering Miss Havisham's room.
23. Pers. comm., DPN-79-F.
24. Ladwig 2011: 24.
25. Interview, ZMO-31-M.
26. Pers. comm., KST-32-M.
27. Patton 2012.
28. Foxeus, personal communication.
29. Burmese sources suspect that the word *zawgyi* derives from the Sanskrit *jogi* or *yogi*.
30. A common belief among present-day *weizzā* devotees is that the some of the *weizzā*, like Bo Min Gaung, are *Gandhārī weizzā*. Devotees believe that in ancient times there was a university in the city of Takkasilā, located in the province of Gandhara (modern-day northern Pakistan and eastern

Afghanistan), that educated its students in obtaining many of the supernatural powers, like flight and creating multiple images of oneself, that are
associated with contemporary *weizzā* path practitioners.

31. The Ten *Siddhi* of the *Maha Gandhārī Weizzā* are: to be free from illnesses; to have
a youthful body; to have a long life; to be invincible to swords and spears; to
be loved by all; to be able to find money easily, as much as you need; to be able
to contract distances; to be able to walk on water; to be able to fly in the air;
to be able to perform miracles.

32. McDaniel 2011: 17, 37, 110 and Hayashi 2000.

33. The lawgiver Manu is always characterized as a *ya-they* (Christian Lammerts,
pers. comm.) Justin McDaniel shows that references to Vedas are "to protective
magical practices or astrological rituals associated with prognostication. While
there are no translations of the Sanskrit *Vedas* in Southeast Asian languages
and the term [*bedin*] does not directly refer to sections of the four Sanskrit *Vedas*
and their commentaries, there are some loose similarities with some of
these practices and practices in various telling of the *Artharva Veda* (AV)"
(2013: 309, n. 12).

The Buddhist hermit vocation that survives in Myanmar and Thailand
(and to a lesser extent in other parts of mainland Southeast Asia) warrants
further study. For instance, the hermits of Myanmar and Thailand wear similarly styled conical hats, the origins of which are unclear. The *bodaw* (venerable grandfather) of Myanmar and *luang pho* (venerable father) of Thailand are
also worthy of further study. My guess is that these strands and lineages have
common origins and have taken on local customs, with Myanmar's *weizzā*
becoming the most organized of the Southeast Asian lineages. For details of
the ordination procedure of a hermit, see Bizot (1988). For details on the life
and practices of hermits in Myanmar, see Jotika (2009).

34. The *vidyādhara* was a standard fixture of Indian fantasy and adventure literature throughout this period. For more on *vidyādhara,* see Snellgrove 2002:
135 and Przyluski 1923: 301–18. See also Von Hinuber 1994: 101–6. Taoist
alchemy may have reached India via maritime routes beginning in at least
the sixth century CE (White 1996: 53). For more on possible *weizzā* connections to Taoism, see Pranke 2010: 453–88.

35. White writes that the "alchemical system" practiced by aspiring *weizzā* "has
a decidedly Taoist stamp to it" (1996: 384, n. 122) and that the *weizzā* "are
indebted at least in part to India for their knowledge of the mercurial" (1996:
48).

36. There are initiation rituals but these are for devotees who wish to become a
member of a particular *weizzā* association and not to become a *weizzā*. See
Keiko Tosa (1996; 2000) on initiations.

37. White 1996: 2.

38. White 1996: 274.

39. Tosa 1996: 241.

40. As is the case with cults, however, they rarely outlive their leader. Schober in
1981–82, for instance, attempted to visit the site of a *weizzā* cult that

Mendelson had written about in the early 1960s (Mendelson 1960, 1961a, 1961b, 1963), only to find it inactive (Schober 2014: 33). Tosa, in her research on *weizzā* associations, also found that most of them were inactive. I visited dozens of *weizzā* chapters throughout Myanmar only to find most inactive as well, usually only a handful of family members or ardent disciples still attending to the main shrine or headquarters for that chapter.

41. Rozenberg 2015: 47.
42. Schober 1988: 23.
43. Foxeus 2011.
44. Turner's research shows that hundreds of Buddhist lay associations were founded in Burma from 1890 to 1920 in an attempt to stem the decline of Buddhism (Turner 2014).
45. The term is not only reserved for *weizzā* groups. It also refers to monastic lineages. For more on this aspect of *gaing*, see Carbine (2011).
46. For more on such practices, see Pranke (1995) and Patton (2012).
47. Carbine 2011: 170.
48. Carbine 2011: 170.
49. Cady 1958: 8.
50. Smith 1965: 21.
51. Carbine 2011: 86. Cady notes that when the laity realized that they could not save the monarchy, lay and clerical leaders from Mandalay and Yangon attempted to get the British to "establish a religious primate for all Burma and undertake to support his authority" (1958: 152).
52. Turner 2014: 81.
53. The British licensed the sale of liquor and opium and made hefty profits from their trade. As a result, drinking and opium use had increased among the Burmese population, and Buddhists at the turn of the century responded with their own calls for temperance. For more on the perceived dangers of alcohol by these lay associations, see Turner (2014).
54. Chie Ikeya (2011) shows how initially good Buddhists had become corrupted by the non-Buddhist influences of British culture.
55. Braun 2013.
56. Turner 2014.
57. Maung 1980: xv.
58. Turner 2014: 138.
59. See especially Jordt 2007, Braun 2013, and Turner 2014. For a discussion of the move from a hierarchical and segmented Buddhism to one "flattened" and based upon a doctrine for the masses, see Kirichenko 2009.
60. Interview, UKH-88-M.
61. Aung-Thwin 2011: 4.
62. Harris 2012: 181.
63. Mendelson 1975: 208.
64. Aung-Thwin, per. comm., 2015.
65. See Foxeus (2011) for a thorough discussion of how the *weizzā* associations function in terms of money, leadership, strategic decisions, dissemination

programs, etc. As far as I am aware, however, no study has been published on how *weizzā* leadership formed and functioned in social terms, especially who these leaders were, their access to technology, and their ability to garner social assent.

66. Some associations, such as the Pathamam Congregation, also allowed "project" or "auxiliary" groups made up of smaller congregations devoted to the worship of *nat* (guardian spirits) that were called upon to do their part in safeguarding the *sāsana*.

67. Foxeus 2011: 150.

68. *PTM* 1, no. 2 (1948): 5.

69. For more on militaristic aspects of Christian associations, see Davis (2007).

70. For discussions of such orders developing in Europe and North America, see Bullock (1996). For their development in colonial Burma, see Turner (2014)

71. The founder of the association Foxeus studied even referred to himself as a Knight Templar. Turner shows how European and indigenous social reformers' attempts to regulate behavior were "part of the spirit of the age in Southeast Asia and around the Victorian colonial world" (2014: 89).

72. Rozenberg 2015: 167.

73. *Pathamam* here is the Pāli meaning "first," but in this context can mean "first/foremost" or even be a reference to an esoteric meaning of the word *pathamam* that is often used in *weizzā* discourse.

74. PTM 1, no. 2 (1948): 2.

75. Consider, for example, the "Tactical Encirclement Group." Rozenberg studied this group in the early 2000s and learned that they believed they were acting as the frontline defense for Myanmar should any foreign power decide to invade (2015).

76. King Mindon had a printing press installed in the country as early as 1870, and print culture became important first in lower Burma, especially, as Braun notes, "under the relatively free market of print capitalism under colonialism" (2013: 68). With the annexation of Upper Burma in 1885 and influenced by the intense Christian missionary use of print culture, individual Buddhists and larger associations began harnessing the power of print media for their own propagation goals.

77. Pinney 2004: 52.

78. Sadan 2014: 299.

79. Sadan 2014: 301.

80. McDaniel 2011: 165.

81. Francesca Torroco makes a similar argument in her discussion of photographic portraits of Chinese Buddhist masters. "In Buddhist Chinese, xiang (像) means 'similar,' 'semblance,' but also 'image,' 'portrait' and 'form.' Xiang (相) is an 'attribute,' a 'mark,' or a 'distinctive feature.' . . . These semantic layers seem to come to the surface in the understanding of photographic portraits of Buddhist masters and perhaps, more generally, in all photography-related terminology in modern China" (2011: 635).

82. McDaniel 2011: 165.

83. Turner (2014: 79–80). Clare Veal, in her study of charisma and photography in Thailand, explains how the display of images of high-ranking military officials is thought to bestow some of their charismatic power, both supramundane and worldly, "onto the person displaying it merely by making explicit visually and physically the association between the two" (Veal 2013).

84. Morgan 2012: 316.

85. Pranke 2008: 12.

86. Blackburn 2010: 336.

87. Morgan 2012: 316.

88. McDaniel 2011: 200. While I saw these *weizzā* grouped together as if assembled for a school yearbook photograph, McDaniel, examining similar pictures of ensembled monks from Thailand, noticed that such individuals "never knew one another, came from different sects and from different regions, but they are grouped together in one poster like members of an all-star monastic football team" (2011: 200).

89. Pers. comm., U Kyaw Min-75-M.

90. Pers. comm., U San Lwin-65-M.

91. Hagiographic collections of these eight *weizzā*, as well as others not included in this group, are popular in Myanmar. See Moṅʻ Panʻʼ Hmveʼ (2013), ʾOṅʻ Mrat ʻ ū" (2016), Kyoʻ Saṃ Lan ʼʼ (2015a, 2015b) and Saṅʻ ū" (2013) for examples of this genre.

92. VM 2, no. 4 (2009): 188.

93. Jotipala 1952: 13.

94. Smith 1991.

95. Poʻ Ū", Ū" 1949: 69.

96. Poʻ Ū", Ū" 1949: 103.

97. Poʻ Ū", Ū" 1949: 109.

98. Poʻ Ū", Ū" 1949: 143–44.

99. Nattier 1991: 119. This theory can be found in the *Manorathapūraṇī* commentary on the *Aṅguttara Nikāya Aṅguttara Aṭṭhakathā*.

100. For an overview of stories of decline in Buddhism, see Nattier (1991).

101. Turner 2014; Frasch 2013.

102. Foxeus 2011: 202. For a concise and thorough discussion of U Nu's plans for Buddhist revivalism, see Mendelson (1975: 262–76). Pranke notes how a cult of charisma surrounding various monks thought to be *arahants* developed around this time, most likely part of the hopefulness surrounding newly won national independence in 1948 and the 2,500th anniversary of the Buddha's *parinibbāna* in 1956 (Pranke 2012).

103. See Houtman (1990: 84) for a more detailed analysis of this schema. Turner (2014: 29–37) provides valuable information on a theory of decline from the *Anāgata Vamsa* (History of the future) that discusses the eventual arrival of the next buddha, Metteyya. She illustrates how popular and widespread it was among Buddhists in Myanmar during the colonial era. A common belief among members of some *weizzā* associations is that they can, through various practices learned along the *weizzā* path, prolong their lives so that they

can be around when Metteyya arrives. My recent ethnographic work has shown that such a view is not as common as it may have been in the twentieth century.

104. Foxeus 2011: 202.

105. Foxeus 2011: 202. Houtman (1990) and Jordt (2010) indicate that this second, cyclical theory of decline was well known and discussed among non-*weizzā* associations and communities of the time.

106. Foxeus 2011: 203.

107. See, for example, Po' Ū″, Ū″ (1949: 63). Members of the *Ariya Weizzā* association believed the Liberation Era had already commenced in about 1957 (Foxeus 2011: 196). Houtman shows how this cyclical schema of the *sāsana* lasting over two cycles of 2,500 years after the Buddha's demise, in which the focus of Buddhist action deteriorates from that of *vipassanā* meditation to carrying out acts of charity, to make place for an upturn during the twentieth century with *vipassanā* again, was accepted by most *vipassanā* meditation communities (Houtman 1999). Schober (2012), drawing on Pranke's (2010) article on *vipassanā* meditation and the *weizzā* phenomenon, writes that "the formation of weikza practices in Burma occurs in concert with the rising popularity of rational vipassanā (insight) meditation practices . . . thus situat[ing] the construction of weikza practices within a broader discourse of the Burmese encounter with modernity in the 19th century" (2012: 282–83).

108. "Thathana ta-wek, min-kaung ta-kyek." As the author of one popular 1949 book with strong *weizzā* overtones wrote, starting from the moment when the pagoda "finial and its bells were broken" (referring to the deposing of King Thibaw in 1885 by the British), the Burmese have been hoping for a "royal defender of the faith" (B. *thathana-pyu-min*) to arrive (Po' Ū″, Ū″ 1949: 5).

109. "Thathana ta-wek, min-kaung ta-sek." Sarkisyanz notes that such prophecies were popular during his visit to Myanmar in the 1950s (1961: 55).

110. Frasch 2013.

111. I thank Dr. Tin Maung Kyi for bringing this book to my attention and for providing me with valuable notes on this work. For an excellent discussion of Bo Bo Aung's appropriation by Burmese Buddhist nationalist groups, see Houtman (1999: 238–40).

112. For more on this weapon, see Foxeus (2011: 309).

113. Zöllner 2010: 7.

114. Po' Ū″, Ū″ 1949: 4. The Liberation Era is the sixth of ten 500-year periods until the complete disappearance of the Buddha *sāsana*.

115. PTM 1, no. 1 (1948): 5–6. The fact that Bo Min Gaung's name contained the words *min-gaung* (noble king) was certainly not lost on the devout. Bo Min Gaung was also considered by his devotees to be Buddha Metteyya in the form of a *phaya laung,* or "imminent buddha." He and Bo Bo Aung (mentioned above) were considered the foremost of *weizzā* by most *weizzā* associations.

116. Jordt 2007: 30.

117. Frasch 2013.

118. Brohm 1957: 395. The religious figure dressed in white robes (B. *hwet-pyu-shin*) is almost always a reference to the wandering religious mendicants, or *bodaw*, associated with the *weizzā* path. They are often seen, as well as portrayed in iconography, carrying a staff or long walking stick. Mendelson too sees messianic Buddhist elements in this account, especially in that the mysterious white-clad mendicant was "intimately related with the idea of the Sangayana [Buddhist Council]" (Mendelson 1977: 273).

119. Foxeus 2011: 204. Apart from the Sixth Council itself, the Buddha Jayanti celebrations during the mid-1950s inspired a host of other activities elsewhere in the Buddhist world, most notably in Sri Lanka where, as George Bond notes, "millennial expectations characterized the Buddhists' interpretations of the Jayanti anniversary" (1988: 75). Frasch (2013) points out that the Sixth Council in Myanmar provided an impetus for Buddhists in other parts of Asia to attempt to spread the *dhamma* across Asia, such as in India.

120. Pranke notes that subsequent publications by the Ministry of Religious Affairs that discuss the *sāsana*'s lifespan omit reference to the theory (2010: 466).

121. Foxeus 2011: 176. According to a 1962 newspaper editorial, General Ne Win's government "issued a decree prohibiting the production of any film depicting nats, ghosts, witches, etc. as 'part of the Revolutionary Government's effort to remove the obscurantist influence of superstitious beliefs on the people'" (*Nation*, August 3, 1962). Quoted in Ho 2009.

122. Foxeus 2011: 81.

123. Tosa 1996: 241.

124. Houtman 1990: 184.

125. Keiko Tosa. Pers. comm. 2006.

126. Foxeus 2011: 350. Rozenberg (2015: 145–46) also notes anti-Muslim rhetoric in the *weizzā* groups he studied: "Isn't it the case that, by means of this imaginary Muslim menace, Buddhists see their religion as in peril, even close to getting swallowed up completely, thereby persuading themselves of the necessity for everyone to engage in its defense and so allowing for the active perpetuation of Burmese identity? In this war, which is considered one only to them, they reveal their haunted fear of the decline of the practice of Buddhism in society and their anguish at a possible collective inability to face up to it. This fear and this anguish, knowingly maintained, are so strong that they induce paranoid fantasies, a method of self-perpetuation based on a pathology in which collective violence becomes a foundational part of the community.
    "Kyaukpadaung is mentioned as Buddhism's last stronghold, high point of the resistance against a chimerical peril. And the four *weikza* become war heroes, because heroes are needed for this fabricated war, in which fictive aggressors, although defeated from time to time, still see their existence spared, as though better to fulfill their original function: to serve as a specter for Buddhists." Kyaukapdaung is the site of Mount Popa, which is the refuge of *weizzā*.

127. Foxeus 2011: 386.

128. Pers. comm., AD-33-M.

2. THE BUDDHA'S CHIEF WIZARD

1. Moṅ' sve" khvyan' 2013: 139–40.
2. Brac de la Perrière 2012: 156.
3. For accounts of Bo Min Gaung's life written in English, see Foxeus (2011: 67–73) and Mendelson (1963a).
4. Sarkisyanz (1968: 34). Bo Min Gaung figures prominently in the work of Michael Mendelson (1961b, 1963a) as well as in parts of Melford Spiro (1982). The Pathamam Taya Weizzā Association's agenda was to propagate the life story of Bo Min Gaung throughout the country in the late 1940s.
5. Mendelson 1963: 782.
6. Berglie 2005: 51.
7. Interview UBT-85-M conducted by U Khin Maung Than (1997).
8. Interview UBN-70-M conducted by U Khin Maung Than (1997).
9. Foxeus 2011: 69.
10. Interview UBN-70-M conducted by U Khin Maung Than (1997). Interview UBT-85-M conducted by U Khin Maung Than (1997).
11. Interview UBT-85-M conducted by U Khin Maung Than (1997).
12. For more on the ways Bo Min Gaung was viewed during this time by the villagers of the area, see NRK 108 (1995): 66–69.
13. Interview UHM-67-M conducted by U Khin Maung Than (1997). Stories of other *weizzā* saints being imprisoned, interrogated, or shot at by Communist, Japanese, and British soldiers are quite common among devotees. Dhammacariya U Aung Kyaw Moe's account of *weizzā* Abha Pyu and Bodaw Pyu surviving drowning and assassination attempts by Japanese soldiers is one such example (VM 1, no. 6 [2008]: 43–47).
14. Foxeus 2012: 214.
15. Interview UKS-88-M conducted by U Khin Maung Than (1997).
16. Deboick 2011: 44, quoting Caciola 1996: 301.
17. Arnold and DeWald (2012). The entire issue of *Modern Asian Studies* 46, no. 1 (2012) provides insight into this phenomenon. Rozenberg (2010) also points out the emphasis his *weizzā* devotee informants placed on modern technology when relating the miraculous feats of their saint. For example, many devotees possessed photographs of one of their *weizzā* standing on the hood of a jeep. Others relished telling stories about how the *weizzā* could outwalk a car going at full speed or a person's camera would fail to take a photo of a *weizzā* if permission was not obtained first. Rozenberg's interpretation is that a photo constitutes a "literal representation" of the *weizzā* over such technology (2015: 65) and that science has "been put in the service of the weikza and its power domesticated" (2015: 64).
18. We will see in chapter 4, for example, the Bo Min Gaung-related "catastrophe pagodas" were meant to protect the surrounding areas from war, famine, and natural disasters.
19. Kyaw Myaing 2009.
20. Interview UKS-88-M conducted by U Khin Maung Than (1997).
21. Houtman 1997: 322.

22. Houtman 1997: 322.
23. This successive rebirth motif is a long-standing one for major figures found in all Buddhist traditions. The *Jātaka* (genre of literature chronicling the previous lives of the Buddha) are the most well-known and revered throughout the Buddhist world.
24. In chapter 2 we saw that an adult Bo Min Gaung was said to have convened the *weizzā* executive council meeting in 1885 even though he would have been about five years old at the time.
25. Reynolds 1976: 3.
26. One devotee who was familiar with Tibetan Buddhism told me that Bo Min Gaung was exhibiting "crazy wisdom." See DiValerio's *The Holy Madmen of Tibet* for a thorough discussion of the topic. Interestingly, the second most revered *weizzā* in Myanmar today, Yat-kan-sin Taung Sayadaw, was also thought to be "mad." He is remembered for offering food to a large group of stray dogs as if they were monks on alms round.
27. Similar ideas can be found among pilgrims at China's Wu Tai Shan, where it is thought that the bodhisattva Manjushri takes the form of homeless people, madmen, and the like. For more on this, see Kieschnick 1997.
28. Interview with AKS-88-M conducted by U Khin Maung Than (1997).
29. Interview UL-70?-M.
30. Devotees of Bo Min Gaung would often ask me, "What kind of experiences did you have of him?" or "How did you encounter him?" Even when corresponding with devotees by email or letters, they would first ask me about any encounter I might have had with Bo Min Gaung, and then would excitedly relate their experiences.
31. Orsi 2005: 62.
32. Orsi 2005: 113.
33. Interview UTS-48-M.
34. *Vijjādhara*, as discussed in the previous chapter, being the Pāli for the Burmese *weizzā-dho* [bearer of wisdom]. *Mahā-gandhārī* refers to the highest class of *weizzā*.
35. Brac de la Perrière notes the steady increase in the number of devotees, and by extension the "numerous new representations of Bo Min Gaung flourishing everywhere [at Mount Popa]," commissioned and donated particularly by Muslims of Kokan "who come from Mandalay and reinvest in religious donations part of the benefits they have made after taking a vow in front of the *weikza*" (2014: 59).
36. See Foxeus 2011: 170 for a detailed, philological explanation of this term. Jordt glosses it nicely when she explains that *patthan-set* "demonstrates the donor's cosmic affinity" to an individual "thought to be evidence of prior kammic affiliation and therefore a shared path in spiritual striving" (2010: 103).
37. Interview UTW-41-M.
38. Interview SKM-30?-M. Foxeus came across one informant who said that "those who do not put their trust in and believe in Bo Min Gaung will face their destiny in accordance with their habit. Those who do believe in Bo Min Gaung, i.e., his adherents who have the particular *patthan-hsek* relation with

him, will be protected and 'saved' by him." According to Foxeus, "the belief in Bo Min Gaung could, according to this informant, be a way of counteracting the effects of accumulated unwholesome *kamma*, a way of bypassing the otherwise rigid law of co-conditioned genesis" (2011: 170).

39. NRK 98 (1994): 18–29.
40. Foxeus 2011: 116.
41. Interviewees who knew Bo Min Gaung during his lifetime commented that he would sometimes make comments about people being related to him: "To one he liked most, he would offer a cup of tea. No one else could touch the teacup except the one he offered it to. If somebody touched it, he growled at him, saying, 'Are you related to me?'" Interview UKS-88-M conducted by U Khin Maung Than (1997).
42. Rozenberg 2015: 125.
43. Interviews TPN-34-M; DP-42-F; DS-38-F; SG-84-F.
44. Morgan and Promey 2001: 16.
45. Orsi 2013.
46. Orsi 2007: 49.
47. Interview AK-41-M.
48. Again, calling to mind the importance of Ann Taves's research on the centrality of nonordinariness in the study of religion (Taves 2009, 2012).
49. The *Buddhānusati Gāthā* being a verse listing the supreme qualities of the Buddha.
50. Mraṅ" Thvan'" 1996.
51. Pinney 2004: 190.
52. Interview SL-85-F.
53. None of the biographies I have consulted contains details of visual representation.
54. Deboick 2011, 38.
55. Interview UNW-38-M.
56. Foxeus encountered similar instances during his fieldwork with *weizzā* associations in upper Myanmar: "Sometimes, I was told, Bo Min Gaung's spirit enters this statue and dwells there. When the statue was cast a miracle occurred at the workshop, of which there is a photograph on the wall. It shows a table with a couple of small statuettes of Bo Min Gaung and a *kadaw-pwe* offering, from which two streaks of smoke are rising. That was a manifestation of Bo Min Gaung, who, as a bodiless *weizzā*, was demonstrating his mystical power with his mental factors" (2007: 10).
57. NRK 93 (1994): 156.
58. The number nine being a particularly auspicious number in Burmese Buddhism. See chapter 5 for more on this.
59. Quoted in Veal 2013: para. 23. Italics in the original.
60. Tarocco 2011: 640.
61. Pinney 2004: 193.
62. Pinney 1997: 111. Italics mine.
63. Wallace 1966: 61.
64. Morgan 2012: 316.

65. Morgan 2012: 311.
66. Morgan 2012: 311.
67. Interview, UL-58-M.
68. Interview, ULY-55-M.
69. McDaniel 2012: 188.
70. Hughes 2016: 59.
71. Hayes 2011: 8.
72. Orsi 1996, 113.
73. Pinney 2004: 190–91.
74. Others engage in a deintensification of involvement with a saint, often after getting what they wished for or if moving on to a new religious practice. One married couple told me they had outgrown belief in such saints after they had achieved a certain level of wealth that they had requested in their earlier years as devotees. They still have statues of Bo Min Gaung on their altar at home and continue to make offerings of water, incense, and flowers to him "just in case," for "we can't turn away from him completely." Interviews DMO-45-F and UHT-46-M.
75. Houtman 1981: 176.
76. Hughes 2016: 59.
77. Pinney 2004: 191.
78. Swearer 2004: 11–12.
79. Swearer 2004: 12.

3. WOMEN OF THE WIZARD KING

1. NRK 100 (1994): 37.
2. NRK 100 (1994): 38.
3. The term used for these people is *vedanā-shin*, which literally means "possessor of pain and suffering."
4. NRK 100 (1994): 38. In this context, the word used to describe her is *sayama-lay*, literally "little teacher," a term often used with *thilashin* (Burmese Buddhist nuns) and with young women worthy of respect.
5. NRK 100 (1994): 38.
6. Such a diagram is a drawing made up of Burmese characters compiled in such a way as to produce images of buddhas, holy figures, and animals. See Patton (2012) for a more detailed discussion of the role of these diagrams among *weizzā* devotees.
7. NRK 100 (1994): 39–40.
8. NRK 100 (1994): 39.
9. A *longyi* is a skirt worn by men in Myanmar.
10. This change is further evidenced by the pronouns used. As Ma Myin, she referred to herself as *kyama*, which is the female pronoun for "I." When possessed by Bo Min Gaung, she used the words *nga* ("I," but as a senior would use to a junior) when referring to himself and *nga mye* ("my granddaughter") when referring to Ma Myin in the third person.

11. The term, *dhat-si*, will be discussed below.
12. NRK 100 (1994): 39–40.
13. Interestingly, the two words *dhat-si* and *pat-lan* (circuit) are combined to refer to an electric circuit, or current, thus further supporting the electrical analogies mentioned throughout this book.
14. Interview. KYH-75-M. This is an admittedly sophisticated explanation, one that most informants could not (or would not) give in such words. I have had to rely solely on oral sources for most of my information on this phenomenon because none of the vast number of Burmese books on the *weizzā* subject offers an analysis of the inner workings of *dhat-si*.
15. Interview, KYH-75-M.
16. Hayes 2011: 34.
17. NRK 104 (1995): 34, 38; interview SML-24-F.
18. NRK 102 (1995): 17. Although less common, the phrases *win-si*, "to enter and flow," and *nam-hkyin*, "bridging the *nāma*," can be used as synonyms to describe the phenomenon. Ma Myin, for example, is also called "she who approached Bo Min Gaung's *nam*." Still another uncommon term, as encountered by Brac de la Perrière during her fieldwork, is *nam-kein*, "the mental is staying" (2012: 169).
19. NRK 102 (1995): 18.
20. This, of course, was one of the criticisms of these mediums—that they are practicing self-suggestion or are faking the event entirely. None of the critics, however, discounted the existence of *weizzā*. On the contrary, they all firmly believed in their existence but doubted the authenticity of the mediums' claims of being in contact with them.
21. For detailed studies on such forms, see Brac de la Perrière (1989 and 2009).
22. Interview KSL-21-M.
23. Htin Paw, U. 2004.
24. *Hnoke* being "lips" and *si*, as we saw before, "flow" or "ride."
25. Interview AY-40?-M.
26. Brac de la Perrière 2014: 70.
27. Coderey 2011.
28. Interview MTT-27-F. Coderey's informants also make reference to *amyin dhat hpwin*, "the skill of seeing is opened," as evidence of a *weizzā*'s contact with a medium (Coderey 2012: 192).
29. See Brac de la Perrière (2011a, 2011b, and 2009) for especially illuminating studies on the subject.
30. Rozenberg 2014.
31. NRK 100 (1994): 42.
32. NRK 100 (1994): 133–137.
33. NRK 101 (1994): 33–38.
34. An example of this being expressed by a *weizzā* devotee can be seen here:
    Sayama: "At 7 p.m., I received [the *weizzā*'s] *dhat*."
    Author: "How do you two have a karmic relation with each other?"
    Sayama: "In a previous life I was his daughter." NYK 104 (1995): 38.
35. Pers. comm. UKM-75-M.

36. Foxeus (2011) notes that this kind of possession is usually temporary, but in some rare circumstances it can be permanent, in the sense that the *weizzā* uses the medium's body until it dies, then leaves to find another body to inhabit.

37. NRK 102 (1995): 113–116.

38. Elias 2012: 203.

39. Elias 2012: 200.

40. This concern with healing and alleviating pain became such a central element of people's relationships with the *weizzā* that the organized cults that developed around specific *weizzā* identified themselves as healing associations. Such cults focus much of their practices on healing people who suffer from illnesses thought to stem from witchcraft or black magic. Members undergo a lengthy training program to become "faith healers" (B. *payoga saya*) and receive copies of training manuals that act as a beginner's guide for curing a wide range of ailments. Although I found used copies of some such handbooks in Yangon bookshops, most of my informants who were members of these associations obtained their copies at the time they officially enrolled at their local branch. Patrick Pranke's seminal article, "How to Become a Buddhist Wizard," is based on his translation of one such handbook (Pranke 1995).

41. I visited one such healer who had set up shop inside a pagoda compound in Mandalay. With a small signboard in red letters that read, in Burmese, "HIV-AIDS Cure," taped on the front of a small table, he sat there in front of a statue of the Buddha every day.

42. Following Coderey, I prefer to speak of "indigenous/local medicine" instead of "traditional medicine," for as Coderey (2012: 186–87) reminds us, " 'traditional medicine' is a phrase generally used in the literature and by the Burmese Anglophones, because the term 'traditional' has been criticized as it refers to something fixed, immutable and for this reason is considered unsuitable to define this kind of medicine which undergoes constant changes under the influence of social, historical, political forces. The idea of 'indigenous/local medicine' better translates the vernacular designation *taing-yin hsay pyinnya*, 'knowledge of indigenous/local remedies.' "

43. NRK 93 (1994): 37.

44. NRK 93 (1994): 37.

45. Skidmore (2008: 198) makes note of the high frequency of bowel cancer in Myanmar that necessitates surgery and then the use of colostomy bags.

46. NRK 113 (1995): 13–15.

47. Oliver Sacks, in his book *Hallucinations,* shows how common they are and why they happen. Visual hallucinations are overwhelmingly (when they are not basic geometric, color, etc. as happens in some blind people) culturally decipherable: Christians see angels, Buddhists the Buddha, etc. But he stops there. I feel we can go much further in terms of how hallucinations are generated, perceived, and interpreted, and how the interpretations are disseminated among people who share a certain cultural context (sociocultural structured frameworks of reference as guides for action, aka "culture"). And of course, Sacks is telling us interesting things about how culture works at the most basic

level of the brain receiving sensory signals and transforming them into understanding according to experience and more importantly, culturally transmitted and learned frameworks that the individual brain has internalized and adopted for its use.

48. Pers. comm. USL-56-M; DKT-49-F.
49. Such healing and conversion narratives are, of course, not restricted to *weizzā* devotees in Myanmar. Strikingly similar kinds of stories are found in similar types of popular media, such as with Catholic Saints (Orsi 1996) or Guanyin in Taiwan (Reed 2003). Take, for example, the narrative of the Taiwanese woman dying of a gastrointestinal disease (stomach ulcer) in 1952. The woman's daughter had a dream of the bodhisattva Guanyin appearing and giving medicine to cure her mother (Reed 2003: 198).
50. VM 1 (2006): 63.
51. Interview DMM-50?-F.
52. Orsi 2002: xx–xxi.
53. McDaniel 2011: 104–105.
54. The following reflects my reading of Edward Shorter's "Paralysis: The Rise and Fall of a 'Hysterical' Symptom" and Ethan Watters's *Crazy Like Us: The Globalization of the American Psyche.*
55. Shorter 1986: 549.
56. Watters 2010: 29.
57. Soe Thein 1979: 37–47; 53–57; 76–78.
58. Supp-Montgomerie 2015: 341.
59. For more about how the mass media and related popular culture are more likely to spread cultural ideals of health, see Featherstone (1991). See also Freund, McGuire, and Podhurst (2003) for a study of how officially promulgated ideals, whether promoted by heads of governmental health agencies or by school curricula, are likely to reflect political agendas (e.g., the deflection of responsibility for health maintenance away from state-sponsored social services and community preventive efforts and onto the individual or immediate family).
60. Such views are inspired by and adapted from my readings of anthropologist Pierre Bourdieu's *Outline of a Theory of Practice* (London: Cambridge University Press, 1977). In addition to our six senses, Bourdieu suggests that humans also experience life through "social senses." These are learned and are not identical across cultures. Although he was using the term in reference to how dominant groups within a culture literally "inculcate, em-body, beyond the grasp of consciousness," a form of reality that is in their best interests, I have adjusted it in this context to refer to a repository of psychophysical ailments and ways of dealing with them through religious encounters with *weizzā* saints.
61. NYK 100 (1994): 41. This taking in of disease and illness was a common practice among the healers I met. One female hermit from Sagaing reported in a magazine interview that, when healing her patients, the disease usually leaves the person through the ear or mouth and enters into her own mouth. NYK 102 (1995): 113–116; DTM-F-60-Sagaing.

62. "Besides," she says, "this ability to heal people will disappear at the end of five years. After that I will be able to devote my life to propagating the Buddha *sāsana*." NRK 100 (1994): 41. *Weizzā* working through devotees for five-year periods was a common theme shared with me by mediums.

63. This seems to agree with Brac de la Perrière's recent findings that prior to 1992, the role of medium was "clearly conceived as a masculine one" and that "in the more formalized session presented [in her article], the mediums are women in an ancillary position compared to the masters of the cult group." After 1992, however, "when the cultic group became more institutionalized, embodiment of the *weizzā* was abandoned by new male leaders, in want of differentiating themselves from mere devotees, and left to female members. Thus gender distribution of the role may be reversed according to contextual status of possession by the *weizzā*" (2012: 176).

      Rozenberg (2015: 3) recorded the story of a twenty-five-year-old female *weizzā* medium who, in 1952, was suffering from unspecified menstrual problems. When she first channeled the *weizzā*, her medical problems ceased, and she gained supernatural powers of healing.

64. See, for example, Brac de la Perrière (2012); Rozenberg (2012); Foxeus (2011); Spiro (1982).

65. Collins 2014: 226.

66. Schober 2012: 286.

67. NRK 116 (1996): 34–37.

68. NRK 143 (1998): 97.

69. NRK 102 (1995): 113–116. For some fascinating parallels of sexuality and tension with family members in Chinese societies, see Sangren (2000).

70. KTS-F-48-Yangon; NZ-F-32?-Mandalay.

71. Ikeya 2011: 51.

72. Pattana Kitiarsa makes a similar claim with regard to Thai spirit mediums: "Popular religion is engendered, framed and practised along the existing gender divisions. . . . Popular religion is never gender-less. Instead, it reflects the pattern of gender construction widely adopted and practised in Thai society, where most active roles in the Buddhist Sangha have been traditionally reserved for men, and women have long been conventionally engaged in the spirit cult" (2005: 222). For a comparative perspective in Sri Lanka, see Obeyesekere (1981).

73. McGuire 2008: 173.

74. Pattana (2005: 221) proposes something similar with regard to spirit mediums in Thailand who work within "specific religious channels" so as to "get themselves out of their socially and economically marginal positions." Similar instances of positive life transformations were reported by Vietnamese spirit mediums (Fjelstad and Maiffret 2006).

75. Interview MAA-28-F. As stated above, *Abha*, or "grandfather," is a term of endearment for Bo Min Gaung.

76. Gold 1999: 84.

77. This fits with Ikeya's findings that "economic prowess enabled women to undertake merit-making activities such as contributing donations to pagodas" (2011: 51).
78. KMT-F-42; MML-F-45; KSA-F-48.
79. NRK 143 (1998): 101.
80. Ong 1988: 28. Pattana Kitiarsa's fieldwork among Thai female spirit mediums uncovered similar themes. For example, one of his informants indicated to Pattana that she had gone insane after her husband left her for another woman. The woman's mental health returned soon after she allowed a spirit to use her as a medium. Pattana notes that "her life has gradually improved and returned to normalcy as she accepted her new identity as a female spirit medium. . . . For [her] Spirit mediumship can be seen as her new gender and self identities (identity) were born out of life crises and suffering. Experiences of encountering the deity provide her with an organized framework to contemplate her past and present existence" (Pattana 2005: 218).
81. Rozenberg (2015) refers to such individuals as "vulnerables," in that they are mainly poor, uneducated villagers who find their newfound vocations of mediums and healers to be avenues to fame and fortune. Pattana (2005: 218) calls the urban counterpart, "urban marginal population."

4. PAGODAS OF POWER

1. *Times Herald,* XCVIII, no. 132, June 5, 1958.
2. *Times Herald,* XCVIII, no. 132, June 5, 1958.
3. For Burmese Christians, this is a common expression meaning evangelism or mission.
4. Brac de la Perrière 2012: 159.
5. *Dhat* from, as we saw earlier, *dhātu.*
6. NRK 106 (1995): 31–32.
7. Tosa 2013. A shrine can also be a "power place," but the term originally referred to pagodas. Shrines began to proliferate after the death of Bo Min Gaung and are almost always connected to a pagoda on the premises.
8. During the 1940s, devotees of a Bo Min Gaung association were said to have erected more than 128 pagodas throughout Myanmar (Jotipala 1952: 32–33).
9. PTM 2 (1948). One article said that the following must be done for everlasting peace to come to Myanmar: People should erect and gather at Bo Min Gaung pagodas and other holy sites associated with him. It seems that these pagodas act as conduits for his spirit to work through.
10. Keiko Tosa (2014: 134) refers to such *weizzā*-inspired structures as "nonstandard religious buildings."
11. A 1952 biography of Bo Min Gaung states that Bo Min Gaung and Yatkansin Taung Sayadaw urged the public to build "nine cubit feet pagodas" throughout the whole country, to observe moral precepts, and to meditate (Po' Ū″, Ū″ 1952: 13). It is doubtful that such pagodas originated with Bo Min Gaung or

his cult, however. In 1944 a *weizzā* monk by the name of Yarkyaw Sayadaw published a book that discussed the erecting of such pagodas to protect the country from various catastrophes. See NYK 179 (2001) for more on this book and Bo Min Gaung's connection with it.

12. PTM 1, no. 5 (1948): 14–16. I came across many of these *ko-na-win* pagodas during my travels, but the majority had fallen into disrepair. Those that were still in daily use by *weizzā* practitioners were located in Yangon, Mandalay, and Mawlamyaing.

13. PTM 1, no. 5 (1948): 27. Although I have been unable to find it, I was told that a comic book about the *weizzā* was published in 1994 that told the story of how the *weizzā* banded together to have pagodas built that would, through their sacred powers, repel non-Buddhist religion from entering the country as well as keeping other dangers from affecting the peace and prosperity of the country and *sāsana*.

14. See Patton 2012 for more on this.

15. Oxford English Dictionary.

16. PTM 1, no. 2 (1948): 31; PTM 1, no. 3 (1948): 1; cover of PTM 1, no. 6 (1948) and PTM 1, no. 8 (1949): 37 are just some examples.

17. *Zedi* here being the Burmese pronunciation of the Pāli *cetiya*. Here and throughout, I am using *zedi* and *pagoda* interchangeably, as is done in the source material. Another word commonly associated with this class of religious structures is "stupa," but it is rarely used in vernacular Burmese. See Moore (2016) for a thorough discussion of the various types of pagodas in Myanmar.

18. PTM 1, no. 3 (1948): 34.

19. PTM 1, no. 9 (1949): 1.

20. The former is also sometimes referred to as a "world power place pagoda" (*B. kambha dhat-pannek zedi*).

21. NYK 218 (2004): 17–21.

22. Pers. corr. KMZ-32-M while on a pilgrimage to attend the 56th anniversary of Bo Min Gaung's exit from this world.

23. Po' Ū″, Ū″ 1952: 45–46.

24. Po' Ū″, Ū″ 1952: 47. I thank Dr. Tin Maung Kyi for analyzing this obscure folk song for me.

25. The three catastrophes being famine, war, and disease. See Moṅ' sve″ khvyaṅ' 2011 for more information on these diverse pagodas.

26. NYK 153 (1999): 46; NYK 174 (2001): 255; NYK 120 (1996): 335–37.

27. Tosa 2014: 135.

28. VM 2, no. 6 (2009): 39.

29. PTM 1, no. 10 (1949): 19. Another article, says that *ko-na-win* pagodas: 1) offer general protection to the country (from what, it doesn't say); 2) help one in his or her practice along the *weizzā* path (it doesn't say how); 3) keep the country safe from heretical/evil forces; 4) help quicken the success of the spread of the *sāsana*; 5) sustain *weizzā* and other persons of virtue who subsist on the power of the pagodas; and allow them to progress along the path (1, no. 2 (1948): 27.

30. Moore 2014: 392–93.
31. Tosa 2014: 114–15.
32. *Kalingabodhi Jātaka*, as quoted in Strong (2004) and Griswold (1974).
33. PTM 1, no. 7 (1948): 47.
34. Such a specialist imbuing the pagoda with the power of success through ritual chanting can be seen in the following video documenting the construction of the pagoda, translated into English as, "108 orchid mountain for friendship and aversion of calamities." Again, notice the reference to *kona-win* with the number 108. Accessed March 2016. https://www.youtube.com/watch?v=rFA6dvYHLB0 4:56–5:20; 8:10–8:20; 8:55–11:15; 14:05–14:25 mark.
35. Rozenberg 2015: 156.
36. Pers. corr. DTT-70-F.
37. This matches the information I found about this area in NRK 154 (1999):

    Yathey Hill's original "*Sāsana-pyu Ya-they-gyi* Bho Vannasippalankāra" in 1918 had a dream where a white clad *bodaw* visited him and told him that the area near present-day Kyaiktiyo "is the center of the Buddha *Sāsana* in Myanmar. Erect pagodas on each of the four adjacent hills and enter into an *adhitthana* . . . in order to help make the Buddha *sāsana* shine forth."

38. A monk who gave a sermon at a pagoda consecration ceremony I attended told of the spiritual power of a pagoda: "A young man was being chased by the army when at one point he collapsed from exhaustion and hunger. He couldn't go on and knew he would be killed. When he looked around, his eyes fell upon a pagoda on a distant hill. At that moment, he was shot and died. But as a result of seeing the pagoda, the young man's mind received *pāramī* and immediately after death, he was reborn in a higher realm."
39. Bennett 2010: vii.
40. Hughes 2012: 20.
41. Interview, DTT-70-F.
42. Interview, DM-66-F, 2009.
43. Interview, DM-66-F. There is a Bo Min Gaung Aung power place in the eastern Shan State town of Kyain-Tone. A monk by the name of U Javana had it built in 1948 after having a dream of a *weizzā* telling him to do this as part of his *sāsana* work (NRK 167 [2000]).
44. Tosa 2014: 130.
45. Kalay-wa Sayadaw is considered by his devotees to be a *weizzā*, and many believe him to be the reincarnation of Bame Sayadaw, a monk popularly considered to be something akin to a patron saint of *yantra*.
46. NRK 107 (1995): 89–92. See also NRK 110 (1995).
    Such *sāsana-pyu* trips are similar to pilgrimages, except that there is more focus on donating money for specific activities. They are modeled after the *sāsana-pyu* trips Bo Min Gaung was believed to have gone on in the years before his residency at Mount Popa. Individuals or associations travel to certain locales donating money or erecting or repairing pagodas.
47. Tosa also notes the importance of dreams in the lives of devotees she studied: "According to U Aung, his donation was made in response to a dream his

mother had in 1989. . . . She saw a pagoda on which the famous *weikza*, Bo Min Gaung [who "exited" in 1952], was standing alone. She realized that this was a revelation but was unable to act upon it because she did not recognize the place in the dream" (2014: 121).

48. NRK 116 (1996): 34–37.

49. http://www.mmtimes.com/index.php/national-news/16360-minister -promises-christians-removal-of-dream-inspired-stupa.html (accessed May 10, 2017).

50. http://morningstarnews.org/2016/05/christians-in-burma-patiently -endure-building-of-pagodas-on-church-lands/ (accessed June 2017).

   http://muslimnews.co.uk/news/south-east-asia/myanmar-muslim -leader-urges-calm-amid-incitement-buddhist-monk/ (last accessed June 11, 2017).

   http://www.bangkokpost.com/news/asean/950337/myanmar-monk -builds-pagodas-in-church-and-muslim-area (last accessed June 2017).

51. Thynn Thynn 2011: 3.

52. Thynn Thynn 2011: 3.

53. This pagoda was "lost" for decades, and rumors circulated among the U.S. Burmese diasporic communities that there was such a pagoda somewhere in New York State. They were eventually able to track down its location but were barred from visiting the pagoda by the owners of the land. They were eventually able to visit and photograph the site in 2015, and the land was finally purchased by a group of Burmese shortly thereafter. Refurbishing of the pagoda is now under way.

54. Aung 2005: 1.

5. WIZARDS IN THE SHADOWS

1. Rozenberg (2015: 140) notes that "[My interlocutor] also worried about the unflattering picture of Burmese Buddhism that my work might offer foreigners. Were readers to come away from it with a lack of respect for Burmese religion, the help he had given me would turn into a negative act, with predictable karmic consequences over the course of his future lives."

2. Crosby 2014: xxii.

3. Houtman 1999: 331.

4. Houtman 1997b.

5. Houtman 1999: 332.

6. *Vipassanā* has been actively promoted and supported by government authorities because it espouses the development of magical powers while also inculcating in the practitioner the idea that nothing can be done to change the current state of affairs, which is all part of the rise and fall of impermanent phenomena.

7. Ledi Sayadaw 1965: 62. Pranke points out that modern critics have used this historical information to link the *weizzā* path to a sect of allegedly heretical monks at ancient Pagan known as the Ari, who are reviled in Burmese

chronicles for their moral corruption and addiction to magic and spirit worship (Pranke 2010/11: 478).

8. Jordt 2007: 228.
9. Houtman 1999: 273.
10. Pranke 2010/11: 454.
11. Pranke 2010/11: 454.
12. Crosby points out that *vipassanā* has become one of Myanmar's major tourist attractions as well, but "not so *weikza*. While *vipassanā* had moved centre-ground, *weikza* has been left quietly to one side, in the marginalia" (2014: xxii). This is supported by Houtman (1997: 79), who writes: "Apart from people entering the country in the capacity of government diplomats, or aid officials, only [*vipassanā*] allows foreigners to get into Burma for a period of more than the one week standard tourist visa. Indeed, I was allowed to visit any [*vipassanā* meditation] centre I chose, but not to visit areas famous for the practice of unorthodox concentration."
13. Houtman 1988.
14. Tarling 1999: 217.
15. On the last page of a *weizzā* tract, *Wonders of Mebegon Village* (Phe Myint, Zaw Win, and Kunsal Kassapa 2005), for example, the author makes clear that the goal of their *weizzā* cult is propagation of the *sāsana* and not criticizing the government.
16. "How the Ariya *Weizzā* group (known as the White Head Missionary Group), led by a bogus monk, Nai Maung Hla, recruited prostitutes as infiltrators," *The New Light of Myanmar* IX, no. 3 (March 1995).

    Another *weizzā* association leader, Maung Aye, was arrested sometime in the 1960s for engaging in unlawful sexual relations with female members of his group (see Ferguson and Mendelson 1983 and Foxeus 2011 for more on this incident).

    Schober notes that such events were supposed to be "interpreted as a warning for charismatic virtuosos and their communities to keep a low profile. However, most weikza-inflected practices merely receded from public visibility and were not silenced altogether" (2012: 291).

    Pranke found that, since the military coup of 1962, the public profession of millenarian ideology had been banned, and no *weizzā* associations or individuals openly made such claims out of fear of reprisal. Pranke's interlocutors indicated that General Ne Win allegedly banned military personnel from joining *weizzā* associations on the grounds that such membership undermined the chain of command (2010/11: 469).
17. Tin Maung Maung Than 1993: 18.
18. Schober 2012 and Tin Maung Maung Than 1993.
19. Kyaw Zaw Oo, "Ne Win's family claims 'bodaws' were used to help plan coup plot," *Myanmar Times*, March 18–24, 2002. U Ne Win suddenly recovered after his grandson telephoned Yangon and asked his friends to entreat a *bodaw* to intervene on his grandfather's behalf. The author of the article does not indicate the year in which this incident occurred.

20. Pers. comm. KTL-19-M.
21. Pers. comm. DSS-65?-F.
22. Stadtner 2011: 68.
23. McDaniels 2011: 227.
24. Houtman 1990: 332.
25. Schober 2012.
26. "Coup plot thwarted," *Myanmar Times* 6, no. 107 (2004). The *bodaw*'s name was Myo Myint Aung, alias Setkya Aung Pwint Khaung, alias Saya Lay. Another military official, General Khin Nyunt's chief astrologer, Bodaw Than Hla, was imprisoned after the former prime minister and military intelligence chief was arrested in 2004.
27. Pranke 2010/11: 475.
28. Uttamasara 1989.
29. Pers. corr., DTT-70-F.
30. Pranke 1995; Foxeus 2011.
31. Pranke 2010/11: 480.
32. *Visuddhimagga* 378. Vijjādharādīnaṃ vehāsagamanādikā pana vijjāmayā iddhi. Yathāha: "katamā vijjāmayā iddhi? Vijjādharā vijjaṃ parijapitvā vehāsaṃ gacchanti, ākāse antaḷikkhe hatthimpipa dassenti, assampi dasseti, rathampi dasseti, pattimpi dasseti, vividhampi senābyuhaṃ dassentī"ti.
33. Mahasi Sayadaw 1997: 33. Two *weizzā* devotees have told me that, in a commentarial notation on a section of the book dealing with supernatural powers, Mahasi Sayadaw highlights the supernatural powers of the early twentieth-century *weizzā* Yatkansin Taung Sayadaw, and how he made use of these powers only for noble purposes. I have been unable to locate this reference, however.
34. *Paramatthadīpanī-Theragāthā Aṭṭhakathā.* "Commentary on the stanza of Pilindavaccha Thera." Trans. unknown. http://www.aimwell.org/LediSayadaw/Theragatha%20Commentary/
35. *Commentary on Visuddhajana-Vilāsinī Apadāna Aṭṭhakathā, Portion II: Commentary on Biography of the Thera Mahākaccāna.* Trans. U Lu Pe Win. http://www.aimwell.org/LediSayadaw/Apadana%20Commentary/
36. *Paramatthadīpanī-Theragāthā Aṭṭhakathā:* "Commentary on the stanza of Uttaratthera." Trans. unknown. http://www.aimwell.org/LediSayadaw/Apadana%20Commentary/
37. Crosby points out that other soteriological systems similar to those found among *weizzā* practitioners (sacred diagrams, chanting of mantras, alchemy, longevity practices, etc.) within the Theravada world came to be marginalized in the nineteenth and twentieth centuries due to their perceived unorthodoxy (Crosby 2014).
38. Some association members, especially of the Mano-seito-pad Association, wish to prolong their life spans in order to hear Gotama Buddha's final sermon at the moment of the re-gathering together of his relics at the end of this current *sāsana.* See Strong (2004: 223) and Pranke (1995) for more on this.

39. A seminal text for the *weizza* association, the *Manomaya Gaing*, has at its beginning a disclaimer saying that the association is not involved in black magic sorcery, but rather in allowing one to achieve nirvana. Keiko Tosa explains this situation in terms of intersecting axes:

> The *weikza* beliefs and the practices are diverse. To find some form in this diversity it is useful to imagine two axes. One axis would be the acquisition and practice of *weikza* arts, comprising alchemy, astrology, folk medicine, esoteric drawing, and mantra. The second axis is aligned along Buddhist practices, such as strictly maintaining moral precepts and engaging in insight (*wipathana*, P. *vipassanā*) or concentration (*thamahta*, P. *samatha*) meditation. Although *weikza* arts are classified as this-worldly knowledge (*lawki pyinnya*) within the Buddhist dichotomy of this-worldly (*lawki*) and other-worldly (*lawkoktara*), most congregation members or individual *weikza* path practitioners insist that becoming a *weikza* ultimately depends on religious (*lawkoktara*, P. *lokuttara*) practice. (2014: 120)

40. Interview ZMU-33-M.
41. Interview UMM-43-M.
42. Braun 2013: 80–81.
43. Braun 2013: 165–68.
44. Crosby 2014: xxiv.
45. Everyone was well aware of the *vipassanā* export to the world, and Burmese from all over the country were proud of this. Echoing the 1950s, there is still a sense that Myanmar is a stronghold of pure Theravada and especially *Abhidhamma*. Even *weizzā* practitioners wish not to tarnish this reputation. For more on the development of *Abhidhamma* influence in Myanmar, see Braun 2013.
46. Seekins 2006: 152–53.
47. Schober (2012) posits that this refusal may have been due to the fact that many military commanders at the time participated in some aspect of these practices.
48. In Burmese, it is "atu tit-taung, ayaung tit-thein, asit tit-yauk."
49. Brac de la Perrière 2012: 162.
50. Houtman 1980: 184. One way editors and writers have gotten around the problem of censorship has been to publish their stories under the guise of fictional accounts (Leehey 2010).
51. Kaṃ Lū ṅve 2008: 198.
52. Some examples include: Bhun'" Teja. 2013, Man'"Gvat' 2014, Moṅ' sve" khvyan' 2013, Jo' Thak' (labha) 2013, Bhaddanta Kosalla 2013, 2014.
53. "The 62th [*sic*] Popa Aung Min Khaung Nat Spirit Festival," Myanmar Celebrity, accessed June 2016; https://www.youtube.com/watch?v=B7UDm9coEks.
54. Pers. comm. DMM-62?-F.
55. Pers. comm. DMA-65-F.
56. Pers. comm. DSS-70-F.
57. Pers. comm. DSS-70-F.
58. Pers. comm. UTT-75-M.
59. Meyer 2012: 98.

CONCLUSION

1. NRK 103 (1995): 20.
2. NRK 103 (1995): 21–22.
3. Orsi 2007.
4. Orsi 2007.
5. Schaefer 2015: 35.
6. Supp-Montgomerie 2015: 343.
7. Supp-Montgomerie 2015: 343.
8. Morgan 2012a: 147.
9. It is true that those who follow the *weizzā* path or belong to a *weizzā* association enjoy putting on a front of a mysterious aura, and unless one is initiated into the path or association, it is often difficult to make sense of the teachings and writings associated with the *weizzā*. It is not difficult, however, to decode such teachings by employing the help of an expert or by studying any number of handbooks and magazine articles that provide instructions. In that sense, then, it is esoteric, but in the way that, as Steven Collins puts it, James Joyce's *Finnegan's Wake* is esoteric: it is not easily understandable to an uninitiated reader, but one can nonetheless go to any bookshop and purchase the book, take a course on it, read any number of websites devoted to it, or seek out the help of an expert on Joyce's writings (Collins 2014: 224). In the same way, *weizzā* materials are easily accessible but are often confusing, with the words and phrases written in code.
10. "In Search of Burma's Wizard-Saints," BBC News, October 6, 2016, http://www.bbc.com/travel/story/20161003-in-search-of-burmas-wizards-saints.

    "Magic in the Air: Myanmar Wizardy Flourishes," Agence France-Presse (AFP), 2017; http://frontiermyanmar.net/en/magic-in-the-air-myanmar-wizardry-flourishes.
11. Pinney 2004: 190.

REFERENCES

ABBREVIATIONS

NRK   *Nakkhatta Ron Khrann Maggajaṅ'*
PTM   *Pathamam Tara Maggajaṅ'"*
VM   *Vijjā Con' Maggajaṅ'"*

BURMESE LANGUAGE MAGAZINES AND JOURNALS

Mrat' Pan" Ra Guṃ [Noble forest of flowers] 2008.
Nakkhatta Ron Khrann Maggajaṅ'" [Rays of stars magazine] 1994–2016.
Pathamam Tara Maggajaṅ'" [Foremost dharma magazine] 1948–1949.
Vijjā Rasa Con' Maggajaṅ'" [Weizzā essence magazine] 2009.

MANUSCRIPT AND OFFICIAL DOCUMENT COLLECTIONS

U Bho Thi Library, Thaton, white parabaik ms 1.
Universities Central Library (Yangon) shelfmark 11180vijjādharas
Ūh Ññāṇa. Vebhan-kyoṅh Charā. 1888. Mahesara bhesaya kyam·h (Buddhistische
    Mythologie)—BSB Cod. birm. 286.

BURMESE SOURCES

Bha Gyamʻ". 2000. ʾAlaṅkā Kyoʻ Cvā Kātvanʻ" Vijjā Ūʺ Bha Gyamʻ" e* Bha Gyamʻ", Hāsarasa Kātvanʻ" Nhaṅʻ" Vatthu Cu Caññʻ"mhu. Ranʻ Kunʻ: ʾOṅʻ Khuiṅʻ la cañʻ.

Bhaddanta Kosalla. 2013. Abha ʾOṅʻ Maṅʻ"Khoṅʻ Kvanʻ" Chakʻ Myāʺ. Ranʻ kunʻMruiʹ : Okāsa Cā pe.

———. 2014. Siddhi Guṇʻ Roṇʻ Mahiddhi Guṇʻ Soṇʻ BhuiʺtoʻʾOṅʻ Maṅʻ"Khoṅʻ. Ranʻ kunʻMruiʹ : Okāsa Cā pe.

Bhunʻ"ʾ Teja. 2013. Bhuiʺ toʻ ʾOṅʻ Maṅʻ"Khoṅʻ hnanʻ vijjācakhanʻ" vijjālamʻ." Ranʻ kunʻ: Ahreʾ bhakʻ koṅʻ" kanʻ.

Joʻ Thakʻ (labha). 2013. Bo Min Gaung te . . . He. Ranʻ kunʻ Myui: Zaw Tet Sa pe.

Jotika, ʾA Rhaṅ. 2009. Rase' Kyanʻ" Vatʻ Rase' Dhale'. Ranʻ kunʻ Myui: Naingan Daw Pariyatti Sasana Takkathui.

Jotipala, ʾA Rhaṅ. 1952. Bhuiʺ To e* atthuppatti hmatʻ tanʻ'" ʾOṅʻ Maṅʻ"Khoṅʻ Krīʺ Vijjā Vanʻ Samuiṅʻ.'" Mandalay: Myousay Press.

Kaṃ Lū ṅve. 2008. "siddhi rhaṅʻ cacʻ tamʻ"." Mratʻ panʻ" ra guṅ. (198: 37–45).

Kyoʻ Saṃ Lan '". 2015a. Sāsanā pru mahiddhi siddhi pugguil thuʺ krīʺ myaʺ. Ranʻ kunʻ Mruiʹ: Majjhima Cā pe.

———. 2015b. Sāsanā pru mahiddhi siddhi pugguil thuʺ krīʺ myaʺdutiya tvai. Ranʻ kunʻ Mruiʹ: Majjhima Cā pe.

Manʺ"Gvatʻ. 2014. Kambha tay may taung puppa: hnan abha aung min gaung e* parami phray bhava kha ri. Ranʻ kunʻ Myui: Shwe khit sa pe.

Moṅʻ Panʺ' Hmveʺ. 2013. Mran mā khetʻ a shakʻ shakʻ vijjā ponʻ'" khyupʻ krīʺ (pathama tvai). Ranʻ kunʻ Mruiʹ: to vanʻ'" Mruiʹma Cā pe.

Moṅʻ sveʺ khvyanʻ. 2013. Pāramī lamʻ pra Abha Bhoʺ Minʻ Gaung Abha Bho Min Gaung e* siddhi mahiddhi sain ra swamʺ ranya thuʺ myaʺ. Ranʻ kunʻ Myui: Kam. Taw nat ranya sa pe.

Moṅʻ sveʺ khvyanʻ. 2011. Yak-kan:-sin Taung Sayadaw-gyi e' sasana-pru kvanʻ'" myāʺ hnanʻ sayadaw u lokatinna e' thuʺ khrāʺ so bha va pratʻ sanʻ hnanʻ kyianʻ san myāʺ. Ranʻ kunʻ Mruiʹ: Majjhima Cā pe.

Mramma ʻEʺ, Bhuiʺ toʻ. 1959. Buddha raja Theruppatti. [ci Cañ` Reʺ saʺ su Bhuiʺ toʻ Mramma ʻEʺ]. Ranʻ kunʻ Mruiʹ, Khettara Pum nhipʻ tuikʻ.

———. 1962. Lokī Vijjā paññā Nhaṅʻ" Gandhārī Samatha Pra naññʻ. Ranʻ kunʻ: Myui"Vaṅʻ "Cā pe.

Mraṅʻ" Thvanʻ'". 1996. Mahiddhi pugguilʻ thūʺ myāʺ e* ʾaṃ phvayʻ phracʻ rapʻ chanʻ" myāʺ. Ranʻ kunʻ: Takʻ Lamʻ" Cā pe.

Ñāṇa, Ūʺ. 1939. Bhui Bhui Oṅʻ hnanʻ Hasʻ Ta Lā. Ranʻ kunʻ: Toke-pe-ye-tana.

ʾOṅʻ Mratʻ ūʺ. 2016. Mahāgandharī re shanʻ kharīʺ hma pugguilʻ thuʺ myāʺ hnan prasʻ rapʻ shanʻ'" myāʺ. Ranʻ kunʻ Myui: kon khranʻ'" konʻ" ca pe.

Poʻ Ūʺ, Ūʺ. 1949. Buddha rājā Maṅʻ" Cakrā Suikʻ ʾa Phre Nhaṅʻ" Ūʺ Kyoʻ Lha Saṃ Khyui ʾa Phre. Ranʻ kunʻ: Mranʻ māʹ Sippaṃ Cā puṃ nhipʻ tuikʻ.

———. 1952. Vijjādhuirʻ ʾOṅʻ Maṅʻ"Khoṅʻ e* thvakʻ rapʻ pokʻ raja vanʻ 'atthuppatti. Ranʻ kunʻ: Mibamettā puṃ nhipʻ tuikʻ.

Saṅʻ, ūʺ. 2013. Pathamam Twak rap pok vijjā pugguilʻ kri mya. Ranʻ kunʻ Myui: Ahreʾ bhakʻ koṅʻ" kanʻ.

Thanʻ Poʻ. N.d. Pathamaṃ siddhi pokʻ joʻgyī kyamʻ ". Ranʻ kunʻ Mruiʹ: Kyaʺ-Piṭhakatʻ Cā upʻ chuinʻ krī ".

Vepullārāma Cha rā toʻ. 2006. *Vijjā Ca kā″ Vuiṅʻ″ Nhaṅ″ Vijjā Rhaṅʻ″ Tamʻ″ (Khoʻ): Vijjadhara Pakāsanī Kyamʻ″ Ranʻ kunʻ: Sa pre Ññui Cā pe.*

———. 2004. *Cakravaḷā Siddhi Kyamʻ″.* Praññʻ: Vepullārāma Kyoṅʻ tuikʻ.

———. 1998. *Pai Khū″ Tuiṅʻ″—Praññʻ Mruiʻ Gaī hā toʻ ʾA Phvaṅʻʻ Kyamʻ″.* Praññʻ: Vepullārāma Kyoṅʻ″.

NON-BURMESE SOURCES

Ahmed, Sara. 2004a. "Affective Economies." *Social Text* 79, 22, no. 2: 117–39.

———. 2004b. "Collective Feelings; or, The Impressions Left by Others." *Theory, Culture and Society* 21, no. 2: 25–42.

———. 2004c. *The Cultural Politics of Emotion.* New York: Routledge.

Arnold, David and Erich DeWald. 2012. "Everyday Technology in South and Southeast Asia: An Introduction." *Modern Asian Studies* 46, no. 1: 1–17.

Aung, Steven KH. 2005. "The Quest for Universal Healing, World Peace and International Harmony." *Heartbeat* 8, no. 2: 1, 3.

Aung-Thwin, Maitrii. 2011. *The Return of the Galon King: History, Law, and Rebellion in Colonial Burma.* Athens: Ohio University Press.

Bastian, Adolf. 1866. *Reisen in Birma in den Jahren 1861-1862.* Leipzig: O. Wigand.

Bennett, Jane. 2010. *Vibrant Matter: A Political Ecology of Things.* Durham: Duke University Press.

Berglie, Per-Arn. 2005. "Shamanic Buddhism in Burma." *Shaman* 13, nos. 1, 2.

Best, Susan. 2011. *Visualizing Feeling: Affect and the Feminine Avant-Garde.* New York: I. B. Tauris.

Bizot, F. 1988. *Les traditions de la pabbajjā en Asie du Sud-Est.* Göttingen: Vandenhoeck & Ruprecht.

Blackburn, Anne M. 2010. "Buddha-Relics in the Lives of Southern Asian Polities." *Numen* 57, no. 3/4: 317–40.

Bond, George Doherty. 1988. *Buddhist Revival in Sri Lanka: Religious Tradition, Reinterpretation, and Response.* Columbia: University of South Carolina Press.

Brac de la Perrière, Bénédicte. 2014. "Spirits versus Weikza: Two Competing Ways of Mediation." In *Champions of Buddhism: Weikza Cults in Contemporary Burma,* ed. B. Brac de la Perrière, G. Rozenberg, and A. Turner, 54–79. Singapore: NUS Press.

——. 2011a. "From Weikzahood to Mediumship: How to Master the World in Contemporary Burma." Religion Kompass, Wiley Online Library.

——. 2011b. "Being a Spirit Medium in Contemporary Burma." In *Engaging the Spirit World: Popular Beliefs and Practices in Modern Southeast Asia*, ed. Kirsten W. Endres and Andrea Lauser, 163–84. New York, Oxford: Berghahn Books.

——. 2009. "Les naq sont là! Représentation et expérience dans la possession d'esprit birmane." *Archives de sciences sociales des religions* 145: 33–50.

——.1989. *Les rituels de possession en Birmanie: du culte d'Etat aux cérémonies privées.* Paris: Editions Recherche sur les Civilisation, ADPF.

Brohm, John Frank. 1957. "Burmese Religion and the Burmese Religious Revival." PhD diss., Cornell University.

Bourdieu, Pierre. 1977. *Outline of a Theory of Practice.* London: Cambridge University Press.

Buddhaghosa, Caroline A., F. Rhys Davids, and Pali Text Society. 1975. *The Visuddhi-Magga of Buddhaghosa.* London: Pali Text Society; London, Boston: Routledge and Kegan Paul.

Buddhaghosa, Eugene Watson Burlingame, and Charles Rockwell Lanman. 1921. *Buddhist Legends.* Cambridge, Mass.: Harvard University Press.

Bullock, Steven C. 1996. *Revolutionary Brotherhood: Freemasonry and the Transformation of the American Social Order, 1730-1840.* Chapel Hill: University of North Carolina Press.

Caciola, Nancy. 1996. "Through a Glass, Darkly: Recent Work on Sanctity and Society. A Review Article." *Comparative Studies in Society and History* 38, no. 2: 301–9.

Cady, John F. 1958. *A History of Modern Burma.* Ithaca: Cornell University Press.

Carbine, Jason A. 2011. *Sons of the Buddha: Continuities and Ruptures in a Burmese Monastic Tradition.* New York: Walter de Gruyter.

Coderey, Céline. 2012. "The Weikza's Role in Arakanese Healing Practices." *The Journal of Burma Studies* 16, no. 2: 181–211.

——. 2011. "Les Maîtres du 'reste' : La quête de l'équilibre dans les conceptions et les pratiques therapeutiques en Arakan (Birmanie)." PhD diss., Université de Provence.

Collins, Steven. 2014. "What Kind of Buddhism Is That?" In *Champions of Buddhism: Weikza Cults in Contemporary Burma*, ed. B. Brac de la Perrière, G. Rozenberg, and A. Turner, 216–27. Singapore: NUS Press.

Commentary on Visuddhajana-Vilāsinī Apadāna Aṭṭhakathā, Portion II: Commentary on Biography of the Thera Mahākaccāna. Trans. U Lu Pe Win. http://www.aimwell.org /LediSayadaw/Apadana%20Commentary/

Crosby, Kate. 2014. "The Other Burmese Buddhism." In *Champions of Buddhism:* Weikza Cults in Contemporary Burma, ed. B. Brac de la Perrière, G. Rozenberg, and A. Turner, xxi–xxvii. Singapore: NUS Press.

Davis, Maryellen. 2007. "Mary as Media Icon: Gender and Militancy in Twentieth-Century U.S. Roman Catholic Devotional Media." In *Religion, Media, and the Marketplace*, ed. Lynn Schofield Clark, 123–53. New Brunswick, N.J.: Rutgers University Press.

Deboick, Sophia. 2011. "Image, Authenticity and the Cult of Saint Thérèse of Lisieux, 1897–1959." Thesis, University of Liverpool.

Dickens, Charles. 2000 (1861). *Great Expectations.* Hertfordshire, UK: Wordsworth Editions Limited.

DiValerio, David M. 2015. *The Holy Madmen of Tibet.* New York: Oxford University Press.

Elias, Jamal J. *Aisha's Cushion: Religious Art, Perception, and Practice in Islam.* Cambridge, Mass.: Harvard University Press.

Fausbøll, V. and Dines Andersen. 1877. *The Jātaka: Together with Its Commentary, Being Tales of the Anterior Births of Gotama Buddha.* London: Published for the Pali Text Society by Luzac.

Featherstone, Mike. 1991. "Consumer Culture, Postmodernism, and Global Disorder." In *Religion and Global Order (Religion and the Political Order Volume IV)*, ed. R. Robertson and W. R. Garrett. New York: Paragon.

Ferrars, M., and B. Ferrars. 1900. *Burma.* London: S. Low, Marston & Co., Ltd. http://www.archive.org/details/cu31924023498557

Figlerowicz, Marta. 2012. "Affect Theory Dossier: An Introduction." *Qui Parle: Critical Humanities and Social Sciences* 20, no. 2: 3–18.

Fjelstad, Karen and Lisa Maiffret. 2006. "Gifts from the Spirits: Spirit Possession and Personal Transformation Among Silicon Valley Spirit Mediums." In *Possessed by the Spirits: Mediumship in Contemporary Vietnamese Societies*, ed. Karen Fjelstad and Nguyen Thi Hien, 111–26. Ithaca: Cornell SEAP Publications.

Foxeus, Niklas. 2011. "The Buddhist World Emperor's Mission: Millenarian Buddhism in Postcolonial Burma." PhD diss., Stockholm University.

Freund, Peter, Meredith B. McGuire, and Linda Podhurst. 2003. *Health, Illness, and the Social Body: A Critical Sociology.* Upper Saddle River, N.J.: Prentice-Hall.

Gold, Daniel. 1988. "Approaching Some Householder Yogis: To Visit or Move In?" *Journal of Ritual Studies* 2, no. 2: 185–94.

Grady, Denise. 2012. "Gut Infections Are Growing More Lethal." *New York Times,* March 19.

Green, Alexandra. 2005. "Deep Change? Burmese Wall Paintings from the Eleventh to the Nineteenth Centuries." *The Journal of Burma Studies* 10: 1–50.

Gregg, Melissa and Gregory J. Seigworth. 2010. "An Inventory of Shimmers." In *The Affect Theory Reader*, ed. Gregory J. Seigworth and Melissa Gregg, 1–28. Durham: Duke University Press.

Griswold, A. B. 1974. *What Is a Buddha Image?* 3rd ed. Bangkok: Fine Arts Dept., B.E. 2517.

Harris, Ian. 2012. "Buddhism, Politics, and Nationalism." In *Buddhism in the Modern World*, ed. David L. McMahan, 177–94. New York: Routledge.

Hayashi, Yukio. 2000. "Spells and Boundaries in Regional Context: *Wisa* and *Thamma* Among the Thai-Lao in Northeast Thailand." In *Dynamics of Ethnic Cultures Across National Boundaries in Southwestern China and Mainland Southeast Asia: Relations, Societies, and Languages*, ed. Yukio Hayashi and Guangyuan Yang. Kyoto: Center for Southeast Asian Studies, Kyoto University.

Hayes, K. E. 2011. *Holy Harlots: Femininity, Sexuality, and Black Magic in Brazil.* Berkeley: University of California Press.

Hickey-Moody, A. Malins, P. 2007. *Deleuzian Encounters: Studies in Contemporary Social Issues.* London: Palgrave Macmillan.

Ho, Tamara C. 2009. "Transgender, Transgression, and Translation: A Cartography of Nat Kadaw Notes on Gender and Sexuality Within the Spirit Cult of Burma." *Discourse* 31, no. 3: 273–317.

Houtman, Gustaaf. 1999. *Mental Culture in Burmese Crisis Politics: Aung San Suu Kyi and the National League for Democracy.* Tokyo: Institute for the Study of Languages and Cultures of Asia and Africa, Tokyo University of Foreign Studies.

——. 1997a. "Beyond the Cradle and Past the Grave: The Biography of Burmese Meditation Master U Ba Khin." In *Buddhist Sacred Biography in South and Southeast Asia*, ed. Juliane Schober, 310–44. Honolulu: University of Hawai'i Press.

——. 1997b. "Burma or Myanmar?: The Cucumber and the Circle." *IIAS Newsletter* 12 (Spring).

——. 1990. "Traditions of Buddhist Practice in Burma." PhD diss., School of Oriental and African Studies, University of London.

Htin Paw, U. 2004. "Multi-part series—Part III—An Engineer in the Mystic World." Accessed March 3, 2009. http://www.ex-rit.org/rit.asp?i=6&f=Part%20VIII%20 -%20Living%20in%20Harmony%20with%20Nature.htm

Hughes, Jennifer Scheper. 2016. "Cradling the Sacred: Image, Ritual, and Affect in Mexican and Mesoamerican Material Religion." *History of Religions* 56, no. 1: 55–107.

——. 2012. "*Mysterium Materiae*: Vital Matter and the Object as Evidence in the Study of Religion." *Bulletin for the Study of Religion* 41, no. 4 (November 16–24).

——. 2010. *Biography of a Mexican Crucifix: Lived Religion and Local Faith from the Conquest to the Present.* Oxford, New York: Oxford University Press.

Ikeya, Chie. 2011. *Refiguring Women, Colonialism, and Modernity in Burma.* Honolulu: University of Hawai'i Press.

Jaini, Padmanabh S. 1965. " 'Mahadibbamanta': A 'Paritta' Manuscript from Cambodia." *Bulletin of SOAS* 28, no. 1: 61–80.

Jordt, Ingrid. 2007. *Burma's Mass Lay Meditation Movement: Buddhism and the Cultural Construction of Power.* Athens: Ohio University Press.

Kieschnick, John. 2008. "Material Culture." In *The Oxford Handbook of Religion and Emotion,* ed. John Corrigan. New York: Oxford University Press.

——. 1997. *The Eminent Monk: Buddhist Ideals in Medieval Chinese Hagiography.* Honolulu: University of Hawai'i Press.

Kirichenko, Alexey. 2009. "From Thathanadaw to Theravada Buddhism: Construction of Religion and Religious Identity in Nineteenth- and Early Twentieth-Century Myanmar." In *Casting Faiths: Imperialism and the Transformation of Religion in East and Southeast Asia,* ed. Thomas DuBois. New York: Palgrave-Macmillan.

Kyaw Kyaing. "Bo Min Gaung—one of the most popular weizzars in Myanmar." Weizzar Lan. July 2, 2009. Accessed June 13, 2018. http://weizzarlan.blogspot.com /2009/07/bo-min-gaung-one-of-most-popular.html

Kyaw Zaw Oo. "Ne Win's Family Claims 'Bodaws' Were Used to Help Plan Coup Plot." *Myanmar Times*, March 18–24, 2002.

Ladwig, P. 2011. "Can Things Reach the Dead?: The Ontological Status of Objects and the Study of Lao Buddhist Rituals for the Spirits of the Deceased." In *Engaging the Spirit World: Popular Beliefs and Practices in Modern Southeast Asia*, ed. Kirsten W. Endres and Andrea Lauser, 19–41. New York, Oxford: Berghahn Books.

Lammerts, Dietrich Christian. 2010a. "Notes on Burmese Manuscripts: Text." *Journal of Burma Studies* 14: 229–53.

——. 2010b. "Buddhism and Written Law Dhammasattha Manuscripts and Texts in Premodern Burma." PhD diss., Cornell University.

Ledi Sayadaw. 1965. *Manuals of Buddhism*. Rangoon: Union Buddha *Sāsana* Council.

Leehey, Jennifer. "Open Secrets, Hidden Meanings: Censorship, Esoteric Power, and Contested Authority in Urban Burma in the 1990s." PhD diss., University of Washington, 2010.

Maung Maung, U. 1980. *From Sangha to Laity: Nationalist Movements of Burma 1920-1940.* Australian National University Monographs on South Asia No. 4. New Delhi: Manohar.

McDaniel, Justin. 2017. *Architects of Buddhist Leisure: Socially Disengaged Buddhism in Asia's Museums, Monuments, and Amusement Parks.* Honolulu: University of Hawai'i Press.

——. 2013. "This Hindu Holy Man is a Thai Buddhist." *Southeast Asia Research* 21, no. 2: 191-210.

——. 2011. *The Lovelorn Ghost and the Magical Monk: Practicing Buddhism in Modern Thailand.* New York: Columbia University Press.

McGuire, Meredith. 2008. *Lived Religion: Faith and Practice In Everyday Life.* Oxford: Oxford University Press.

McLain, Karline. 2016. *The Afterlife of Sai Baba: Competing Visions of a Global Saint.* Seattle and London: University of Washington Press.

Mendelson, Michael. 1975. *Sangha and State in Burma: A Study of Monastic Sectarianism and Leadership.* Ithaca: Cornell University Press.

——. 1963. "Observations on a Tour in the Region of Mount Popa, Central Burma." *France-Asie* 19: 780–807.

——. 1961a. "The King of the Weaving Mountain." *Journal of the Royal Central Asian Society* 48: 229-37.

——. 1961b. "A Messianic Buddhist Association in Upper Burma." *Bulletin of the School of Oriental and African Studies* 24, 3: 560-80.

——. 1960. "Religion and Authority in Modern Burma." *The World Today* 16: 110-18.

Meyer, Birgit. 2012. "Religious and Secular, 'Spiritual' and 'Physical' in Ghana." In *What Matters?: Ethnographies of Value in a Not So Secular Age,* ed. Courtney Bender and Ann Taves, 86-118. New York: Columbia University Press.

Morgan, David. 2012a. *The Embodied Eye: Religious Visual Culture and the Social Life of Feeling.* Berkeley: University of California Press.

——. 2012b. "The Look of the Sacred." In *The Cambridge Companion to Religious Studies,* ed. Robert Orsi, 296-318. Cambridge; New York: Cambridge University Press.

Morgan, David and Promey, Sally M., eds. 2001. "Introduction." *The Visual Culture of American Religions,* 1-20. Berkeley: University of California Press.

Moore, Elizabeth. 2016. "The Social Dynamics of Pagoda Repair un Upper Myanmar." *Journal of Burma Studies* 20, no. 1.

——. 2014. "Patronage and Place: The Shwedagon in Times of Change." In *Colonial and Contemporary Encounters, Buddhism Across Asia*, ed. T. Sen and G. Wade, 631–59. Singapore: Institute of Southeast Asian Studies (ISEAS).

Nattier, Jan. 1991. *Once Upon a Future Time: Studies in a Buddhist Prophecy of Decline.* Berkeley: Asian Humanities Press.

The New Light of Myanmar IX, no. 3 (March 1995). Obeyesekere, Gananath. 1981. *Medusa's Hair: An Essay on Personal Symbols and Religious Experience.* Chicago: University of Chicago Press.

Okell, John. 1971. *A Guide to the Romanization of Burmese.* London: Luzac [for] The Royal Asiatic Society of Great Britain and Ireland.

Ong, Aihwa. 1988. "The Production of Possession: Spirits and the Multinational Corporation in Malaysia." *American Ethnologist* (Medical Anthropology) 15, 1: 28–42.

Orsi, Robert A. 2013. "Holy Cards." In Reverberations: New Directions in the Study of Prayer. April 8, 2013. http://forums.ssrc.org/ndsp/2013/04/08/holy-cards/#more-2590.

——. 2007. "2+2 = 5, Can We Begin to Think About Unexplained Religious Experiences in Ways That Acknowledge Their Existence?" *The American Scholar* (Spring). http://www.theamericanscholar.org/when-2-2-5/.

——. 2005. *Between Heaven and Earth: The Religious Worlds People Make and the Scholars Who Study Them.* Princeton: Princeton University Press.

——. 1996. *Thank You, St. Jude: Women's Devotion to the Patron Saint of Hopeless Causes.* New Haven: Yale University Press.

Orwell, George. 1950. *Burmese Days: A Novel.* New York: Harcourt, Brace.

Paramatthadīpanī-Theragāthā Aṭṭhakathā. "Commentary on the stanza of Pilindavaccha Thera." nd. Trans. unknown. http://www.aimwell.org/LediSayadaw/Theragatha%20Commentary/

——. nd. Commentary on the stanza of Uttaratthera. Trans. unknown. http://www.aimwell.org/LediSayadaw/Apadana%20Commentary/

Pattana Kitiarsa. 2005. "Magic Monks and Spirit Mediums in the Politics of Thai Popular Religion." *Inter-Asia Cultural Studies* 6, no. 2 (2005): 209–25.

Patton, Thomas. 2012. "In Pursuit of the Sorcerer's Power: Sacred Diagrams as Technologies of Potency." *Contemporary Buddhism* 13, no. 2.

Phe Myint, Zaw Win, and Kunsal Kassapa. *Wonders of Mebegon Village.* Banglamung (Pattaya), Chonburi, Thailand: Nagamasa Center, 2005.

Pinney, Christopher. 2004. *'Photos of the Gods:' The Printed Image and Political Struggle in India.* London: Reaktion.

——. 1997. *Camera Indica: The Social Life of Indian Photographs.* Chicago: University of Chicago Press.

Pranke, Patrick. 2010 [2011]. "On Saints and Wizards—Ideals of Human Perfection and Power in Contemporary Burmese Buddhism." *Journal of the International Association of Buddhist Studies* 33, 1–2: 453–88.

——. 1995. "On Becoming a Buddhist Wizard." In *Buddhism in Practice*, ed. Donald S. Lopez Jr., 343–47. Princeton: Princeton University Press.

Przyluski, Jean. 1923. "Les Vidyaraja." *Bulletin de l'Ecole Francaise d'Extreme-Orient* 23: 301–18.

Reed, Barbara E. 2003. "Guanyin Narratives—Wartime and Postwar." In *Religion in Modern Taiwan: Tradition and Innovation in a Changing Society*, ed. Philip Clart and Charles B. Jones, 186–203. Honolulu: University of Hawaii Press.

Reynolds, Frank E. 1976. "The Many Lives of Buddha: A Study of Sacred Biography and Theravada Tradition." In *The Biographical Process: Studies in the History and Psychology of Religion*, ed. Frank Reynolds and Donald Capps. The Hague: Mouton.

Rozenberg, Guillaume. 2015. *The Immortals: Faces of the Incredible in Buddhist Burma*. Honolulu: Hawai'i University Press.

——. 2014. "Powerful Yet Powerless, Powerless Yet Powerful." In *Champions of Buddhism: Weikza Cults in Contemporary Burma*, ed. B. Brac de la Perrière, G. Rozenberg, and A. Turner, 188–215. Singapore: NUS Press.

Sacks, Oliver W. 2012. *Hallucinations*. New York: Knopf.

Sadan, Mandy. 2014. "The Historical Visual Economy of Photography in Burma." Bijdragen tot de Taal-, Land- en Volkenkunde 170: 281–312.

Sangren, P. Steven. 2000. *Chinese Sociologics: An Anthropological Account of Alienation and Social Reproduction*. London: Athlone.

Sarkisyanz, Manuel. 1965. *Buddhist Backgrounds of the Burmese Revolution*. The Hague: M. Nijhoff.

Saya U Htin Paw. 2004. "Multi-part series—Part III—An Engineer in the Mystic World." Rangoon Intsitute of Technology Alumni Newsletter. http://www.ex-rit.org.

Schaefer, Donovan O. 2015. *Religious Affects: Animality, Evolution, and Power.* Durham: Duke University Press. Schober, Juliane. 2012. "The Longevity of the Weikza and Their Practices." *Journal of Burma Studies* 16, no. 2.

——. 1988. "The Path to Buddhahood: The Spiritual Mission and Social Organization of Mysticism in Contemporary Burma." *Crossroads: An Interdisciplinary Journal of Southeast Asian Studies* 4, no. 1: 13–30.

Scott, James George. 1896. *The Burman, His Life and Notions*. London; New York: Macmillan.

Sedgwick, Eve. 2003. *Touching Feeling: Affect, Pedagogy, Performativity*. Durham: Duke University Press.

Seekins, Donald M. 2006. *Historical Dictionary of Burma (Myanmar)*. Lanham, Md.: Scarecrow Press.

Shorter, Edward. 1986. "Paralysis: The Rise and Fall of a 'Hysterical' Symptom." *Journal of Social History* 19, no. 4 (Summer).

Skidmore, Monique. 2008. "Contemporary Medical Pluralism in Burma." In *Dictatorship, Disorder and Decline in Myanmar*, ed. Monique Skidmore and Trevor Wilson, 193–207. Canberra: ANUE Press.

Smith, Donald Eugene. 1965. *Religion and Politics in Burma*. Princeton: Princeton University Press.

Snellgrove, David L. 2002. *Indo-Tibetan Buddhism: Indian Buddhists and Their Tibetan Successors*. Boston: Shambhala.

Soe, Thein. 1979. "A Study of the Shwe Yin Kyaw and Mano Mayeiddi Schools of Traditional Burmese Healing." Trans. Tin Maung Kyi. B.A. thesis, University of Mandalay.

Spiro, Melford E. 1970. *Buddhism and Society: A Great Tradition and Its Burmese Vicissitudes.* Berkeley: University of California Press.

Stadtner, Donald Martin. 2011. *Sacred Sites of Burma: Myth and Folklore in an Evolving Spiritual Realm.* Bangkok: River Books.

Strong, John. 2004. *Relics of the Buddha.* Princeton: Princeton University Press.

——. 1992. *The Legend and Cult of Upagupta.* Princeton: Princeton University Press.

Supp-Montgomerie, Jenna. 2015. "Affect and the Study of Religion." *Religion Compass* 9/10: 335–45.

Swearer, Donald. 2004. *Becoming the Buddha: The Ritual of Image Consecration in Thailand.* Princeton: Princeton University Press.

Tarling, Nicholas. 1999. *The Cambridge History of Southeast Asia.* Cambridge: Cambridge University Press.

Taves, Ann. 2012. "Special Things as Building Blocks of Religions." In *The Cambridge Companion to Religious Studies,* ed Robert Orsi, 58–83. Cambridge; New York: Cambridge University Press.

——. 2009. *Religious Experience Reconsidered: A Building Block Approach to the Study of Religion and Other Special Things.* Princeton: Princeton University Press.

Tin Maung Maung Than. 1993. "Sangha Reforms and Renewal of *Sāsana* in Myanmar." In *Buddhist Trends in Southeast Asia*, ed. Trevor Oswald Ling, 6–63. Singapore: Institute of Southeast Asian Studies.

Torrocco, Francesca. 2011. "On the Market: Consumption and Material Culture in Modern Chinese Buddhism." *Religion* 41, no. 4: 627–44.

Tosa, Keiko. 2014. "From Bricks to Pagodas: Weikza Specialists and the Rituals of Pagoda Building." In *Champions of Buddhism: Weikza Cults in Contemporary Burma,* ed. B. Brac de la Perrière, G. Rozenberg, and A. Turner, 113–39. Singapore: NUS Press.

——. 1996. "Biruma niokeru weikza shinko no ichikosatsu: gaing nitotteno Lawki and Lawkoktara" (A consideration of *weikza* belief in Burma: the meaning of *lawki* and *lawkoktara* for the *gaing*). *The Japanese Journal of Ethnology* (Japanese Journal of Cultural Anthropology) 61, no. 2: 215–42.

Turner, Alicia Marie. 2014. *Saving Buddhism: The Impermanence of Religion in Colonial Burma.* Honolulu: University of Hawai'i Press.

U Aung Thein Nyunt. 2014. "Preservation of Cetiya or Pagodas in Myanmar." International Buddhist Conference on "Promotion, Protection and Preservation of Buddhist Cultural Heritage." Part II. Papers on World Buddhist Heritage, Buddhist Culture, Buddhist Education System, 54–59. Lumbini, Nepal: The Sacred Birthplace of the Buddha, 15–18 November. Theravada Buddhist Academy, Sagaing, Nepal: Sitagu International Buddhist Academy.

Uttamasara, U. 1989. *The Buddhist Way of Daily Life / Sayadaw U Uttamasara; with the Introductory Message of Dhammacariya U Htay Hlaing; Translated by Saya Ba Kyaw.* Rangoon: Voice of Buddha Sarpay.

Van der Linden. 2014. "On the Relationship Between Personal Experience, Affect and Risk Perception: The Case of Climate Change." *European Journal of Social Psychology* 44 (5): 430–40.

Veal, Clare. 2013. "The Charismatic Index: Photographic Representations of Power and Status in the Thai Social Order." *Local Culture/Global Photography* 3, no. 2.

Von Hinuber, Oscar. 1994. "The Vidyadhara's Sword." In *Selected Papers on Pāli Studies*, 101–6. Oxford: The Pāli Text Society.

Wallace, Anthony. 1966. *Religion: An Anthropological View.* New York: Random House.

Watters, Ethan. 2010. *Crazy Like Us: The Globalization of the American Psyche.* New York: Free Press.

White, David Gordon. 1996. *The Alchemical Body: Siddha Traditions in Medieval India.* Chicago: University of Chicago Press.

Zöllner, Hans-Bernd. 2010. "Introduction." In *Working Paper No. 10:15 Material on Four Books About Germany.* ed. Hans-Bernd Zöllner. University of Passau, Department of Southeast Asian Studies.

INDEX